The Bottom Line

Also by Andrew Zimbalist

Baseball and Billions: A Probing Look Inside the Big Business of Our National Pastime

Sports, Jobs and Taxes: The Economic Impact of Sports Teams and Stadiums (written and edited with Roger Noll)

Unpaid Professionals: Commercialism and Conflict in Big-Time College Sports

The Economics of Sport I & II (edited)

May the Best Team Win: Baseball Economics and Public Policy

National Pastime: How Americans Play Baseball and the Rest of the World Plays Soccer (with Stefan Szymanski)

In the Best Interests of Baseball? The Revolutionary Reign of Bud Selig

The Bottom Line

Observations and Arguments on the Sports Business

ANDREW ZIMBALIST

Temple University Press
PHILADELPHIA

For Jeff, Mike, Alex, Ella, Manuel, and Olivia
and
for Sam and Naima

ANDREW ZIMBALIST is Robert A. Woods Professor of
Economics at Smith College. He is the author or editor of sixteen
previous books, is a member of the editorial board of *The Journal
of Sports Economics,* and has consulted extensively in the sports
industry for players' associations, leagues, cities, and owners.

Temple University Press
1601 North Broad Street
Philadelphia PA 19122
www.temple.edu/tempress

Text design by Lynne Frost

⊗ The paper used in this publication meets the requirements of the
American National Standard for Information Sciences—Permanence
of Paper for Printed Library Materials, ANSI Z39.48-1992

Library of Congress Cataloging-in-Publication Data

Zimbalist, Andrew S.
  The bottom line: observations and arguments on the sports business /
Andrew Zimbalist.
    p. cm.
  Includes index.
    ISBN 1-59213-512-9 (cloth : alk. paper) — ISBN 1-59213-513-7
(pbk. : alk. paper)
      1. Sports—Economic aspects. 2. Sports—Finance.
3. Professional sports—Economic aspects. I. Title.

GV716.Z56 2006
338.4'7796—dc22   2005046690

2 4 6 8 9 7 5 3

ISBN 13: 978-1-59213-513-4

Contents

PART IV. Antitrust and Labor Relations

Introduction

The essays in this collection span a decade and a half of exciting action in the sports industry. They represent a selection of op-eds and journalistic pieces I have written for numerous newspapers and magazines.[1]

While the examples change, the environments mutate, and the dollars grow, the basic dilemmas and dynamics of the sports industry remain very much the same. Dollar growth is the easy part to document. Between 1990 and 2004, Major League Baseball's gross revenues increased roughly from $1.3 billion to $4.3 billion (annual growth rate of 8.7 percent), the National Basketball Association's revenues increased from $843 million to $2.9 billion (annual rate of 10.1 percent), the National Football League's revenues rose from $1.3 billion to $5.3 billion (annual rate of 11.4 percent), and the National Hockey League's revenues grew from $518 million to $2.2 billion (annual rate of 11.9 percent).[2] NASCAR and golf witnessed even more rapid growth.

Elucidating the underlying economic dynamic of team sports leagues is more challenging. Team sports leagues are different from other industries in one fundamental way. The teams (companies) that compete against each other on the playing field must also cooperate with each other to a certain degree as businesses. General Motors can produce cars by itself; it does not need Chrysler. The Yankees, however, cannot play a game of baseball without another team. In the team sports industry, then, it takes at least two companies to produce the desired output.

Moreover, the two teams must be sufficiently balanced so that the outcome of each game is uncertain. In practice, of course, there will be many more than two teams in each league, because it is not only the outcome of each game that

---

[1]The essays have been edited slightly to avoid redundancy, to provide greater clarity, and occasionally to update material. One entry comes from testimony I gave before the U.S. Congress.

[2]These figures are all estimates from *Financial World* and *Forbes*. They are given here only to suggest the general magnitude of growth. Major League Baseball's figures represent fourteen years of growth, while the other three sports represent thirteen years. Hockey's faster growth rate in large measure results from the more rapid expansion in the number of its franchises (from twenty-one to thirty teams) over the period. Adding the four sports together, total estimated revenues grew from $4 billion in 1990 to $14.8 billion in 2004, for a 10.3 percent annual growth rate.

is at stake, but the outcome of the competitive season, as well. A league that functions effectively will also be one where the outcome of each season is uncertain and where the fans in most cities believe that their team has a reasonable chance of making it to post-season competition.

The car industry could function effectively if Toyota sold 50 percent of the cars, GM sold 30 percent, and Chrysler and Ford each sold 10 percent. That is, it would be OK, other things equal, if Toyota dominated the other companies year after year. Such an outcome, however, would not lead to a very successful sports league.

If teams in a sports league were not allowed to cooperate economically, then there would be a very strong tendency for big-market teams to dominate. A team in a market of 8 million people would be able to generate several times more revenue than a team in a market with 1 million people. Yet the two teams would go to the same players' market to sign up talent. While there is not a perfect correlation between team payroll and performance, having a higher payroll certainly increases a team's chances of winning.

These market imbalances are exacerbated by the different ownership circumstances on each team. Owners have different motives for buying teams. Some are interested solely in the sport. Some see the sport as programming to support their other investments (e.g., media outlets, stadiums or arenas, concessionaire companies, car- or jet-rental businesses, etc.). The latter group of owners may treat the team itself not as a profit center but, rather, as a means to generating profits for their other investments. When these owners go to the players' market to sign players, they may be asking multiples questions: How much revenue will the player generate for the team? How much will he generate for the owner's regional sports channel, for the planned real-estate–development project, and so on? The team's success will also enhance the owner's standing in the community and, hence, his or her ability to make new deals with other executives, investors, and politicians.

This latter group of owners is likely to perceive more potential value from star players. Thus, Tom Hicks, owner of the Texas Rangers, Clear Channel Communications, a major international investment firm, and the rights to develop 250 acres around the team's stadium and to sell naming rights to the ballpark, believed that the potential contribution of Alex Rodriguez to his investment universe was huge. Accordingly, he offered A-Rod a prodigious and unprecedented contract: ten years for $252 million plus bonuses. Had Hicks been thinking only about A-Rod's contribution to the Rangers, he never would have offered such a sum.

Because of these inequalities in market size and ownership synergies, teams appraise players' worth in vastly different terms. Without a league-imposed constraint, some teams may outspend others by a margin of nine or ten to one. Indeed, this happens today in baseball, even though the league imposes a luxury tax of up to 40 percent on that portion of the team's payroll that exceeds the threshold. In the NBA until 2002, some teams had payrolls above $100 million while others had payrolls below $30 million.

These disparities are not conducive to either the promotion of competitive balance or financial stability. Hence, owners seek constraints on the players' market. (Owners, though, must be careful how they impose constraints, lest they run afoul of the nation's antitrust laws.) Players, in contrast, seek free markets and the highest possible salaries. Each of the four major team-sports leagues in the United States today employs at least one artificial mechanism to constrain salaries. The NFL, the NBA, and the NHL (with the new 2005 labor agreement) have salary-cap systems. MLB has a luxury tax on high team payrolls, an extensive revenue-sharing system that reduces a player's net value to a team, and team debt limitations. Each of these systems has imperfections and produces tensions among owners as well as between owners and players that are discussed in the essays in Parts II and IV.

Major League Soccer has organized itself as a putative "single-entity" league, which means that the teams have common ownership. The principal goal of this system of organization is to avoid competition among teams for players and thereby to reduce players' salaries. MLS has succeeded in maintaining low salaries, but it has failed to attract the world's best players. The top players go to Europe, where player markets are open and salaries frequently rise to several million dollars a year or higher. In consequence, soccer fans generally perceive MLS to be a minor league, and the league's attendance numbers reflect this perception. At the same time, the league's owners are losing money and are understandably reluctant to risk quadrupling or quintupling their payrolls to hire the world's best players. The league's business model, thus, appears to be caught in a rut.

MLS, like the big four U.S. team-sports leagues, is a monopoly. It is the only top-level producer of its sport in the country. Similar to the NHL prior to 2005, however, MLS, despite being a monopoly, does not generate profits. To some this may appear anomalous—monopolies are supposed to generate above-normal profits. While this is valid in general, it is not true for industries that are poorly managed or have insufficient demand for their product.

In contrast, MLB, the NFL, and the NBA are all economically healthy leagues. This is not to say that all teams in these leagues are always profitable. There are some inefficiently run teams, particularly those in smaller markets, that may experience unprofitable years. But even in these leagues the owners of the profitable teams may not experience abnormally high rates of return. This is because (1) the players have been able to capture some of the monopoly rents via higher salaries or (2) the monopoly value of teams has already been reflected in the team's sale price. Nonetheless, the fact that franchise values have risen over time (and done so at a rate considerably above the increase in the Standard and Poor's 500) is strong evidence that owning franchises in these leagues is a good economic investment. These financial considerations are illustrated by the essays in Parts I and III.

One of the most important factors that has contributed to franchise profitability is the phenomenon of publicly funded stadiums. As monopolies, the leagues can artificially reduce the number of franchises below the demand for them from economically viable cities. This scarce supply thrusts cities into competition with each other and results in large public subsidies to attract or retain a team. Over $20 billion of public money has been spent on new facilities for teams during the past fifteen years, with an average of approximately 70 percent of the construction cost being publicly defrayed. Politicians and other stadium supporters have claimed that this public investment pays off because the city will get more back in taxes from the increased economic activity associated with the new facility. Independent studies by economists, however, find that such a payoff cannot be anticipated, and the justification for any public financial support has to be found in quality-of-life, not economic, benefits. These arguments are discussed and illustrated in the essays of Part III.

While college sports bear multiple similarities to their professional counterparts and are linked to them because they provide free training and simplified scouting opportunities to the pro leagues, the educational, economic, and moral issues raised by college sports are entirely different. College sports are run by a monopoly, the National Collegiate Athletics Association. The NCAA, in turn, is divided into three divisions, basically according to each school's financial commitment to its athletics program. Division I is the most commercially oriented of the three, and within Division I, Division IA stands out. Division IA includes 115 schools. These programs, despite extensive commercial ties and top coaches' compensation rising above $1 million, benefit from the same tax-exempt treatment as the educational programs at the university. The football and basketball players are not directly compensated in financial terms, but they have a special status among the students, receiving extensive tutoring, blinkered advising, privileged access to a watered-down curriculum of courses, often separate living and dining conditions, under-the-table payoffs, and so on.

Notwithstanding the assertions that this is all amateur sports intended to provide a healthy balance to the intellectual life of the college student, male athletes are showered with many more resources than female athletes. Title IX is supposed to rectify the gender imbalance. Yet while women have made significant progress over the years, particularly from 1992 to 2000, Title IX has not been vigorously enforced since 2001 and has come under attack from various sources.

There is little question that the college sports system has elements that are both hypocritical and corrupt. In the vast majority of cases, it is also financially burdensome for the schools. The educational, ethical, and money issues surrounding college sports are presented in the essays of Part V.

Part VI includes pieces on the media and doping in sports. The area of media has witnessed the most radical transformation of any since 1990.

The telecommunications revolution, along with the advent of the Internet and fourth-generation cell phones, have provided a proliferation of channels, including specialized sports and niche networks, and new viewing options. The introduction of a new national network, Fox, in the 1990s meant increased competition for sports programming and higher rights fees. The innovation of Tivo and similar products challenged the traditional advertising model by making it easier for viewers to record programs and skip over the ads. At the same time, it put a premium on the telecasting of sporting competition, which viewers strongly prefer to watch live. The sports with stronger television allure, such as football and baseball, benefited the most from these changes, while hockey was left behind. In the NFL in 2005, the average teams received over $110 million in annual television-rights fees (with the number slated to rise to around $140 million in the coming years). In contrast, in the NHL, the average team in 2005–2006 will earn less than $3 million from centralized television-rights fees.

Finally, the integrity of sporting competition has been called into question by the anabolic-steroid and performance-enhancing–supplements scandal of recent years. The matter was brought to a head by the publication of Jose Canseco's book *Juiced* in early 2005 and then the March 2005 congressional hearings. Several essays deal with the evolution and complexity of the doping issue and suggest that the problem will be with us for some time to come.

One of the more remarkable aspects of the doping scandal in baseball is that fans, while curious, seem unperturbed. Attendance and television ratings continue to grow. If nothing else, this is testimony to the intensity of sports fandom in the United States. In our increasingly automated and visual culture, sports represent one of the few opportunities for communities to find identity and to come together. It is hard to imagine our society without spectator sports. Whether or not one is a fan, then, it makes sense to try to understand the sports business and what makes it tick. By presenting vignettes and interpretations of important events in the sports industry over the past fifteen years, this collection, I hope, will contribute to such an understanding.

I

Team Management, Finances, and Value

So You Want to Own a Big-League Ball Team?

Richard Jacobs bought the Cleveland Indians with his now deceased brother David in 1986 for $35 million. Two weeks ago, the Indians issued a prospectus detailing plans to sell 4 million ownership shares in the team at a projected price of between $14 and $16 a share.

With this deal, Jacobs is the first to take advantage of a new Major League Baseball (MLB) policy to allow direct, albeit partial, public ownership of its franchises. With increasing corporate ownership of baseball teams, it seemed only a matter of time before MLB would allow teams to sell stock to the public. As with corporate ownership, public ownership provides capital and boosts franchise values. The new MLB policy, however, does not permit the public to own more than 10 percent of the voting rights in any club. Jacobs's plan adheres to this constraint with a vengeance.

What's Being Sold

The structure of the deal is baroque, but here are the essential details. The ownership of the team will be through a partnership. The partnership, in turn, will consist of a general partner owning 51 percent and a limited partner owning 49 percent. Jacobs will keep the ownership of the limited partner for himself. As the limited partner, he has virtually no legal liability with his ownership.

The 51 percent general partnership is being sold to the public. On the surface, it appears that Jacobs is selling 51 percent of the team. If each share sells for $16, then 4 million shares are worth $64 million, and the implied value of the entire franchise appears to be $125.5 million.

But reality is different. In addition to the 4 million shares being offered to the public, the general partner will also consist of 139,376 shares to be given gratis to Jacobs and 2,283,957 special "Class B" shares also to be awarded gratis to Jacobs. After the initial public offering (IPO), or stock sale, then, the general partner will consist of 6,423,333 shares. The 4 million shares sold to the public would make up 62.27 percent of the general partner, which in turn would own 51 percent of the team.

During the first year, there will be an additional potential 700,000 shares offered as stock options to the Indians' executives (including Jacobs). After the stock options are exercised, the public would hold 56.15 percent of the general partner and 28.64 percent of the team. Jacobs would own the balance (apart from 8,000-odd shares owned by his colleague Martin Cleary), including the entire 49 percent that is the limited partner.

At a projected price of $16 a share (the actual offering price could be higher or lower), the 4 million publicly issued shares would be valued at $64 million. Since these shares represent 28.64 percent of the team, the implicit value of the team is $237.4 million. However, in March 1998, just prior to registering his public offering, Jacobs took out $49.2 million from the team. Thus, the franchise, prior to Jacobs's withdrawal, had a price, implicitly valued by this deal, of $286.6 million (or $244.7 million at $14 a share).

Since reported team revenues were $140 million in 1997 (after deducting $7.2 million the Indians paid to the league under MLB's new revenue-sharing plan), the implied team value is approximately two times team revenues. This would not be an unreasonable multiple for an MLB franchise were it not for other aspects of the deal.

The Indians are playing in a new, state-of-the-art ballpark with an excellent lease. Following a horrendous four decades, the team has been successful on the field since 1994 and holds the major-league record for consecutive sell-outs (232 through May 17, 1998). In 1997, the team went to game seven of the World Series, and net post-season revenue was $6.8 million. While the Indians might benefit from larger national television contracts or baseball's international expansion in the future, local revenue seems to be currently maximized, and other risk factors will potentially have an impact on the franchise's economic performance in coming years.

Who's in Control and Who Benefits

The stock sold to the public will carry one vote per share, while the special "Class B" shares held by Jacobs will carry 10,000 votes per share. This stipulation confers to Jacobs 99.9 percent of the voting rights. He will have total control over the team and the appointment of its directors.

The prospectus explicitly states that the Indians do not intend to pay any cash dividends in the foreseeable future. It would be understandable for a growth company to reinvest all its profits and pay no dividends, but the Indians are not a growth company, and the team faces no major capital investments. To be sure, the Indians cannot be expected to continue to win their American League Central Division every year and proceed to the World Series. As team performance inevitably wanes, revenues might also diminish. Under such circumstances, normal stockholders should anticipate a dividend. Indeed, the Boston Celtics of the NBA is a partnership with public ownership. Its stock trades on the New York Stock Exchange for around $20 a share and pays a $1 dividend. The other professional-sports franchise that is partially publicly held, the Florida Panthers of the NHL, does not pay a dividend but has engaged in an active program of investment outside the hockey business.

Since Jacobs will control all aspects of team operations, since he owns a number companies that do business with the Indians, and since he will receive handsome income (in excess of $715,000 a year along with stock options as chief executive officer and a director), expenses, and perquisites, he will be able to manipulate the reported income per share while he also takes his return through related businesses he owns.

Jacobs owns and manages thirty-nine shopping malls, nine office buildings, three operating hotels, and twenty-three hotels under development, inter alia. Through some of these businesses Jacobs leases office and warehouse space to the Indians. He also owns companies that provide legal, consulting, and accounting services to the Indians and received $2.4 million from the club during 1995–97. Significantly, Jacobs benefits from heavily subsidized naming rights to the Indians' ballpark, Jacobs Field.

Jacobs, according to the pro forma (projected operation of the club going forward), will also lay claim to 49 percent (the limited partner's share in ownership) of the pretax operating income, which in 1997 came to $9.554 million.

Bottom Line

This is a lopsided deal. With it, Jacobs is cashing out part of his ownership for approximately $64 million, plus the $49.2 million he withdrew prior to the registration of this offering with the Securities and Exchange Commission. Jacobs will retain majority ownership and total control over the club, which will continue to provide him with a rich income stream while he minimizes his financial liability under the new partnership arrangement. Public shareholders can expect no dividends and slow company growth, at best.

Advice: If you are an incurable baseball fan with a lifetime dream to own a team, then buy one share of stock and hang it over your fireplace.

Capital Needs, Political Realities Fuel New Interest in Sports Offerings

The ownership landscape in professional team sports is undergoing a significant transformation. Including minority positions, there are now sixty-seven public companies that have investments in teams in the NHL, the NBA, or MLB. Most of these companies have come on board in the 1990s. The NFL has long proscribed such owners, but Commissioner Paul Tagliabue has indicated that the league's policy may soon change.

In the past two years, a new trend seems to be emerging that entails direct public stock offerings by sports teams. In November 1996, the NHL's Florida Panthers sold 7.3 million shares at $10 apiece, with the majority owner, H. Wayne Huizenga, maintaining firm control. The Green Bay Packers, taking advantage of an exemption granted by the NFL back in the 1930s, is issuing 400,000 shares at $20 each.

In September 1997, MLB approved a policy allowing public issuance of stock as long as the incumbent owner retained 90 percent voting control over the franchise. In early 1998, after experiencing political difficulty with his maneuvering to induce New York City to erect a $1 billion-plus facility over the West Side Railyards in midtown Manhattan, George Steinbrenner hinted that he might consider a minority public offering to raise the capital toward a substantial private contribution for stadium construction. The Pittsburgh Pirates' ownership has also stated that it is studying a public offering. And earlier this month (June 1998), the Cleveland Indians sold 4 million shares at $15 a share, representing approximately 29 percent of ownership but less than 1 percent of voting rights.

Public ownership of sports franchises is not new. There are, after all, several publicly traded companies that own sports teams: Time Warner (the Atlanta Braves), News Corporation (the Los Angeles Dodgers), Tribune (the Chicago Cubs), Disney (the California Angels), Ascent (the Denver Nuggets and Colorado Avalanche), Comcast (the Philadelphia 76ers and Fliers), Anheuser-Busch (the St. Louis Blues), among others. An irrepressible fan can buy stock in one of these companies and indirectly own a piece of a sports team. But the team is usually a very small part of the company's holdings.

Nor is it new for there to be direct public ownership of sports franchises ("pure plays"). Stock in the Cleveland Cavaliers had been publicly traded from 1970 to 1984; likewise with the New England Patriots from 1960 to 1976, the

Baltimore Orioles from 1954 to 1979, and the Milwaukee Bucks from 1968 to 1979. Prior to the Panthers offering in 1996, however, the only existing pure play was the Boston Celtics, which issued approximately a 40 percent ownership stake to the public in 1986.

How can we understand this renewed interest in public stock offerings? First, the stock market represents an important source of capital for most businesses in the United States beyond a certain size. As the sports industry has grown, its need for capital has grown, too. It would be hard to imagine the U.S. economy today if there were a requirement that General Motors, Boeing, Pfizer, and IBM all had to be owned by a family or partnership. As sports franchises have appreciated in value, the sports industry needs to tap more sources of capital to sustain and enhance that value.

Second, an economic theory known as Tobin's Q (after the Nobel Prize-winning Yale economist James Tobin) points to the greater attractiveness of new investments and public stock offerings when the stock market overvalues an asset relative to its replacement cost. With the price–earnings ratio of the Standard and Poor's 500 hovering above a heady 22 today (implying a below 5 percent return on a risky investment), the stock market is a very alluring venue to seek asset valuation. Like everyone else, team owners want to take advantage of the buoyant U.S. stock market.

Third, sports teams are a natural for public ownership. Sports fans have a special relationship to their teams that is quite unlike the relationship between the public and typical manufacturing or service companies. This relationship comes not only from their emotional bond to the team but also from the multi-million-dollar annual public subsidies provided to sports teams. Going public gives fans an opportunity to put their money where their hearts are, and it gives owners an opportunity to broaden and deepen the support base for their teams.

Fourth, the post-1950 trend toward growing public subsidies to build stadiums is being challenged. In he past two years, stadium referenda have failed in Minnesota, Pittsburgh, and North Carolina and have passed by razor-thin margins in San Francisco and Seattle (though the legitimacy of the vote in each case is being questioned by citizens' groups). Owners in New York, Miami, Los Angeles, Chicago, and Boston have failed to muster sufficient political support for their stadium initiatives. In this context, owners have been compelled to assign larger shares of their new stadium revenue streams to help finance construction. Capital from the stock market can be used to supplement or replace the commitment of stadium revenues.

As in other industries, the trailblazers get the highest return. As long as public offerings in sports are a novelty, owners can expect a premium. That, of course, is bad news for prospective shareholders. The Celtics stock sold for $19 a share at issue in 1986; today the stock sells for $20, or about $13.50 in 1986 prices. The Indians sold their shares for around $15. Their prospectus warns investors not to expect any dividends and that the company has likely maxed out on local revenues—that is, don't expect this to be a growth company with revenues already at baseball's apex above $140 million a year. The incumbent owner, Richard Jacobs, however, will do very well: He pulled out $49.2 million prior to the offering; nets more than $50 million from the stock sale; receives more than $715,000 a year in various forms of compensation; benefits from heavily subsidized naming rights to Jacobs Field; extracts net income as minority partner; enjoys profitable related business transactions with his other investments; and maintains complete control over the team.

The largest potential premium, though, goes to the Green Bay Packers. Prior to its offering, the Packers split the existing stock 1,000 to 1, yielding 4.6 million shares. Then the team offered 400,000 new shares at $200 a piece, which implicitly values the team at $1.006 billion!

The only case where there has been a payoff to the investor is the Florida Panthers. And this return has come because the company has diversified rapidly since the IPO, buying at least six other properties in the entertainment and resort industries. Whether the Panthers' stock price will continue to increase remains to be seen.

But the pure plays have not paid off. As the novelty wears off, as more franchises do public offerings, and as investors see they have no control and no return, having a framed Indians' stock certificate in one's den will have all the cachet of a laminated rookie card of Todd Van Poppel. At such a point, team IPO deals may become structured in an economically more realistic manner.

A Miami Fish Story

Far from losing $30 million in '97, the Marlins made a hefty profit. So why did their owner destroy the team?

How could a baseball team in a major media market win the World Series and lose $34 million? The owner of the Florida Marlins, Wayne Huizenga, claims that is just what his team did last year. He hoped that his proclamation of penury would shame Broward and Miami-Dade counties into building him a new, retractable-roof ballpark. When it didn't, he went ballistic. Putatively to stop the team's financial bleeding, he conducted the most radical fire sale of players in baseball history, lowering the Marlins' payroll from $53 million in 1997 to $13 million in mid-July 1998 and leaving many baseball fans wondering exactly what Bud Selig was doing in the commissioner's office. At the same time, Huizenga tried to arrange a sale of the Marlins to his longstanding associate and team president, Don Smiley, for $169 million.

As the Marlins stumbled through the season, losing 108 games, Huizenga refused to provide any details about the team's 1997 finances. However, Smiley issued a confidential report on the team to prospective partners in his effort to complete the purchase. Smiley's "Private Placement Memorandum" reports a variety of financial information for 1997 as well as projections for 1998 and beyond. Based on these projections, payroll figures from MLB, and my own calculation of ticket sales (actual attendance multiplied by the average ticket price), the picture for 1997 looks like this:

Revenues (in millions)	Costs (in millions)
Ticket sales: $23.9	Payroll: $53.5
Broadcasting: $23.2	Team operations: $18.9
Concessions: $1.8	Player development: $5.1
Other: $10	Scouting: $5.1
Total: $58.9	Latin American operations: $0.6
	Stadium expenses: $5
	Total: $88.2

These numbers suggest an operating loss of $29.3 million. Quibbling over a few million dollars aside, what's the problem? Did Huizenga's Marlins really lose around $30 million? Of course not. Huizenga is employing an accounting trick as familiar to sports-franchise owners as Mark McGwire's home runs are to viewers of ESPN's *SportsCenter*.

Huizenga owns Pro Player Stadium and the team's cablecaster, Sportschannel Florida. Pro Player was built in 1987 and is amply stocked with all the revenue-generating accouterments of a modern sports facility. Yet there is no mention in the team's reported revenues of income from luxury boxes, even though Pro Player Stadium has 195 suites that rent for between $55,000 and $150,000 a year. Nor is there mention of income from club seats, although the stadium has 10,209 club seats selling for between $900 and $3,500 a year.

Bob Kramm, president of the stadium corporation, estimates that in 1997, an average of 65 luxury suites and 5,000 club seats per game were sold. Assuming that the average suite rented for $100,000 and the average club seat sold for $2,000, the gross revenue from these two sources would be $16.5 million. Huizenga attributes none of this revenue to the Marlins and all of it to his separate business entity, Pro Player Stadium.

Similarly, Huizenga sells naming rights to the stadium, worth, by conservative estimates, about $2 million a year. Since the stadium is shared with the NFL's Miami Dolphins (also owned by Huizenga), let us attribute half of this value to the Marlins. Parking for approximately 788,000 cars during the baseball season at $5 a car in 1997 brought an estimated $3.9 million. Sales of signs and advertising at the park and in the team program produced an estimated $6 million. (The Cleveland Indians' signage and ad sales at Jacobs Field yielded $8.8 million in 1997 on an average attendance of about 44,000.) Sales of merchandise brought in something like $3 million in net income. (The Indians' figure was $4.5 million.) All told, that's $13.9 million in ballpark revenue attributed to the stadium company, not to the Marlins.

Further, the revenue from concessions appears to be substantially understated. Fans spend an average of $10 on concessions, with about 40 percent of that going to the team. With total 1997 attendance of 2.4 million, the Marlins should have had net concessions income of about $9.4 million. Yet the team is credited with only $1.8 million, a discrepancy of $7.6 million. In all, $38 million in revenues are credited to the stadium rather than to the Marlins ($16.5 million from luxury and club seating, $7.6 million from concessions, $6 million from signage, $3.9 million from parking, $3 million from merchandise, and $1 million from naming rights).

Even though the Marlins receive only a small portion of stadium revenue, they still are charged $5 million to cover "stadium expenses." These expenses presumably are used to pay off Huizenga's debt service on the county industrial bonds that he assumed when he purchased the park. The yearly service on this debt has been estimated at around $5 million, but since the stadium is also the home facility of the Dolphins and the site of special events throughout the year, the Marlins' share of this debt should be no more than half.

Huizenga plays the same game with Sportschannel. According to Smiley's prospectus, an independent appraiser estimated that the Marlins' contract with the cable station is undervalued by more than $2.1 million a year. Herein lies a powerful reason why Huizenga wanted to sell his team to Don Smiley. Huizenga's deal with Smiley included an extension of the Sportschannel contract through 2024. Under that contract, the Marlins were to receive rights fees well below market value. While that didn't help the Marlins, it increased the station's value from an estimated $85 million to $125 million.

Unfortunately for Huizenga, the deal fell through when Smiley's fundraising efforts came up $50 million short. So in August, Huizenga began to talk to John Henry, a Boca Raton commodities trader and minority owner of the New York Yankees. They reportedly have reached a deal for $150 million plus other considerations worth, by my calculations, about $50 million. But all is not lost. Apparently, Henry acceded to a ten-year extension of the Sportschannel contract.

Adding the $2.1 million in lost cable revenues to the $38 million in lost stadium revenues brings the total earned by—but not credited to—the Marlins in 1997 to $40.1 million. But that's not the end of it. Smiley's prospectus suggests "other" revenues of $10 million. No details are provided. In 1997, the Marlins beat the Indians in the seventh game of the World Series. The Indians reported net post-season ticket revenues of $6.8 million. Presumably, this is part of the "other" $10 million for the Marlins.

Then there is roughly $2 million that comes from Major League Baseball Properties as licensing and sponsorship income. This leaves only $1.2 million for all "other" sources of revenue: roughly fifteen pre-season games at the Marlins' publicly financed spring-training ballpark; special functions; net income from the team store in Fort Lauderdale (since closed); and so on. Finally, in the "Private Placement Memorandum" Smiley reports that he intends to lower general and administrative expenses by $3 million a year, suggesting there is that much padding in the current budget.

In short, if the Marlins' financial statement is adjusted for related-party transactions and bloated costs, what appears to be a $29.3 million operating loss in 1997 becomes instead an operating profit of $13.8 million (adding $40.1 million in revenues and $3 million of bloated costs). Why else would Don Smiley, who as team president knows its financial predicament as well as anyone, have wanted to buy the team?

Why does Huizenga want to sell a profitable team? Perhaps the same reason he sold Blockbuster to Viacom: He can get a good price for it with a nice capital gain and he can control the terms of the deal to benefit his other holdings, including Sportschannel and the Pro Player Stadium corporation. Further, Huizenga has owned the Marlins since 1993 and by now has used up his player-amortization allowance (a tax benefit that allows an owner to set aside up to 50 percent of franchise value and then depreciate this sum, usually over five years). Thus, the substantial tax-shelter value of the club is exhausted.

Meanwhile, the team finished the 1998 season with a payroll of $13 million. Seven million dollars of this was from the insured contract of the pitcher Alex Fernandez, who was on the disabled list all season. As such, the insurance company was responsible for at least 70 percent of the $7 million, so the actual payroll disbursements for the 1998 Marlins were probably below $10 million.

With average attendance at Pro Player down from 29,555 in 1997 to 22,157 in 1998, ticket revenue fell by around $6 million. Auxiliary stadium income also took a proportional hit, but the player payroll was down by more than $40 million—more than offsetting lower stadium income. Thus, Huizenga's Marlins were even more profitable losing in 1998 than they were winning in 1997.

Take Stock in the Tribe

Back in June, before the Indians' IPO, I advised *Sports Business Journal* readers to buy Cleveland Indians stock only if they were incurable baseball fans with a lifelong dream to own a share of a franchise—and even then, to buy only one share and hang it above their mantelpiece.

The target price for a share prior to the IPO was $14–$16, yielding an implied franchise value in the neighborhood of $250 million. There was nothing wrong with that implied value. First, the Indians had gross revenues of $147 million in 1997. With a standard sales multiple of two, the implied franchise value would be more than $290 million. With long-term liabilities of around $40 million, the net value would exceed $250 million.

Second, the Texas Rangers had just sold for $250 million, and the Indians had to be worth as much as the Rangers. After all, the Indians sell out Jacobs Field every game and had done so dating back to the beginning of the 1996 season, whereas the Rangers sold approximately 70 percent of their seats in 1996 and 1997—and the Indians' average ticket price was $2 higher than the Rangers' in 1997. Both teams play in excellent new facilities, but Jacobs Field is smack in the middle of downtown while the Rangers play in the Dallas suburb of Arlington. Moreover, the Indians had a fully sold season-ticket base of 25,000, with a waiting list of 8,000; thirty-six luxury boxes sold through 2000, sixty-one through 2002, and twenty-four through 2003, with a waiting list of 100; and all its club seats committed through either 2000 or 2002.

The main problem with the Indians' IPO is that there was no way for the public shareholder to participate in the financial success of the Indians. The prospectus stated that no dividends were anticipated, and an exception precluded stockholders from sharing in the team's capital gains if the franchise were sold.

Jacobs has announced that he will change this exception at the next annual meeting in early 1999. This means that if someone bought the stock at the IPO price of $15 and Jacobs sells the team two years from now for, say, $300 million, the shareholder will be given the option of selling his or her stock for roughly $21.50 a share. So team financial performance is now linked to the value of the stock.

But the real plus is that the stock, which was issued at $15 a share, today (October 9, 1998) closed at 6^{1}/8. Since the public holds 28.64 percent of outstanding stock, the implied value of the entire Indians franchise is only $85.5 million. This, sports fans, is a steal.

Further, Jacobs and his business managers are pursuing a variety of investment-diversification alternatives, including facility and event management, complementary sports and entertainment businesses, and hotels. Such diversification activity spiked the stock price of the Florida Panthers up from $12 a share to well over $20 last year.

The final kicker is that when the Rangers were sold for $250 million, it was in the pre-McGwire–Sammy Sosa era. Baseball has catapulted itself back onto its cultural pedestal. Ratings and attendance are up, and word has it that CBS is itching to get a piece of the next national television contract. Look for a sizable increase in rights fees.

I didn't recommend the stock at $15 in June. It turns out that this was good advice at the time. Now, at 6¹/₈, it's a whole new ballgame.

*[**Note:** When the Indians were finally sold to Larry Dolan in November 1999, each share of public stock was worth approximately $22.50. Those who had heeded the advice of this and my previous article in Sports Business Journal on the Indians' public offering made a hefty return. With a batting average of 1,000, I decided to end my career as a stock analyst.]*

Has Milstein Lost His Mind?
Not Hardly

First the Browns sell for $530 million; now the Redskins sell for $800 million. What's next: the Cowboys for $1 billion?

Funny thing. Owners have been complaining for years that escalating player salaries are out of control. The NFL's 1995 expansion teams paid $140 million each for their franchises. Paul Allen in 1997 paid $200 million for the Seattle Seahawks. Then the Browns; now the Redskins. Let's see: Franchise prices increased from $140 million in 1995 to $800 million in 1999. That's almost a sixfold increase in four years, or an annual growth rate of 54.6 percent. Anybody remember the last time player salaries grew at that rate over a four-year period?

What's the connection between players' salaries and franchise values? Simple. Give the owners artificial constraints on how much they can pay the players and their profits soar (as do coaches' and executives' salaries). Soaring profits lead to soaring franchise values.

The NFL currently has a salary-cap system that limits team payrolls to 63 percent of the average team's defined gross revenues (DGR). DGR is not all football revenue by a long shot. It excludes revenue from stadium signage, concessions, luxury boxes, club seats, parking, and naming rights (except spillover). The NFL salary cap is not impermeable. There are some loopholes, one of the most popular being the practice of signing a star player for a non-guaranteed, long-term contract with a big signing bonus. The signing bonus is prorated over the life of the contract for cap-accounting purposes. Since the contract is not guaranteed, it can be nullified after the first year and then done all over again, with another large signing bonus the next year.

With the loopholes, the players have managed to get the average team payroll up to almost 70 percent of DGR in recent years. This converts to approximately 60 percent of all football revenues.

The new NBA cap at 55 percent of basketball-related income (BRI)—with a player escrow tax to reimburse the owners for any payments between 55 percent and 60.5 percent of BRI, along with an onerous 100 percent tax on individual owners for overspending if the excess tax does not cover the overage—comes very close to a hard cap. NBA profits were already healthy under the old system. With this new system, look for them to soar. And guess what will happen to franchise value? One indication is the publicly traded Boston Celtics' stock, whose share price has risen from around $10 to more than $17 (on January 15) since the agreement between the owners and players was reached on January 6.

Now, what about Howard Milstein, who is buying the Redskins: What does he get for his $800 million? In addition to the team, he gets the 1997 John Kent Cooke Stadium. And what a stadium! Among other features, it has 80,116 seats, 280 luxury boxes, 15,044 club seats, and six restaurants. The seats and suites alone could bring in close to $90 million–$100 million a year. Overall stadium revenue could easily reach $110 million–$120 million. Add to this another $75 million from the NFL central fund (national television, radio, and properties income) and a few million more for local radio and pre-season television, and the Redskins could be grossing in the $170 million–$200 million neighborhood. *[**Note:** Milstein's purchase was never consummated.]*

On the cost side, team salary caps should rise into the $50 million–$60 million range for the next couple of years and then head higher. Team travel, insurance, publicity, front office, stadium operations, and other expenses should not surpass another $35 million–$40 million. Let's say that total operating costs are $90 million–$100 million. Milstein, then, should be able to clear $70 million–$80 million or more annually.

That is, Milstein's yearly net financial return should approach 10 percent. But there's more. First, assuming he holds the team as either a partnership or subchapter S corporation, Milstein will benefit handsomely from the use of the team as a tax shelter. According to existing practice, the Internal Revenue Service allows a team's owner to presume that up to 50 percent of the team's purchase price ($400 million) is attributable to the inherited player contracts. This amount is then generally amortizable over the next five years, allowing Milstein to deduct $80 million from his taxable income each year and saving him some $32 million a year in tax payments to the federal government. (Some of this gain may be later recaptured.)

Second, Milstein will accrue the pleasures, perquisites, and power of owning an NFL team in our nation's capital. Milstein's ability to entertain the nation's leaders in his luxury suite can only help secure him legislative favors for his expanding business empire. Howard Milstein did not get where he is today by throwing money at frivolous investments.

So repeat after me: "Players' salaries are going through the stratosphere. Soon they will bring ruin to professional sports."

If the Redskins Are Worth $800 Million ...

What's it worth to own a ball club in Texas? As with all professional sports teams, it depends on the value of the expected stream of future economic benefits the club will generate. To an owner, these benefits include team profits; owner income from salary, consulting fees, and loan interest; enhanced profits in companies related to the sports team under the same owner; tax-sheltering opportunities; capital gains, perquisites; prestige; power; and plain old fun. Each of these items depends on how well the team is managed, the owner's other businesses, and the owner's personality, among other things. Thus, a sports franchise may be worth different amounts to different prospective buyers.

Further, because an owner can take some of his economic return in the form of improving the performance of his other business (e.g., a cable channel) or can choose to earn some of this return on capital in the form of interest income rather than profits, the reported bottom line is not always a meaningful guide to a team's worth. For this reason, analysts often use a multiple of team revenues (rather than reported profits) to estimate a team's value. The multiple that is chosen varies by sport and by team, depending on the expected future performance of each.

Two teams, each with $100 million in revenue, may have quite distinct market values. For instance, one team may be about to enter a new stadium with an expected revenue increase of $30 million per year and favorable lease terms or about to sell naming rights to an existing ballpark for $5 million a year. The team with higher expected revenue in the near future will have a higher value, despite having identical revenue today.

Similarly, if the two teams had the same revenue but were in different sports, they would likely have different values. One sport may have just signed a new multiyear television deal under which revenues per team might grow at 15 percent per year over an eight-year period. Using this year's revenue alone in this case will give an inadequate gauge of the team's future profitability. Or one sport may have recently entered into a long-term labor agreement, guaranteeing labor peace with restrictions on the growth of players' salaries, while the other is on the precipice of a protracted work stoppage. Here, too, the two sports' projected profitability will diverge substantially, and hence, so will team values.

Thus, franchises in baseball, football, basketball, and hockey tend to have different sales-price-to-revenue multiples, and teams within each sport also differ, all depending on expectations for the future. In what follows, I consider present and expected future revenues (and the sources of these revenues) to estimate the value of baseball's Rangers and Astros; football's Cowboys; basketball's Mavericks, Rockets, and Spurs; and hockey's Stars. In all cases, I am estimating the value of the team's assets, not its equity. That is, I am not considering the amount of team debt.

The Rangers

Consider what baseball did for George W. Bush. He contributed approximately $600,000 toward the purchase of the Texas Rangers for around $85 million in 1989. He owned roughly 1 percent of the team but was selected as its managing partner. With his father in the White House, George W. was actively involved in derailing the early 1990s efforts of Senator Howard Metzenbaum to lift baseball's antitrust exemption. He was also involved in developing the plans for a new baseball stadium in Arlington, a project that he acknowledged was in part a land play (*Fort Worth Star-Telegram*, October 27, 1990). For his efforts, George W. had a deal with his partners that his ownership share of the team would rise to nearly 10 percent.

Getting the new ballpark and control over the 270 acres of land around it entailed a lot of politicking. First, a referendum on contributing public money for the $191 million construction had to be approved by the voters. Second, state legislation was needed to grant Arlington bonding authority. Third, the Arlington Sports Facilities Development Authority (ASFDA) had to be created and endowed with eminent-domain power. With the latter accomplished in April 1991, the ASFDA condemned thirteen acres of land around the ballpark site and had the land appraised at $1.52 million. Then the ASFDA offered the owners only $817,220 for the land. The owners refused and sued. It was ultimately determined that the land was worth $4.98 million.

No matter. The condemned thirteen acres became part of the 41.6 acres owned by the Texas Rangers. In addition, the Rangers were granted control over 230 more acres around the park, along with an option to buy the land.

Politics also seems to be involved in the following oddity. The Rangers' 41.6 acres are appraised at $10.88 million, on which the team paid a 1998 property tax bill of $148,989. The team's new owner, Tom Hicks, however, has told the news media that of the $250 million he paid for the team in 1998, the value of the land earmarked for development was $50 million. Something is off.

The Bush ownership group, of course, got not only the land. It also got a loaded new ballpark in 1994 with a sweetheart lease. The ballpark in Arlington has 115 luxury suites rented on an annual basis, plus twenty-three more sold on a game basis, as well as 5,386 club seats, each selling for more than $1,200 per season. The Rangers contributed only $30 million of the $191 million construction cost, and much of that, along with the annual rent, comes back to the team in various schemes. According to *Forbes* magazine, the Rangers' venue revenues at the ballpark in Arlington equaled upward of $80 million in 1998, compared with venue expenses of only $5.5 million.

The same ballplayer produces more value in a newer ballpark. Team owners with new facilities thereby can make more competitive bids for the top players and enhance team quality. Improved on-field performance, along with the cachet and comforts of a new park, set the franchise on an upward cycle. The economic result in this case was that the Bush–Rose partnership group saw the franchise value more than triple, as George W. saw his share in equity multiply. His initial $600,000 became nearly $15 million, and his political star was rising all the while. Baseball, then, has treated George W. Bush very well, and if he gets to the White House, look for him to return a few favors.

Tom Hicks is also poised to experience growth in his $250 million investment. First, baseball's popularity has surged since he bought the team, thanks largely to the McGwire–Sosa heroics of the 1998 season. Baseball's new network contracts after next year should grow handsomely. Second, Hicks plans to sell multiyear stadium naming rights for some $100 million. Third, Hicks's annual rent is scheduled to fall by $1.5 million in a few years, after the stadium's bond obligations are met. Fourth, Hicks's packaging of the Rangers and Dallas Stars, together with his media entities, will at the very least generate more competition for his sports programming, appreciably raising his local media revenue. Fifth, if handled properly, the land development around the ballpark offers more than a modest return.

Exactly how much the Rangers are worth depends on the success and organizational structure in Hicks's forthcoming land-development and sports-media projects. It also depends on MLB's ability to find a way to deal with its financial and competitive imbalance problems without engendering another devastating work stoppage after the 2001 season. With team revenues around $120 million and rising, a current value in the neighborhood of $280 million–$300 million seems reasonable.

The Astros

Drayton McLane Jr. bought the Houston Astros in 1992 for a reported $115 million. Playing in the Astrodome in 1998, the team generated approximately $90 million in revenues. Even without a new stadium in the year 2000, applying the standard industry sale price to revenue multiple of two would suggest that the franchise today would be worth about $180 million.

If the construction schedule for the new ballpark at Union Station is met, the Astros will be playing in a HOK-designed state-of-the-art facility next year. The ballpark at Union Station will have a retractable roof and 42,000 seats and will cost at least $248 million to build (68 percent of which is coming from public coffers). There will be higher attendance at higher ticket prices, more luxury and club seats, more signage, more concessions and merchandising income, naming-rights revenue, and so on. Not only will the Astros reap all revenues generated at the new downtown stadium, but their estimated venue costs will decrease from $8 million to $7 million a year. Look for the new park to increase team revenues by $25 million–$30 million a year and for franchise value to jump to $250 million or higher. Thus, the value of McLane's investment will have more than doubled in less than ten years—not as good as George W., but a gusher all the same.

The Cowboys

There is no question that the Cowboys have been the premier team in the NFL during the 1990s. The team has led the league in revenues, with the Washington Redskins at a close second over the past two years. According to the Cowboys' vice president of marketing, George Hays, "If the Washington Redskins can sell for $800 million, then the Dallas Cowboys are worth over a billion. We are a helluva lot more profitable than they are." There may be some hyperbole mixed in with Hays's hubris, but he's not far off.

Consider the following: Texas Stadium has approximately 400 sold-out luxury suites. No other stadium in professional sports has more than 212 suites. Some of the suites at Texas Stadium sell for as much as $1.5 million over the term of the lease, the Cowboys' owner, Jerry Jones, gets all that revenue. Indeed, except for parking, Jones's master lease gives him all the revenue generated at the stadium, with 8 percent going back to the city of Irving as rent.

Jones also successfully challenged the NFL's attempt to monopolize company sponsorships in certain categories. League rules prohibit teams from having local deals with companies that compete with the NFL's national sponsors. Nonetheless, Jones signed deals with Pepsi, American Express, and Nike, despite NFL deals with Coke, Visa, and other apparel manufacturers. The Pepsi deal alone is worth a reported $40 million. Jones claimed that his local deals were not between the team and the companies but between the stadium and the companies and hence did not violate NFL policy. He ultimately prevailed.

Now Jones and the city of Irving are in discussions to finance a $200 million expansion and renovation of Texas Stadium, including an increase in seating capacity to more than 100,000, a new grass field, and a retractable roof.

Also working for Jones are the NFL's economics of labor peace and its abundance of network television revenues. Commencing with the 1998 season and going through 2005, the NFL's new network television contracts will bring in an average of $2.2 billion a year (with thirty teams, that's more than $73 million per team annually). The four-year deal that ended with the 1997 season was less than half this size.

As NFL revenues from the media and new stadiums skyrocket, labor costs are controlled by the salary cap set at 63 percent of defined gross revenues. a term of art that excludes much of the revenue generated at the stadium by premium seating and the like. Thus, labor costs don't grow as rapidly as revenues, and profits grow disproportionately. Even better, the current collective-bargaining agreement goes through 2003 and, judging by past experience, is likely to be extended before it terminates.

Combine this happy state of affairs with the extensive revenue sharing among the NFL owners and the resulting competitive balance on the field, NFL team values are doing a good imitation of the loftiest Internet stocks. If the league could just find some way to stop being sued every other week, it might be officially claimed an investment nirvana.

So would the Cowboys really sell for $1 billion? I doubt it. One important advantage that the Redskins have is Washington, D.C. The owner of the Redskins, inviting members of Congress and denizens of the White House to his stadium suite, automatically becomes a power player in the nation's capital. That's what economists call psychic income and what psychologists call ego gratification. There's also the opportunity to influence legislation that may benefit one's other investments.

But maybe Jones could get $900 million for the team. Not too shabby, considering that he bought the franchise in 1989 for $150 million.

The Mavericks

If the NBA used the same system as British soccer, where the top teams in a lower league rise to the next-highest league the following year and the bottom teams in the higher league fall to the next-lowest league, then the Mavericks would be playing Division II NCAA basketball by now. Their woeful on-court performance notwithstanding, the value of the Mavericks increased from $13.3 million in 1979, when they entered the NBA as an expansion team, to $125 million in May 1996, when they were purchased by a group led by Ross Perot Jr. Perot's group includes Roger Staubach, Fred Couples, and Michael Johnson.

Perot and his investors have three important factors working for them. First, the team is slated to be playing in a new arena in the West End Historic District north of downtown Dallas. The $300 million-plus arena is scheduled to open for the 2000–2001 season. The Mavericks will share the arena with Hicks's NHL Stars, and together the teams will contribute around $175 million to the construction cost. It seems that this expense will pretty much be covered, however, by the thirty-year naming-rights deal for $195 million that the teams signed with American Airlines.

The new 20,000 seat arena will contain 100 luxury suites and 2,500 club seats, compared with zero suites and zero club seats in Reunion Arena. Perot also plans to develop the surrounding land to include hotels, office space, and residential and retail properties. The arena should boost team revenues by at least 20 percent.

Second, the NBA signed a new national television deal with NBC and TNT commencing with the 1998–99 season. The guaranteed average revenue per team is $22.8 million annually, compared with $9.5 million in the previous deal.

Third, in January 1999, the NBA owners reached a collective-bargaining settlement with the players after a protracted lockout. Not only does the agreement guarantee seven years of labor peace, but it establishes a much firmer salary cap at 55–57 percent of defined basketball revenue. Thus, as NBA revenues rise at their projected 12 percent per year over the next seven years and players' salaries grow at the same rate or a bit slower, NBA profits are sure to increase rapidly. This is because the owners' other costs, such as air travel, hotels, equipment, front-office personnel, and so on, will likely rise at the economy's rate of inflation (2–3 percent per year).

And maybe, just maybe, one of these years the Mavericks will be able to convert their early draft picks into a winning team. Look for the Mavericks to be worth $200 million or more in their new arena.

The Rockets

Les Alexander bought this NBA franchise in 1993 for a reported $85 million. With a modest payroll, he has been fortunate to field a very competitive team and consistently achieve sell-out crowds. Not a bad accomplishment, given that the top ticket prices at Compaq Center run $575 per game.

But, guess what: Alexander wants a new arena, and Houston's Mayor Lee Brown wants to oblige him. The Compaq Center was built in 1975 and has only twenty luxury boxes, no club seats, and a modest capacity of 16,285. The Rockets' goal is to begin playing in a new arena after its lease at Compaq Center expires in 2003. The first step is to get a referendum on the ballot for the Harris County voters.

Meanwhile, the value of Alexander's franchise will benefit from the new NBA television and labor deals, as well as from the ascendance of the WNBA's Houston Comets. The Rockets' revenues run around $80 million a year and, with basketball's new network contract and favorable labor agreement, the NBA's sale-price-to-revenue ratio averages about 2.5. The team should be worth some $200 million, and rising if Harris County voters cooperate.

The Spurs

Peter Holt, along with twenty-one partners, bought the team in March 1993 for $75 million from Red McCombs. McCombs had bought the team four years earlier for $47 million. The Spurs play in the 1993 Alamodome with only thirty-two luxury suites and 3,172 club seats and where capacity can rise to 34,215. The team keeps most of the arena revenue and pays rent equal to 6 percent of gate receipts.

Holt wants a new basketball-only arena. So far, his efforts to create a special tax-increment financing district or to call a referendum on a sales-tax increase to finance the arena have been rebuffed.

Holt claimed that his team lost $1.9 million in the 1997–98 season to support his assertion that the team needs a new facility. Take the claim with a cube of salt. First, two of Holt's partners are ARAMARK and Clear Channel Communications. ARAMARK also happens to be the concessionaire and caterer at the Alamodome, and Clear Channel Communications (owned by Red McCombs) owns the Spurs' radio broadcaster, WOAI-AM. WOAI can offer below-market rights fees to the Spurs to lower the team's income and then make other arrangements to compensate Holt. Similarly, ARAMARK can claim a larger share of concessions sales, thereby reducing team income. Another partner is a bank holding company, and similar deals can be cut with the team's debt. Second, Holt and his partners may receive healthy compensation for advising management, serving on the board, or capitalizing team operations with their loans rather than paid-in capital. Third, the $13.3 million average annual increase in the NBA's per-team national-television revenue kicked in for the 1998–99 season, and the new labor agreement will provide a further fillip to the team's bottom line. But whatever the Spurs' net income may be, Holt and his partners would always like it to be larger.

Without the new arena, the Spurs' revenues should be around $70 million and rising. The team's value today—maybe $175 million.

The Stars

The Stars are owned by Tom Hicks and are part of the new arena company with the Mavericks. If it sounds like the Stars might be well connected politically, it should. A few months after securing the pledge of $125 million of taxpayer money toward the new arena, Tom Hicks announced that he was hiring City Manager John Ware, with whom he had just negotiated the arena financing deal. And according to the *Dallas Morning News*, Dallas Mayor Ron Kirk stood to earn at least $500,000 from stock options in one of Hicks's companies.

Hicks bought the Stars in 1995 for $85 million. *Forbes* estimates that the team was worth $118 million at the end of 1998. But the synergies with Hicks's emerging sports and media empire and the $300 million new American Airlines arena will lift the team's value considerably above this level.

One important hurdle for the Stars will be the resolution of the NHL's economic woes. The league's diminutive national television package and absence of revenue sharing among the teams have engendered financial difficulties for several small-market teams. Until these problems are resolved at the league level, it is unlikely that the Stars' value will exceed $160 million.

As with all sports franchises and their owners, the Stars' value to Hicks goes beyond what the team earns on the bottom line. The team helps promote Hicks's other business interests, and it brings him pleasure, perquisites, tax writeoffs, greater political influence, and, likely, attractive capital gains.

The Texas wells may be drying up, but its playing fields are still fertile.

The NFL's New Math

Is a new NFL franchise in Houston worth $700 million, or has Robert McNair lost his mind? Recall that the two NFL expansion franchises in 1995 sold for the bargain-basement price of $140 million each. Last year, however, the born-again Cleveland Browns sold for $530 million, and five months ago, the Washington Redskins sold for $805 million. So if the NFL is experiencing an asset bubble, McNair is not the only one to fall for it.

When Daniel Snyder bought the Redskins for $805 million in May, the price included the assumption of $160 million of debt on the team's new stadium. Thus, the team itself cost $645 million. Moreover, the Redskins play in the country's fifth-largest media market, which also happens to be the nation's capital, bringing valuable political connections to the team's owner.

Houston, in contrast, is the tenth-largest media market, and McNair is committing an additional $115 million to help build the team's $310 million new ballpark (the balance of $195 million coming from public funds). Thus, McNair's total bill will be around $815 million (actually somewhat less in present value terms, since his payments are spread out over five years). Further, in contrast to Snyder, who acquired an existing franchise, McNair will have to invest another $30 million–$40 million in startup costs to build his operation, and his team will not begin playing and earning revenue until 2002.

On the positive side, McNair will have a new, state-of-the-art facility with 110 luxury suites, 7,700 club seats, and a 75,000 capacity. These are impressive revenue-generating credentials, but once again, they don't measure up to the Redskins' 280 luxury suites and 80,116 seats. McNair, however, hopes to be able to raise about $75 million–$100 million from the sale of permanent seat licenses, reducing substantially his net outlays for stadium construction.

Once the new Houston franchise begins to play, its annual income statement should include on the revenue side $90 million–$100 million in stadium-related revenues (regular gate, luxury and club premiums, signage, concessions, parking, theme activities, merchandising, sponsorships) and $75 million in NFL central-fund distributions (from national television, radio, and properties income). On the cost side, it should include player payroll costs in the neighborhood of $80 million–$90 million and front office–administrative–team costs of another $40 million–$45 million. Thus, the team could generate some $30 million–$50 million a year in net operating income.

Then there's the curious tax-shelter benefit of owning a professional sports franchise. Assuming McNair holds the team as a partnership or subchapter S corporation, the IRS will allow him to presume that up to 50 percent of the team's purchase price ($350 million) is attributable to the player contracts he will eventually sign. This amount is generally amortizable over five years, allowing McNair to add $70 million annually to the team's costs before calculating its tax liability. (Of course, McNair will also be allowed to expense players' salaries.) Then McNair can transfer any reported losses from the team to reduce his personal income-tax liability, potentially saving him some $28 million a year for five years. (Part of this is later recaptured, unless the capital-gains tax is abolished by 2008.) On top of this, McNair will benefit from the pleasures, perquisites, and power that accrue to the elite owners of NFL teams.

The downside risk appears to be small. NFL teams do not go bankrupt. Labor relations in the league appear cooperative and peaceful. The largest question seems to be what will happen to the national television contracts after 2006. Although high, the NFL's TV ratings are dipping, and competition over the airwaves is ever increasing.

Some are asking whether the NFL has not let short-term greed blind it to the importance of having a team in Los Angeles. The league passed up what apparently was a $550 million offer from Michael Ovitz to bring the expansion team to the country's second-largest media market. Did the NFL owners really forsake Los Angeles for $150 million? Not likely, although the money was hardly irrelevant. The bigger problem with Los Angeles is that the public support for a new stadium was not yet in place.

Besides, it is a good bet that the NFL will find a way to have a team in Los Angeles by the time the new Houston franchise begins to play, or shortly thereafter. It won't be an expansion franchise, but it may be the Arizona Cardinals, the Oakland Raiders, or the Indianapolis Colts. If Ovitz offered the owner of any of these economically less fortunate teams $550 million, he would probably have a deal. The NFL could then vote to allow Ovitz to move the team.

So the deal makes sense after all. Perhaps McNair will get a lower financial return than he would on another investment, but he will gain significant potential for promoting his other businesses and appreciable consumption value from ownership. The key to understanding the value of football franchises is twofold: the sport's immense popularity and the NFL's power as a monopoly to restrict output and raise the price of its teams.

Don't Cry for Woody

Robert Wood (Woody) Johnson IV, heir to the Johnson and Johnson fortune, has purchased the New York Jets for $635 million. Some think Woody Johnson will need more than Band-Aids this time to stanch his bleeding checkbook.

Although the Jets' price is $170 million below last year's sale price for the Washington Redskins and $65 million below the price of the new NFL Houston franchise, each of these franchises came with a new stadium. The Jets' sale price is the highest for a U.S. sports team without a facility.

Not only do the Jets not have a new facility, but they are subordinate tenants at an old facility: Giants Stadium, built in 1976. Their lease requires the Jets to remain at the Meadowlands until 2008, where the Jets pay an abnormally high rent for the NFL of 15 percent of gross ticket receipts and receive a low share of stadium revenues (e.g., only 30 percent of non-scoreboard signage and 25 percent of parking).

For the 1999–2000 NFL year, the Jets' team revenue is projected to be about $105 million, with profits of $12 million. The *New York Times* (January 12, 2000) reported that various sports-finance mavens estimated the Jets to be worth no more than $250 million. *Forbes* magazine's estimate was a bit more generous, at $363 million. With these numbers, Woody Johnson minimally will need some large Ace bandages to salvage his $635 million investment—and I haven't even mentioned Bill Parcells yet.

Fortunately for Johnson, however, an asset is worth what it sells for in the market. At least one other potential investor was also willing to pay more than $600 million for the team. Why?

First, even if the Jets' reported profits this year are only $12 million, the return to ownership is likely much higher. That is, the $12 million may hide salary and consulting or interest payments to members of the owner's family. It may also cover up transactions between the team and other entities held by ownership. More important, whatever profits currently are, they are sure to grow in the coming years. The national television contract grows at about $10 million per team annually through 2006, and only $6.3 million of this goes to the players. This locks in a yearly profit growth of nearly $4 million.

Second, in all likelihood, the Jets will be playing in a new stadium in eight years. At today's prices, a new stadium could add $100 million or more yearly to the Jets' revenue stream. For instance, with 225 luxury suites at $250,000 each ($56.3 million), 18,000 club seats at $3,500 a piece ($63 million), naming rights of $10 million a year, and tens of millions more from sponsorships, signage, and concessions, annual stadium revenues at a new facility in the

New York City area could reach more than $150 million. Depending on the public–private split in financing this facility, the team could find a healthy chunk of these new revenues appearing on its bottom line.

Third, Johnson will get an impressive tax break from his purchase. Present IRS practice allows team owners to attribute half the franchise's purchase price to the value of the team's player contracts, then to amortize this sum over five years. Thus, Johnson will be able to reduce his taxable income by $63.5 million for the each of the next five years. At the top federal tax rate of 42.5 percent (including the FICA obligation), this deduction is worth $27 million annually. (Of course, some of this benefit is potentially recaptured when Johnson sells the team. unless the capital-gains tax has been abolished by then or he passes the team on with his estate.)

Fourth, Johnson will benefit from all the pleasures and perquisites of owning an NFL franchise. There are only thirty-two such owners in the world, and he will be one of two in the world's most glamorous city.

So put the Band-Aids away. There are some risks here for Woody Johnson, but there are also some very significant rewards down the road.

Ticket Prices and Players' Salaries: The Real Story

How many times have we heard owners say that they'll be raising ticket prices because of escalating player salaries? These ownership pleadings are then dutifully regurgitated by much of the local media and assimilated by fans as an economic truism.

Actually, this purported relationship is little more than folklore. To be sure, historically rising ticket prices tend to accompany increasing payrolls. But just because two things move up together, it doesn't mean that one causes the other to go up.

One of my favorite apocryphal stories from teaching introductory economics relates the tale of a man who lives next to the railroad tracks. Every morning his alarm wakes him up at 8 o'clock and, after splashing his face with water, he opens his bedroom window. Within minutes, a train comes roaring by. Does the act of opening the window cause the train to pass? Sign up for Economics 100 to find out.

Suppose you own a local sports team and you want to maximize the return on your massive investment. How high should you set your ticket prices?

The answer is simple. You set your ticket prices to maximize the total revenue from gate, plus net concessions sales, parking, and signage at the stadium. This maximizing price is determined by the fans' demand to watch your team play live games in person.

Consider an example: Suppose that the team's financial officer presents the following estimates for ticket demand. At an average ticket price of $9, the team will sell 42,000 seats a game, generating $378,000 in gate revenue. At an average price of $10, the team will sell 40,000 seats a game, generating $400,000. At $11, it will sell 35,000 and take in $385,000. And at $12, it will sell 30,000 seats and take in $360,000. Ignoring concessions, parking, and signage revenue for simplification, the team will maximize its revenues (and stadium profits, because the extra cost of having an additional fan in the stadium is close to zero) when it charges an average ticket price of $10. This result is entirely dependent on the structure of fans' demand for tickets.

Fans' demand, in turn, is determined by the success of the team and its individual players, by the facility where the team plays, by the efficacy of the team's public relations in the community, by the economic conditions in the area, by the intensity of the local sports culture, and by the weather, among other factors. It does not depend on whether the team pays its shortstop $3 million or $5 million a year.

Hence, based on perceptions of fan demand, the profit-maximizing owner will set the team's ticket prices. If the owner re-signs a star player for a higher salary and then raises the team's ticket prices to recoup the extra salary expenses, then the owner will no longer be maximizing the team's stadium revenues and profits. In the earlier example, if the owner raised the team's average ticket price from $10 to $11 because he is paying his shortstop an extra $2 million, stadium gate revenues would fall by $15,000 a game; concessions, parking, and signage revenue would also decline. That is, by setting ticket prices in response to player salaries instead of fan demand, the owner is shooting himself in his foot.

There is one exception to this analysis. If higher salaries also mean better players or players with more charisma on the team, then fan demand may go up along with team payroll. Or if the owner convinces the media that he must raise prices to cover the higher salaries, and the media then convinces the fans (whether or not the team is better), then the fans' willingness to pay higher ticket prices (fans' demand) may increase. In this case, the fan can thank the local sports reporter and not the star player for the more expensive seats. Ticket prices and player salaries, then, may be indirectly related.

Higher ticket prices in the 1990s, however, have had more to do with the gentrification of stadiums than the increasing popularity of the sports themselves. On average, new facilities built in the past decade have been financed with approximately two-thirds of the money coming from public coffers. The public money, in turn, generally comes from sales taxes or lottery funds— revenue sources that disproportionately burden lower-income groups. Since the incremental benefits from the new facilities go mostly to the high-income and corporate fans (not to mention to the teams' owners and players), it makes more sense to finance construction out of ticket (user) taxes or personal seat licenses than out of general sales levies.

With monopoly sports leagues, fans will pay one way or the other. Blaming the players makes little sense.

Yes, It's about Money

Alex Rodriguez, the twenty-five-year-old all-star shortstop, this week signed a contract with the Texas Rangers that will make him the highest-paid player in the history of sports. The contract—for $252 million over ten years—has drawn harsh criticism as an example of the runaway spending that is ruining the sport.

Yes, the deal is extravagant. Two years ago, Tom Hicks, the Rangers' owner, bought the team, along with the lease on the stadium near Dallas and options on about 200 acres of surrounding land, for $250 million. Is Rodriguez worth more than the team? Crazy as it seems, he almost is.

Hicks is a crafty businessman. The contract itself isn't quite as high as it sounds: It includes long-term deferred money that reduces its net present value to $180 million. But more fundamentally, Hicks is betting that Rodriguez will help fill his 49,000-seat stadium, allowing him to raise ticket prices, sell more concessions, increase parking revenue, and so on.

And there's a kicker. Hicks wants to sell the right to name the ballpark, and he is developing the surrounding acreage. If Rodriguez brings a championship, Hicks's payoff comes in the form of tens, if not hundreds, of millions of additional dollars in real-estate and advertising value.

Like any good capitalist, Hicks is attempting to maximize his profits. He expects that Rodriguez alone will produce well over $25 million a year in value for all his investments. There are no guarantees, of course. Should Rodriguez be injured, his guaranteed contract will leave Hicks hurting. And should Rodriguez stay healthy, Hicks still needs to find some way to strengthen a pitching staff that had one of the worst earned-run averages in the American League last year. Can Rodriguez pitch, too?

While Hicks's deal with Rodriguez might make sense for the Rangers, it may not make sense for Major League Baseball. The imbalances in the revenues of baseball's haves and have-nots have grown acute over the past decade. The top- and bottom-earning teams were $30 million apart in 1989; in 1999, the spread was more than $160 million. Since 1995, out of 189 post-season games, only three have been won by teams with payrolls in the bottom half.

Unlike typical businesses, baseball needs balanced competition. That is not to say that all teams should be equal in their resources and their ability to win games. The most successful league would have the big cities' teams win most often because they lift the television ratings the most.

But it's not healthy for the sport to be dominated by the richest teams. When the biggest city's team wins the championship four of five years and begins to play its crosstown rival for the championship, as happened in the Subway Series, inequality has gone too far. Too many Americans, feeling left out, will yawn and turn away.

New York Times, December 13, 2000

The NFL's Economic Success

America's infatuation with the NFL's product is about to be stoked again by a new season. The league's successful economic model, which includes extensive revenue sharing, protracted labor peace, and effective marketing, is a major factor behind the sport's popularity.

During the off-season, the public learned more about the league's auspicious economic fortunes. As a result of Al Davis's failed suit against the NFL, documents summarizing the teams' financial performance became public. The documents showed that in 1999 only one of the league's thirty-one teams did not have an operating profit. Of the thirty teams that were profitable, twenty-one earned more than $5 million. The single unprofitable team was the New Orleans Saints.

No one should feel sorry for Tom Benson, the Saints' majority owner. The team earned operating profits of $12.4 million, $7.2 million, $2.1 million, and $15.3 million in 1995, 1996, 1997, and 1998, respectively. In 1999, the team lost $849,000, and even that number is suspect. Oddly, the Saints reported $18.9 million in "team expenses" (travel, conditioning, staff, etc.), more than $8.5 million above the league average in this expense category and $13.8 million above the most frugal team (the Titans).

Why did the Saints spend so much more? Not infrequently, the owner or his family benefit handsomely from free jet service, luxury hotel suites, and lavish entertaining. The released documents provided only category summaries, so we do not know whether part of the reported operating costs went into Benson's pocket via executive salary or consulting fees or he was otherwise favored via related party transactions.

Still more to the point, does anyone believe that NFL teams should be guaranteed a profit no matter how poorly they perform on the field and no matter how inadequately they conduct community relations? Benson has been grumbling about the Superdome for years, and his team has provided little excitement. In 1999, the team went 3 and 13, finishing last in their division. The previous three seasons, the Saints were 15 and 33, and the team had not appeared in the post-season since 1992. In that year, the Saints snuck in as a wild-card team and lost their only game. By my book, Benson should be counting his blessings that his team was profitable during 1995–98.

As for the other thirty teams, the NFL argued that the court documents were misleading. The league stated that the documents reflected only operating profits, thereby excluding service cost on stadium or franchise debt, which could turn an operating profit into a book loss. Dean Bonham picked up the

NFL's claim and extended it, alleging that the documents also did not include players' signing bonuses.

Actually, the appropriate figure is operating profit, or EBITDA (earnings before interest, taxes, depreciation, and amortization). There is no reason that a team's economic performance should be affected by whether an owner, for instance, borrowed money to buy his team (occasioning interest costs) or used his own capital. That is why the EBITDA concept is used. And Bonham is just wrong. Players' signing bonuses are amortized over the life of the contract, as they should be.

In fact, the operating profit understates the economic return from owning an NFL team. First, when an individual buys a franchise, he is allowed to amortize the value of the player contracts, up to (a presumed) 50 percent of the purchase price of the team. This is a valuable tax shelter. Second, as with the Saints, it is possible that some returns to ownership are being hidden by the summary nature of the financial documents. For instance, one team spent as little as $4.7 million on general and administrative expenses while another team spent as much as $18.3 million. We know from documents in the 1992 McNeil case that one owner paid himself a salary of $7 million, and several others paid themselves more than $1 million. Such payments to ownership probably account for some of the discrepancy in the general and administrative expenditures reported for 1999.

Third, owners get substantial intangible returns in the form of business and political connections, related-party–transaction benefits, perquisites, ego gratification, enhanced influence, and fun. Fourth, owners have also realized appreciable capital gains when they have sold their teams.

Indeed, it is both the operating profits and the large intangible returns that account for the fantastic spurt in NFL franchise prices over the past several years. In 1997, the Seahawks sold for $200 million, and in 1998, the Vikings sold for $246 million. In 1999, the Redskins sold for $800 million (including stadium), while in 2000, the Ravens sold for $600 million and the Jets sold for $635 million. Expansion-team prices rose from $140 million in 1993 to $476 million in 1998 and $700 million in 1999. These escalating franchises prices can be explained only by increasing economic returns to ownership.

There is no need for the NFL to deny its economic success. Nothing is wrong with a business earning a profit. The question is whether the rate of return on investment is excessive, which seems unlikely at today's franchise prices.

Gene Upshaw and the NFL Players' Association will do their best to keep the rate of return in check. The league and the union are currently negotiating an extension (through 2007) of the present collective-bargaining agreement, which expires after the 2002 season. The expectation is that the cap will rise modestly above its 2001 level of 63 percent of defined gross revenue.

When the extension is finalized, the NFL will be on track to achieve eighteen consecutive seasons without a work stoppage. Are you listening Bud Selig and Don Fehr?

How Much Are the Red Sox Worth?

Last month, the first round of bids came in from would-be owners of the Boston Red Sox. According to Major League Baseball's Blue Ribbon Economic Report, between 1995 and 1999 the Red Sox had operating losses totaling $5.43 million. The team indicates that 2000 and 2001 have been basically break-even years. So why are there at least six ownership groups willing to pay more than $300 million for 53 percent of this team?

If 53 percent of the team finally sells, say, for $340 million, it would imply an equity value of $642 million for the whole franchise, including an 80 percent stake in New England Sports Network (NESN). If we assume that an 80 percent stake in NESN is worth $110 million, the implied value of the team itself becomes $532 million. Until now, the highest price paid for an MLB franchise was $323 million for the Cleveland Indians in 1999.

Moreover, back in 1999 the U.S. economy and the stock market were still booming, and baseball was neither on the precipice of another possible work stoppage nor on the verge of increasing its revenue sharing from high- to low-income teams. It is estimated that in 2000, the Red Sox contributed a net amount of $12 million to MLB's poor franchises. This year, that number will likely approach $15 million. MLB's owners are talking about increasing the tax on net local revenue from 20 percent to 40 percent or more, and the Sox's share would rise accordingly.

So, what is going on here? First, the $15 million in net revenue sharing essentially comes directly off of the Sox's bottom line. Without the sharing, zero operating profits become $15 million profits. Of course, the hope is that the sharing leads to greater competitive balance on the field, which in turn should strengthened the industry in the long run.

Second, zero operating profits do not mean that there is no return to ownership. Owners may take their returns in a number of forms: benefits to related businesses (such as NESN or a concessions company); salaries, consulting fees, or perquisites to owners or members of their family; tax benefits; greater access to politicians and executives of other companies; potential capital gains upon sale of the team; or, finally, prestige, ego gratification, and fun.

Third, the Red Sox are one of professional sports' leading franchises. It is a storied team playing in a wonderful ballpark. It is a team that, despite the long absence of post-season success (need I mention no World Series crowns since 1918?), charges the game's highest ticket prices (an average of $36.08 in 2001, a full $7.18 above the Yankees' average and nearly double the MLB average of $18.86) and still sells out every game. What's more, the ticket price includes no ticket tax, as it does in the vast majority of cases (i.e., the Sox do not have to share ticket revenue with the city). All this is true, despite the fact that the team was languishing in second place when the first round of bids came in on August 15.

Fourth, despite the absence of a new facility, the Sox's revenues have been growing by leaps and bounds—from $117 million in 1999 to an estimated $170 million this year—and revenues could have risen by another $5 million–$10 million if the team had gone to the post-season. (As I write, the past subjunctive seems appropriate.) When the team gets a new stadium or does an overhaul on Fenway, these revenues should rise by another $30 million–$50 million.

Because reported profits of closely held private businesses can be manipulated with ease, and because a significant part of the return to owning a baseball team is indirect or intangible, it is a common practice in the industry to estimate a franchise's asset value by using a revenue multiple (the ratio of team value to team revenues). For the seven team sales since 1998, the estimated revenue multiples have varied between 1.5 and 2.7. The higher multiples are for teams whose revenues are expected to grow the fastest. Thus, the Cincinnati Reds sold for $183 million, at a 2.7 revenue multiple, in 1999, largely because the team will begin playing in a new stadium in 2003.

Applying this higher multiple of 2.7 to the Red Sox's roughly $170 million in revenues in 2001 yields an asset value of $459 million. Add $110 million for 80 percent of NESN and you get a team value of $569 million. Assuming the Sox have no long-term debt, this is still $73 million below the implied value of a $340 million offer for 53 percent of the team.

While the intangible benefits of owning a franchise in Boston must exceed those of owning one in Cincinnati (justifying a higher multiple), the Red Sox bidders also face the additional risks of a work stoppage, greater revenue sharing, various multiyear contractual liabilities, and an uncertain stadium plan. Thus, if the bidding for the Yawkey share (the portion of the Red Sox up for sale) rises substantially above $340 million, there is a good chance that youthful exuberance, hubris, and the greater fool theory are at work.

MLB in the Aftermath of September 11

First things first. Baseball and football fans should be proud and appreciative of the exemplary behavior of executives, owners, and players in the NFL and MLB in response to the ugly and devastating acts of terrorism on September 11, 2001. The cancellation of games, the extensive relief efforts of the players and coaches, the large donations (including at least $5 million each from MLB, the NFL, the MLBPA, and the NFLPA, and a special contribution of one day's salary from the entire New York Mets team valued at $450,000), the sensitive and compassionate statements, and the pre-game ceremonies honoring the victims, among other actions, deserve our plaudits and gratitude.

And the fans should be proud of themselves. A Boston fan at Fenway holding up an "I Love New York" banner is the ultimate reminder that we are all in this together.

Peter Gammons and others have suggested that, given the massive destruction and the ongoing struggle against terrorism, MLB's owners and players should set aside collective bargaining and extend the existing agreement for another year. Gammons argued that it would be unseemly to haggle over dollars at this time and that the future financial structure of the game should not be decided at a time of such economic uncertainty. He is certainly right about the first point. However, if President Bush is correct that the fight against terrorism will last for years, it is unclear whether there will be more economic certainty in 2002.

Indeed, perhaps this is precisely the time to seek a new collective-bargaining agreement for baseball, when both sides are feeling humbled and cooperative. Might not the owners in the midst of our national crisis be more willing to compromise among themselves, and might not the owners and players be more flexible at the bargaining table?

One of the issues at the bargaining table will be baseball's system of revenue sharing. It is commonly assumed that the high-revenue teams are the principal obstacles to increasing the tax on net local revenue substantially above the current 20 percent level. In this context, it is interesting to contemplate the plans for the Yankees/Nets' new regional sports channel, YES.

According to recent press reports, YES and the Yankees have agreed to a thirty-year deal that will pay the Yankees an annual rights fee of approximately $55 million—almost identical to the fee paid this year to the Yankees by MSG. The *Sports Business Journal* reporter Andy Bernstein wrote that the "YES Network rights fee agreement was recently approved by Major League Baseball"

(September 17–23, 2001, 4). That is, MLB was accepting the $55 million figure as representing fair market value. Yet it is well known that MSG had offered to pay considerably above this sum—perhaps as much as $100 million annually.

MLB's present revenue-sharing plan assesses a tax on a team's net local revenue. When the team owner also owns a business with which the team does business, it is possible for the related business (e.g., a TV or radio station or a concessions company) to underpay the team for the services or goods it is buying. The owner takes the revenue in one pocket instead of the other. Anticipating this, MLB has an agreement that in such cases the fair market value of the contract will be estimated and applied.

So assuming that the news reports are correct, the first question is: Why are the Yankees willing to accept such a substantial underpayment for their television rights? The apparent answer is that this underpayment immediately makes YES a highly profitable company. Based on the reported minority share values, YES has a market value of $850 million, despite the fact that it currently owns no equipment, has no studio, and is not carried on any cable system in the New York metropolitan area. George Steinbrenner retains a large share of ownership in YES, and he walks home with hundreds of millions of cash from his YES investment partners. Better still, Steinbrenner does not have to subject YES income or profits to MLB's revenue-sharing system.

The second question is: Why is MLB willing to allow the Yankees to underestimate the market value of their television rights by tens of millions of dollars a year? One plausible answer is that it is the price that MLB must pay to gain Steinbrenner's support for a more extensive revenue-sharing system and Steinbrenner's pledge not to bring a legal suit against MLB if revenue sharing is passed above his vote.

A similar set of circumstances is at play with the valuation of the Yawkey 53.5 percent share of the Red Sox. The Sox own 80 percent of NESN. The higher the rights fees paid by NESN, the better the Sox's cash flow, the higher the revenue-sharing levy on the team, and the lower the value of NESN. The lower the rights fees, the worse the team's cash flow, the lower its revenue-sharing levy, and the higher the value of NESN.

The Sox sale is further complicated by the 11 acres of land the team owns around Fenway Park. If a new park were built down the street, the Sox would own prime commercial and residential real estate. If the existing park is renovated, there is no real-estate value. Guess why the Sox want a new park down the street.

These complications notwithstanding, the larger issue for the Sox sale will be the immense destruction of wealth since September 11. Some bidders may drop out, and others will grow more cautious. All can take pride in their prospective affiliation with a sport that has served its country with generosity, dignity, and intelligence during the past three weeks.

MLB by the Numbers, but Who's Buying?

Two things always seem to be true about baseball: There is never enough pitching, and no one ever makes any money. Actually, owner-commissioner Bud Selig gave a slightly more nuanced version of the second maxim before the House Judiciary Committee on December 6: Twenty-five of MLB's thirty teams lost money in 2001, and combined, all of the teams suffered a total loss in excess of $500 million.

Are these numbers any more believable than Selig's assertion (*Milwaukee Journal Sentinel*, November 15, 2001)—amid claims that his Brewers team would benefit disproportionately from the contraction of the Twins—that St. Louis is closer to Minneapolis (464 miles) than is Milwaukee (295 miles)? Probably not, but they are convenient for MLB to trot out just before opening labor negotiations and just as it has to explain why it is attempting to reduce industry output by two teams despite the fact that industry revenues have grown from $1.38 billion in 1995 to $3.55 billion in 2001.

If the baseball industry is in such dismal economic shape, how come John McMullen (who sold the Astros in 1992) and Tom Werner (who sold the Padres in 1994) are bidding to be new owners of the Boston Red Sox? And how come Jeff Luria is rumored to want to buy the Florida Marlins after unloading his Expos and John Henry is angling to own the Red Sox after unloading his Marlins?

Selig told Congress that interest in the Red Sox is irrelevant because it is a big-market team. Huh? Isn't the value of the Red Sox affected by the health of the game and the magnitude of the revenue-sharing burden imposed on the team? Doesn't Selig believe his own figure that the Los Angeles Dodgers had the largest cumulative operating loss during 1995–2001 of $165 million?

John McMullen is part of Charles Dolan's reported $405 million bid for 53 percent of the Bosox (and 80 percent of NESN). Allowing a 10 percent discount for minority shares (since minority owners often don't have a management role) and a $140 million value for 80 percent of NESN and the team's real estate, the implied value of the team itself is $588 million. In all likelihood, the new owner will also have to put down another $250 million–$350 million in private money toward a new stadium.

According to Selig's figures, the Red Sox lost $13.7 million in 2001 from baseball operations. As a big-market team, the Sox contributed $16.4 million in revenue sharing last year, and Selig says that number will have to grow significantly in the future to fix the sport economically. That is, the Sox's advantage as a big-market team will shrink.

So, members of the House Judiciary Committee had good cause to inquire: If the Red Sox market value is near $600 million, is baseball really in desperate straits? Before the hearing, Selig promised that MLB finances would be fully divulged and there would be no more secrets.

In fact, Selig provided only four pages of summary revenue and cost data for the thirty teams, and he threatened the players' association with a lawsuit if it shared additional information on the clubs' finances. As anyone at all familiar with the business of baseball knows, any serious examination of the game's economics has to begin with the financial statements of individual franchises—each about fifteen pages in length. After that, one would want to look at payroll forms and financial ledgers describing certain transactions.

Selig expresses alarm that baseball's debt has grown to $3.1 billion, but he doesn't reveal what this debt is for. Certainly, a good portion of it is for new stadiums. If a team has to pay, say, $100 million (for which it issues bonds) out of a $400 million new-facility cost, and that facility generates an additional $50 million of net revenue for the team annually, then by any reasonable reckoning the team is in better shape financially after the deal—despite the fact that the team has increased its debt by $100 million. If all thirty teams did this, Selig could announce that MLB has $3 billion in debt.

Interest on debt and amortization should be taken out of Selig's figures to get a proper gauge of baseball's economic viability. This reduces 2001 losses from the frequently cited $519 million figure to $232 million.

In 2001, baseball's central-fund revenues (from national TV, radio, Internet, and properties) averaged $23.999 million per team, and distributions per team averaged $17.856 million—meaning that baseball's central office kept $6.14 million per team. That is, baseball's central office had a budget of at least $184.3 million compared with an early 1990s budget of less than $25 million. Might there be some bloating in the central office?

Many owners of baseball teams today also own companies that do business with the team. Owners can make revenues and costs appear in either the team or the related entity. If nothing else, MLB's revenue-sharing rules provide an incentive to inflate team costs and deflate team revenues.

Although a wide variety of related-party transactions exist, the most prominent ones occur when the owner of the team also owns the team's broadcasting or cable station. If one uses figures from the industry's authoritative magazine *Broadcasting and Cable*, then the Chicago Cubs' television revenue was $35.4 million greater than is reported in Selig's numbers, and the team's $1.8 million loss in 2001 becomes a $33.6 million profit.

To be sure, many other accounting options, such as expensing instead of prorating signing bonuses for minor leaguers, can elevate reported costs by millions of dollars.

Finally, owners can take their investment returns in a number of ways. For instance, Steinbrenner created a holding company with the NHL's Devils and

NBA's Nets and then formed the YES regional sports network in the nation's largest media market. Reports indicate that the network will pay the Yankees a below-market rights fee, lowering the team's local income and revenue-sharing obligations but raising the network's value to an estimated $900 million—a healthy chunk of which goes to Steinbrenner. And Rupert Murdoch recently admitted that his purchase of the Dodgers has already paid off because it enabled him to prevent Disney from creating a regional sports network in Southern California.

Some owners put themselves or their family members on the team payroll at handsome sums. Others use the team to develop nearby real estate. Still others exploit their community prominence to develop closer ties to politicians and corporate executives. Most enjoy substantial tax benefits, eventual capital gains, alluring perquisites, and the power and glory of ownership.

Increasingly, owners treat sports teams as part of an investment portfolio. Often, the team itself is managed not as a profit center but, rather, as a vehicle for promoting the owner's other investments.

Only when all of these factors are considered can one discern whether buying a baseball team is a good economic investment. The point of all this is not to deny that many baseball teams might be losing money. Nor is it to argue that baseball does not have economic problems. Both are true, but neither is properly addressed by contraction. Baseball needs to modify its system of economic incentives, and there is only one way to do this: start collective bargaining.

Baseball by the Numbers

1. Redefine Operating Income

Bud Selig claims that, combined, the thirty MLB teams lost more than $500 million in 2001. But this figure includes both interest expenses and depreciation charges. The appropriate measure of a business's ongoing viability is operating income, which excludes these items. When this is done, the losses shrink from $519 million to $232 million.

2. Expand Operating Expenses

In 2001, baseball's central-fund revenues (from national TV, radio, the Internet, and property) averaged $24 million per team; distributions to each team averaged $17.9 million. The difference was kept by the central office of MLB, which had a budget of at least $180 million. The budget was less than $25 million in the early 1990s. Why the increase? Bigger salaries for execs and staff, tens of millions of dollars spent on the new MLB website, money stashed away in the event of a future work stoppage. But these aren't operating expenses. Properly adjusted, MLB's operating losses might be reduced to $150 million or less.

3. Pay Yourself Too Little

Many team owners today also own entities that do business with their teams, such as TV stations and stadium concessions. And owners can take investment returns in a number of ways. George Steinbrenner of the Yankees, for instance, formed a holding company called YankeeNets with the Nets of the NBA and the Devils of the NHL and then created the YES regional sports and entertainment network. Reportedly, the network is paying the Yankees an undervalued rights fee, thus lowering the team's local income (and its revenue-sharing obligations to other teams) but raising the network's value to an estimated $900 million—a healthy chunk of which belongs to Steinbrenner. Other owners use teams to develop real estate near stadiums. Others exploit their community prominence to foster closer ties with politicians and corporate executives. Most enjoy substantial tax benefits, eventual capital gains, and the ego ride of ownership.

4. Move Value from One Pocket to Another

According to Selig's figures, in 2001 the Chicago White Sox took in $30.1 million from local TV, radio, and cable contracts. The Chicago Cubs brought in only $23.6 million. A curiosity, to say the least: The Cubs are the far more popular of the two teams, generating consistently higher ratings than the White Sox on broadcast TV and cable. So what's going on? The Cubs are owned by the Tribune Company, which just happens to own WGN Superstation. Most Cubs games, in turn, are shown on WGN, which reaches 56 million homes nationally. The Tribune Company in effect is shifting its profits from one pocket (the Cubs) to another pocket (WGN). According to *Broadcasting and Cable* magazine, the industry's authoritative source, the Cubs' local broadcasting earnings were $59 million. If the Cubs reported this figure instead of $23.6 million, then their reported $1.8 million loss would become a $33.6 million profit in 2001.

5. Charge Yourself Too Much

Owners can readily inflate team costs by expensing rather than amortizing signing bonuses for minor leaguers or by putting themselves or family members on the payroll or by charging costs from other businesses to the baseball team and so on.

The Mets Are Worth More Than $391 Million

How much are the New York Mets worth? The team's two owners could not seem to decide. For Fred Wilpon to buy out Nelson Doubleday's 50 percent share, Robert Starkey, MLB's financial adviser, was hired to do an appraisal. In his April 12, 2002, report, Starkey claimed that the team was worth $391 million.

Doubleday thought that the Starkey estimate was far too low and refused to sell his 50 percent share based on that price. On July 10, Wilpon filed a complaint in U.S. District Court in an effort to compel Doubleday to sell his share. On August 5, Doubleday's lawyers filed a counterclaim with all sorts of juicy contentions. Doubleday's lawyers called Starkey's estimate of $391 million "outrageously low" and accused Starkey of having various conflicts of interest.

How does one determine the value of a baseball franchise? In normal industries, appraisers will use one or more of several methodologies, including multiples of revenues, or EBITDA (earnings before interest, taxes, depreciation, and amortization); comparable sales; and discounted cash flow. In baseball, it is problematic to use discounted cash flow because owners can take financial and nonpecuniary returns in a variety of ways that will not show up in cash flow. The more common practice for valuing baseball teams is to use revenue multiples in conjunction with comparable sales, and this is what Starkey does. So far, so good.

Of course, these valuation methodologies yield only estimates. The best guide in valuing an asset is the market test—what someone would pay for it—but this information is not always available.

Starkey began his analysis by identifying eleven franchise transactions between 1995 and 2002 from which he could identify an appropriate revenue multiple to employ in valuing the Mets. Based on these eleven transactions and using regression analysis, he estimated an equation that he claimed provided a more accurate estimate of value than a simple revenue multiple. The equation was

$$\text{Franchise value} = (2.637)\text{Revenue} - \$16.2 \text{ million}$$

To derive this equation, Starkey needed sales prices for the eleven team transactions. For the recent Red Sox sale, Starkey took $700 million and deducted $300 million, the value he assumed for 80 percent of NESN (the share of the New England Sports Network owned by the Red Sox), yielding a team value of $400 million. This is problematic for two reasons. First, with supplementary agreements and fees, John Henry and his partners probably paid close to $730 million for the team. Second, the more typical price range cited for 80 percent of NESN is $150 million–$225 million. Starkey thereby underestimated the value of the team itself at $400 million, and this produced a downward bias in the equation.

Because franchise value in large part derives from synergy and indirect benefits, teams in large markets offer owners disproportionately more opportunities for gain. For this reason, Starkey's equation might well provide better information than a straight multiple, but he probably could have done even better by using a nonlinear estimate of value.

In any event, in 2001 the Mets' reported revenue after revenue sharing was $166.96 million. When this number is put into Starkey's equation, it yields a value of $424.1 million.

But Starkey did not use that number. Instead, he identified four "most comparable" transactions and, based on these alone, estimated a new equation. Using the new equation, the value of the Mets fell to $400 million.

To estimate the new equation, Starkey again used least-squares regression analysis. The problem is that he had only four data points (and two degrees of freedom), and the high correlation coefficient (that he said validated his estimate) was unreliable. There is, in fact, no statistically or economically sound reason for Starkey to throw out the other seven transactions.

But Starkey's next sleight of hand takes the prize. He decided to adjust team revenue by subtracting stadium operating expenses, which in the Mets' case were $21.7 million in 2001 and considerably higher than for the "most comparable" teams. When he did this, the Mets' value fell to $382 million. Starkey then averaged this with his $400 million estimate to arrive at his valuation of $391 million.

But Starkey needs to choose between doing a revenue-multiple and a cash-flow–multiple analysis rather than arbitrarily combining them. If he is doing the former, which he says he is doing, then it is inconsistent to deduct expenses. If he is doing the latter, then he must deduct all expenses, not just the ones where the Mets are well above the average. In this case, he would have to use a higher multiple.

Forbes magazine in its latest annual survey estimated the Mets' value at $482 million, and its estimates are generally conservative. In his counterclaim, Doubleday asserts that since May 1999 Charles Dolan repeatedly has offered $500 million for the Mets, and these offers were before entertaining competitive bids. If this assertion is true, then it provides the market test and is the best gauge of the Mets' value. Since no competitive bids were engaged, it would establish a minimum team value of $500 million.

I don't know whether Doubleday's allegations about Starkey's conflicts of interest or about the manipulation of his numbers by Selig's office are valid. I do know that Starkey's methodology appears improper and biased and that his resulting estimate makes little sense.

The Sports Franchise Market Is Stronger Than Many Think

The sports media is having a field day writing about the supposed glut of teams for sale on the market. Some writers—seemingly alarmed that the Dodgers and Angels didn't sell within two months—are now claiming that the decades-long sports boom is over.

A more cautious interpretation, however, would be more prudent. First, recall that the Red Sox took seventeen months to complete their recent sale for $720 million (including 80 percent of NESN). A typical team transaction is a complicated affair, passing through several stages: selecting an investment banker; writing a financial prospectus; identifying prospective buyers; conducting due diligence; taking initial bids; vetting by the league office; taking final bids; and ironing out the details of the buy–sell agreement.

Second, sports may have been largely immune to the business cycle thirty years ago when teams relied chiefly on gate revenue. These days, however, successful teams are dependent on the corporate dollar. When economic doldrums and political uncertainty buffet the corporate world, the sports world feels it.

Third, the more or less simultaneous decisions of AOL/Time Warner, Disney, and News Corporation to rid their empires of their diminutive team assets say little about the economic prospects for MLB and the NBA or about the potential synergy between media companies and sports teams. They say more about the travails and shifting strategies of these media giants.

Fourth, potential bidders for baseball teams would do well to take a close look at some very positive developments in the leagues. Among the most promising is MLB.com. For a variety of reasons, the revenue outlook for this enterprise is downright rosy. Reasonable projections are for total revenues to grow from roughly $50 million in 2002 to $70 million–$90 million this year, to $110 million–$130 million in 2004, with healthy growth thereafter. Better still, the net revenue will be equally distributed to each of MLB's thirty teams, promoting financial and competitive balance and lessening the pressure for more revenue sharing in the future.

Consider the following: Last year, MLB.com's largest revenue source was merchandise sales, which probably reached $18 million–$22 million. Advertising on the site yielded another $14 million–$18 million. (MLB.com had approximately 480 million site visits in 2002.) Game audio feeds and other paid services to some 900,000 subscribers generated another $8 million–$12 million.

It is this last category that is about to take off. Full-season audio-service prices are slated to increase 33 percent, to $19.95 for all teams or to $11.95 for a single team. This year nearly 1,000 games will be video-streamed live to out-of-market fans and business travelers. This is a new service that offers decent viewing quality for broadband (T1, DSL, and cable modem) connections. Currently, there are some 20 million homes and 40 million people at work with broadband access, and these numbers are growing by almost 100,000 per month.

MLB.com will offer various video packages. A subscription for live games will cost $14.95 per month or $79.95 for the entire season. Individual games will also be available on a pay-per-view basis, at $3 to $4 apiece. Five- and twenty-minute game-highlight services, along with interactive statistical packages (and much more), will also be sold. The site offers something for every baseball fan.

It does not seem far-fetched to estimate that within a few years there will be 1 million MLB.com customers spending an average of $15 per month and another 3 million fans spending $5 per month during the baseball season. Such traffic would yield $180 million in revenue. Beyond this, soon MLB.com will be selling advertising spots for its streamed games, and in 2004 it hopes to stream games live in Japan.

There is little reason for these packages to diminish baseball's other media contracts. MLB.com employs Internet-locating technologies to ensure blackouts of local games. Baseball's jewels on national television will lose none of their allure.

Bob Bowman and his crew at MLB.com are effectively developing this business. If they can continue to grow the business at 35–55 percent annually, don't be surprised to see a partial public offering down the road.

Now if this weren't enough good news, the IRS—for reasons that are as alien to me as George W. Bush's Iraq policy is to French Prime Minister Jacques Chirac—seems to be ready to sweeten its amortization allowance for player contracts from 50 percent to 60 percent of a team's purchase price.

None of this is to suggest that MLB and the other sports do not have some serious management and structural problems. They do, but this is nothing new.

I expect to see the sports-team market rebound after the economy turns the corner.

Flawed Financial Analysis of NHL Skates on Thin Ice

In early April, Philip Propper, a Los Angeles Kings season-ticket holder and portfolio manager, released his report on the Kings' finances to the media. Propper had observed that there was a serious discrepancy between the Kings' claims of financial losses and an article in *Forbes* magazine estimating a club operating profit of $7 million in 2001–2002.

Propper offered his services to the Kings, and the Kings apparently shared their financial statements with him. Propper's report alleges that the Kings' public statements of losses are accurate. On the basis of his incomplete financial analysis of the Kings and smatterings of publicly available data, Propper goes on to denounce the NHL's economic system and suggest his own alternative. The media widely reported the results of Propper's study.

Propper's study, though not without an occasional insight, is laden with inaccuracies and problems. The first difficulty is that Propper saw only summaries of several of the Kings' revenue and cost items and provides the reader with even less information than he received. It seems that the Kings will not allow Propper (who signed a nondisclosure agreement) to share many of the details, so Propper assures us that he is evenhanded and asks us to believe his interpretations.

He acknowledges that the Staples Center, owned largely by Anschutz Entertainment Group (AEG), which also owns the Kings, is profitable, but he asserts that Staples Center makes less money than the Kings lose. Propper, however, provides no figures to support this claim, nor does he show how AEG allocates various costs between the team and the arena. He argues that the Kings' lease terms at the arena are reasonable because they are the same as the Lakers', but he does not note that AEG also owns a 25 percent share of the Lakers as well as an option to purchase Jerry Buss's 70 percent share of that NBA team. Nor does he observe, as he should, that the Kings' share of arena revenues is well below what many teams receive.

Propper's next faux pas is his contention that the Kings' value today must be below the team's purchase price of $115 million in 1995 because the Buffalo Sabres were recently purchased for $70 million. Sure, and the New York Yankees are not worth $600 million because the Expos sold for $120 million.

Propper then asserts that the Kings' average ticket price of $48.12 is "comfortably below the league average." The opposite is true. According to the newsletter *Team Marketing Report*, the Kings have the sixth-highest average ticket price in the NHL and the fifth-highest fan-cost index (including concession, memorabilia, program prices, etc.). The average league ticket price in 2002–2003 is $41.56—$6.56 below the Kings' price. The Kings' fan-cost index is $280, while the league average is $240.

At one juncture we learn that the "Kings' fan base is simply not large enough," but later we learn that the Los Angeles market has enormous hockey potential and the ownership has failed in its marketing efforts.

Propper switches back and forth between financial categories (operating income and cash flow) so that it is not clear whether his alleged cash losses include all or part of debt service, although it appears that they include all of it. Generally, the appropriate measure of operating income (and financial viability) would exclude debt service. It certainly should in this case, because more than $75 million in debt was used to finance the purchase of the Kings, and then more than 60 percent of the purchase price was claimed to be attributable to player contracts (and was amortized to lower tax obligations).

After mangling the Kings' finances, Propper assesses the NHL. He tells us that, in the NHL, "player compensation is based on a free and open market, and individual teams have very little control over this expense item." Huh? Unrestricted free agency for players doesn't begin until age thirty-one, and team payrolls in 2001–2002 varied between $19.2 million and $64.8 million.

Then, after citing news reports on selected revenues of only two teams (the Colorado Avalanche and the Edmonton Oilers), he writes: "I feel confident that by looking at representative numbers, quite a few teams are losing money." From this he leaps to his punchline: The NHL economic system is broken, and the only viable solution is for four to six teams to be eliminated.

Propper believes that the NHL expanded too rapidly over the past decade, yielding talent dilution, "a slower, less skilled product than what was on display just ten years ago," and "a boring, defensive style" of play. The only evidence Propper adduces to support this curious claim is an erroneous assertion that the "influx of the top European players into the NHL in the late 1980s and early to mid 1990s has mostly ended." So Propper argues that the supply of talent has not grown, but the demand shot up in line with the increase from twenty-one to thirty teams, leading to excessive salary growth.

Here Propper is misleading on two counts. First, he bemoans the "end of the era of the 60 to 80 goals a year scorer" and connects this to talent dilution. But if talent were indeed diluted and, hence, decompressed in the league, then it would promote offensive records as the great scorers were guarded by weaker defenders.

Second, Propper's contention about the supply of European players is just plain wrong. He has their influx "mostly" ending in the mid-1990s. The number of non-U.S. and non-Canadian players in the NHL grew from 156 in 1994–95 to 299 in 2002–2003—an increase of 143 players and a far cry from "mostly" ending. In contrast, the number of foreign players grew from 54 in 1986–87 to 156 in 1994–95—an increase of 102. That is, the increase in the number of foreign players was 40.2 percent greater in the eight years since 1994–95 than during the eight previous years.

The central problem in the NHL is not too many teams; it is too much revenue disparity among the teams. The obvious solution is increased revenue sharing. The NHL shares less than 10 percent of its revenue, compared with 25–35 percent in MLB and the NBA and nearly 70 percent in the NFL. But Propper eschews revenue sharing, saying that it undermines entrepreneurial incentives. If revenue sharing were based not on actual team revenues but on forecast revenues (based on market characteristics), however, there would be no such disincentives.

At the beginning of his study, Propper explains that he is not able to share all the Kings' financial numbers and asks the reader to trust him. By the end of his study, my reaction is: No thanks.

Baseball's New Numbers: Doom and Gloom or Blip and Fit?

Remember last July? After declaring the All-Star Game a dead heat, Bud Selig warned that one franchise might go out of business within the week and another might not finish the season.

As of mid-May, MLB's average game attendance was down roughly 5 percent relative to 2002, and 2002 itself had been down 6 percent relative to 2001. Combine this with news reports that the Angels, just six months from their thrilling World Series triumph over the Giants, sold for only $182 million and one might believe that Selig was on to something.

It's the economy, stupid. Well, maybe, but consider that the economy has been weak since late 2000; that NFL attendance this past season was up 1 percent; and that NBA attendance was off only .5 percent. Also consider that a few months ago, the Boston Celtics sold for $360 million, and last year the Red Sox (along with 80 percent of NESN and Fenway Park) sold for $720 million.

Still, unemployment is higher now than it was last year, and the prolongation of the slump has wearied consumers and investors. And MLB's 2.8 percent increase in average ticket prices (to $18.69) and 3.3 percent increase in the fan-cost index ($148.66 for a family of four) in 2003 does not help.

Then there's the weather. Cold and rain persisted in many baseball cities through the third week in April. While baseball in April has always been somewhat iffy, this year it admittedly was worse than usual. But here, too, it is a stretch to attribute the drop in attendance for the Dodgers, Devil Rays, Padres, As, Astros, Diamondbacks, Brewers, Braves, and Mariners (or, for that matter, the Angels' sales price) to Mother Nature.

Maybe it was the invasion of Iraq. Weren't many baseball fans too preoccupied with the war, its devastation, and its implications for terrorism at home to go to the ballpark? Undoubtedly so. And the scare over severe acute respiratory syndrome (SARS) did not help, particularly in Toronto.

Finally, there is the impact of new stadiums. What? Aren't new stadiums supposed to help attendance? Sure, but only for a few years, and even then usually only for good teams. Since 1992, baseball has gained sixteen new facilities. The teams that got new stadiums in the early and mid-1990s are seeing the honeymoon effect wear off, and the teams that got new stadiums in the past few years forgot to take advantage of their new potential revenues to improve their teams. Their honeymoon effects faded quickly.

Indeed, aided by the experience of team collapse when the NFL Bengals got their new stadium, fans in Cincinnati quickly tired of the Reds' mediocrity this season. The novelty effect of the Reds' new park seems to have lasted just a few weeks: The team's average home attendance after twenty-two games was just 25,979.

Thus, attendance was artificially lifted for several years by the stadium boom. In 2002 and 2003, the bloom is wearing off, and attendance is back to normal levels.

To be sure, part of the 6 percent decline in 2002 was because of the continued collapse of baseball interest in Montreal. And this year's drop would be steeper if the Expos were not playing some of their games in Puerto Rico. The Expos average attendance through mid-May 2002 was 7,749; this year, it is up to 13,794.

So is baseball's attendance problem long term? While some fans may have been turned off by last year's near work stoppage and talk of doom and gloom, it appears the attendance issues are primarily conjunctural. This is not to say that MLB doesn't have some promotional work to do.

What about the Angels? Many analysts, myself included, felt that the team would sell in the neighborhood of $250 million or higher. Clearly, the economy, the stock market, and the war had negative effects on the reported sales price, but isn't $182 million still uncannily low?

After all, since 1995 the seventeen teams whose assets changed hands have sold for values averaging more than 2.2 times the previous year's revenues. No sales price was below 1.5 times revenue, and that was for the then lowly Kansas City Royals. If the 2.2 multiple is applied to the Angels' 2002 revenues of around $120 million, the team would have sold for $264 million.

Given that the Angels are in the country's second largest media market and that the team finally appears to be exploiting some of the market's great potential, it would seem that it should command at least an average sales multiple. Moreover, given MLB's 2002 collective-bargaining agreement and the various new drags it provides on players' salaries, as well as the early success of MLB.com, baseball's franchise values should be somewhat buoyant (though rational buyers will be circumspect about continued growth of local cable revenues).

The first question to ask is whether the Angels indeed sold for the reported $182 million. That is, does that price represent the equity or asset value of the team? If it's the former, then the new owner, Arturo Moreno, also assumed the team's debt. According to Selig's December 2001 report on baseball finances to the U.S. Congress, the Angels paid $4.98 million in interest on debt. The Angels reportedly contributed $80 million to the renovation of Edison Field in 1998. At slightly above an average 7 percent long-term interest rate, the Angels' 2001 interest payments are consistent with a $70 million debt. Thus, if Moreno paid $182 million for the team's equity, he was paying the equivalent of roughly $250 million for the team's assets.

Another factor that could have depressed the Angels' value is the team's long-term local television and cable contracts. Disney signed a ten-year deal in 1998 with FSN West for about $6 million per year and a broadcast television deal worth about $3 million annually through 2005. The contract with Fox may have been accompanied by side deals beneficial to Disney (such as News Corporation's commitment to carry some of Disney's channels on its international satellite-distribution business). But whether or not there were side deals, Moreno is saddled with a very inferior set of local media contracts for several years. These commitments constrain revenues and artificially lower the team's value.

So regarding MLB's franchise values, let's not jump to conclusions until we have more information. Disney's 10Q report in October may tell more of the story. In the meantime, if the good commissioner tries to sell you a used car, keep your hands in your pockets.

Baseball's New Management Culture Is a Work in Progress

What follows is a commentary, not a book review. So let me get the preliminaries out of the way.

Michael Lewis's new book *Moneyball: The Art of Winning an Unfair Game* is a good read and an insightful look into the changing business of baseball. Read it.

The book's teachings, however, need to be tempered in several ways before we can assess their true meaning for the industry.

Lewis presents a clear and compelling case that baseball's traditional system of player evaluation has grown old and inefficient. For instance, fielding percentage and batting average are incomplete measures of defensive and offensive performance. Supplementary information, such as number of assists and putouts per game or walks per at bat is needed.

But it is easier to knock down than to build up. The new Billy Beane System is never fully elucidated by Lewis. Indeed, at one point Lewis writes that Beane's method by its very nature is unsystematic.

According to Beane's statistical analysis, a one-point increase in on-base percentage generates three times as many runs as a one-point increase in slugging percentage. But Lewis never explains the methodology by which Beane and his assistant, Paul DePodesta, arrive at this (or other) conclusion(s). In statistical analyses, the methodology matters.

The value of walks to Beane is not just getting the batter on base. A hitter who takes pitches accomplishes two other important things. First, he makes the pitcher throw more pitches, thus wearing the pitcher down and getting to the bullpen sooner (which on average has weaker pitchers than the starting rotation). Second, it allows the other hitters an opportunity to see more of the pitcher's stuff on that day. These two factors then make the whole offense more potent.

Fair enough, but why is not a similar analysis applied to stolen bases, which are practically banished from Beane's scheme? That is, stolen bases not only represent an additional base, but they force the pitcher to divide his concentration and potentially tire him out both emotionally and physically. And what are we to make of Lewis's claim that Chad Bradford's submarine delivery makes the perceived speed of his pitches increase from 84 to 94 miles an hour due to supposed extended release point? Lewis doesn't tell us that the release point would have to be 7.2 feet closer to home plate for this to be true.

Or what of Lewis's contention that hits allowed by a pitcher is an inferior indicator of pitching prowess because it depends in part on the fielders, unlike walks or strikeouts, which depend only on the pitcher? Would Beane have signed Tommy John?

The Sandy Alderson–Beane approach clearly has value, but Lewis's few anecdotes cannot tell us how much value or help us discriminate among the more and less useful approaches to player evaluation. Lewis spends considerable time describing the As' picks in the 2002 amateur draft but little time explaining how the rosters of the past three years were assembled.

How much of the As' recent success is attributable to the team's excellent starting pitching? How these remarkably proficient hurlers were identified and obtained remains largely untreated by Lewis.

From what I have heard from baseball people, Beane wanted to sign Ben Sheets, but he didn't have the money, so he chose Barry Zito. Tim Hudson was identified by the As scout John Poloni, although Poloni is denigrated by Lewis in the book as the "fat scout." Nor was the record much different for position players. Beane apparently persuaded Alderson to pass over the Colorado slugger Todd Helton in 1995 to sign Ariel Prieto. And Beane's proposition that it is safer to sign college grads than high-school players does not seem to have informed the As' selection of their strongest hitters, Eric Chavez (signed out of high school) and Miguel Tejada (signed at seventeen out of the Dominican Republic).

What is needed in MLB, and what will ultimately emerge, I suspect, is a synthesis of the traditional and new systems of talent evaluation. Player statistics below the double-A level will always be somewhat suspect because the level of competition is uncertain. Scouts have been and will continue to be an integral part of the process. Beware of formulaic quick fixes.

One of the interesting features of the Beane approach is the notion that the general manager should put a money value on each and every player in the major leagues. This is a dubious exercise, scientifically speaking, but perhaps a useful one for owners, as it is likely to take some of the emotion out of bidding for players. Less emotion will lead to lower salaries.

As described by Lewis, another element of Beane's success is that he cheats. MLB rules prohibit teams from negotiating with amateurs before they are drafted. By violating this rule, Beane can make a deal with a prospect and sign an early-round pick—who was not originally projected to be a top selection—for a late-round price.

Too bad for the amateurs who are not protected by a union or the nation's antitrust laws. It doesn't seem to occur to Lewis that this practice might be condemned rather than lauded.

Last but not least, Lewis mocks Commissioner Bud Selig's concern with competitive balance by suggesting that good management can overcome the revenue disadvantages of small-market teams. Good management is important, of course, but so are revenue disparities. The statistical relationship between team payroll and win percentage has been significant at the 1 percent level (read, highly correlated) every year since 1994. Moreover, to the extent that some of Beane's success is systematic rather than serendipitous, it offers little remedy for baseball's imbalance problems.

Not dissimilar to Branch Rickey's initial success with his St. Louis Cardinals farm system in the 1920s, if one team follows a contrarian strategy of player selection, it can reap big rewards. If lots of teams follow the contrarian strategy (as is beginning to happen), any benefits will accrue to all such teams. Competitive balance will be back to where it started—in need of repair.

$53 Million for Pedro?
How Do You Figure?

This week, the New York Mets committed between $53 million and $56 million over four years to the thirty-three-year-old pitcher Pedro Martinez. More than a few commentators have warned that this could be the second coming of Mo Vaughn, an over-the-hill, overpriced, injury-prone, erstwhile superstar. Is the Mets' new general manager, Omar Minaya, trying too hard to make an impression, or does the signing of Martinez make sense financially?

Let's be optimistic. Assume that Pedro stays healthy and pitches well. If he starts sixteen home games and the Mets' average attendance for those games increases by 15,000 from 28,979 (last year's average) to, say, 43,979, the average ticket price is $25, and the average net revenue per fan from concessions, memorabilia, and parking is $8, then Pedro's direct impact on stadium revenues would be $7.92 million. If attendance increases on average by only 10,000 fans at his games, then Pedro's revenue impact would be a more modest $5.28 million.

Alas, matters are more complicated than this, because if more people come to the ballpark, the Mets will also earn more money in the sale of signage and sponsorships. Moreover, Pedro's presence will also lift the Mets in the standings and impress on the fans that the Mets' ownership is serious about winning. So attendance should rise at other Mets home games, as well.

Suppose the Mets sign another superstar (think Carlos Delgado) or two, and the team actually competes for the division championship. (Signing Pedro may even help Minaya to attract other top players who want to play for a winning team.) Mets fever returns, and the team reaches the Yankees' 2004 average attendance of 47,788, representing an increment of 18,809 over the 2003 Mets average. This translates into extra revenue of $50.3 million. If we can attribute, say, one-third of this to Pedro, then his incremental contribution is $16.8 million.

Did we crack the nut? Not quite. Baseball's revenue sharing takes away from the Mets approximately 40 percent of the team's incremental revenue. So if Martinez brings in $16.8 million gross, this is only $10.1 million net—more than $3 million below his average yearly salary of around $13.5 million.

So bad deal, right? Not necessarily. We've left out television. Martinez is not going to make Cablevision's 2005 contracted rights fee payment to the Mets increase, but he can have a major impact on the reception of the Mets' new regional sports channel venture with Time Warner and Comcast.

The Yankees launched their channel in the midst of a protracted string of World Series appearances. The team was hot, so the YES Network was hot.

At its inception in 2001, the channel was valued at about $900 million, more than the team itself.

The New York regional sports network market is flooded: YES, MSG, FSNY, and now the Mets' RSN. There is no guarantee that the Mets' RSN will be successful, but it will help a great deal if the Mets put a compelling product on the field. If Pedro helps the team win and he infuses the team with attitude and charisma, the Mets may create a media asset that generates $250 million in revenue annually (most of which can be hidden from baseball's revenue-sharing system) and is worth more than the team.

The Mets have been down too long. This is the right time for Wilpon to open up his wallet. NHL Commissioner Gary Bettman's fantasies about attaining cost certainty to the contrary, nothing is certain in the sports world. But some gambles are better than others.

Pedro Martinez is a good risk for the Mets in 2005. If the risk fails, Omar Minaya can console himself with the thought that the Yankees will be paying Kevin Brown $16 million next year.

II

League Structure, Design, and Performance

Fewer Families Own Sports Teams: It's OK

Americans often form deep attachments to their sports teams. In return, they expect their teams minimally to try to win and to show some loyalty to the communities. When Walter O'Malley moved his Brooklyn Dodgers to Los Angeles in 1958, it marked the era of disloyal teams and changed the sports world forever. Despite O'Malley's perfidy in the eyes of Brooklyn, for many, family ownership is associated with stability in sports.

Now, Peter O'Malley, Walter's son and the present Dodger owner, is about to sell this storied franchise to Rupert Murdoch, media magnate par excellence, for a reported $350 million–$400 million. (The highest previous sale price for a baseball franchise is $173 million, suggesting that Murdoch views the Dodgers as more than a simple baseball investment.) Murdoch's Fox will thereby joins Disney Corporation (Angels), Time Warner/Turner (Braves), and the Tribune Company (Cubs) as major media corporate owners of Major League Baseball teams.

Walter O'Malley made his name and fortune as a bankruptcy lawyer during the Great Depression and took over for Wendell Wilkie as the Brooklyn Dodgers' lawyer in 1942. Two years later, Walter purchased a minority interest in the club along with the baseball innovator Branch Rickey. Over the ensuing half century, the family presided over the team that introduced Jackie Robinson into baseball in 1947, introduced Major League Baseball to the West Coast in 1958, and introduced Japanese and Korean players into the major leagues in the 1990s.

What does the O'Malley family's departure mean for baseball? Certainly, the days of family ownership of franchises are fading. As franchise prices have skyrocketed from less than $5 million in the 1950s to $10 million–$20 million in the 1970s to in excess of $100 million today, there are fewer families who can afford to be sole proprietors. Instead, there has been a gradual process that began with CBS's purchase of the Yankees in 1964 for $14 million toward corporate partnerships and joint-stock–company ownership.

Fans have nothing to fear in this trend. Family owners have been no more likely to show loyalty to their host city than corporate owners. To be sure, the NFL, which still proscribes corporate ownership, has experienced more franchise movements than either baseball or basketball.

Some express the fear that corporate owners, with their deep pockets, are more likely to spend indiscriminately to monopolize top talent, but Chicago Cubs fans know better. If anyone, it has been the well-heeled family owners such as Ewing Kaufman, former owner of the Kansas City Royals, who have treated their teams as playthings and elevated winning above making profits. Corporate owners are unlikely to subordinate profits to pleasure. And even if they were so inclined, baseball's new revenue-sharing and luxury-tax systems would provide powerful disincentives.

Further, corporate ownership is more likely to be professional and proficient; less likely to be eccentric and errant. Corporate executives are at least responsible to a board of directors. They cannot readily divert funds to other businesses, pay themselves multimillion-dollar consulting fees, publicly berate ethnic groups, or embrace Hitler à la Marge Schott without losing their jobs.

There is, of course, also a potential downside. Large corporations have power, political and economic. A coalition of Disney, Time Warner, and Fox is more likely to lobby successfully for the preservation of the interest exemption on municipal bonds for stadium construction or for baseball's anomalous antitrust exemption. And Fox's Murdoch, if history is any guide, is more likely to lead a confrontation with the players' association (not to mention Ted Turner). Nonetheless, Congress has consistently genuflected before MLB sans Murdoch, and one would like to believe that baseball is sufficiently chastened from the debacle of the 1994–95 strike to resist any call to arms from Murdoch.

If Competitive Balance Spoils the Show, Congress Waits in the Wings

It is by now a cliche to note that the ownership of professional team sports is changing. By one estimate, in early 1998, sixty-six public corporations had direct or indirect ownership interests in sports teams. A large share of these public companies are in the media business. Media business-owned teams often have a different objective from stand-alone teams—namely, the team itself is not necessarily a profit center but, rather, is viewed as software or programming to promote the larger business empire. When Fox decided to pay the thirty-three-year-old Kevin Brown $105 million over seven years two months ago, part of the expected payoff was in the promotion of the Fox Network in the United States and abroad. Just like CBS's gargantuan contract with the NFL, the network is buying football along with its ratings, but it is also buying exposure and status for its other programming. This fall, CBS led the networks in prime-time ratings. It's the first time CBS has topped the charts this deep in the season since 1993, which was the last time CBS had the NFL.

Fifteen million dollars a year for a forty-year-old pitcher seven years into the future is a lot of money and probably would not make sense viewed from the perspective of a single baseball team. Murdoch thinks Brown is worth at least $105 million to News Corporation, and he likely is right, but it is questionable whether Brown is worth this much to the Los Angeles Dodgers baseball team.

About a year ago, the thirty owners of MLB teams were debating whether to allow Murdoch and News Corporation to buy the Dodgers. After their reported unanimous vote to allow the purchase, I asked one owner whether baseball didn't have some serious reservations about this decision. His reply was: "We didn't have a choice." He was referring to the fact that the Fox regional sports network already had local contracts to televise twenty-four of baseball's thirty teams.

But there was another element, as well. Fox was about to offer $310 million for the Dodgers, by far the highest purchase price for a team in baseball's history. Baseball's owners were happy to have Murdoch push up the value of their teams, but now, when Murdoch also breaks the salary scale, the owners cry that he is upsetting competitive balance.

The media-company-as-team-owner phenomenon is just the latest irritant to the competitive-balance mixture in professional team sports. Owners have long argued that teams from larger cities had an advantage over those from smaller cities, and, especially in the 1990s, teams with new facilities generating tens of millions of dollars in additional revenues are seen as having a competitive edge over teams playing in older facilities. That is, a team from a large city or with a new facility or owned by a media conglomerate will be able and willing to outbid other teams in the quest to procure top player talent.

In theory, this argument always made some economic sense. In practice, the advantaged teams were not dominating their leagues (save in baseball during the pre-free agency era). Indeed, some even argued that it would have been in the leagues' best financial interests for the big-city teams to be stronger than they were, because having those teams in the playoffs would raise aggregate fan interest along with television ratings.

Beginning in the mid-1990s, however, the big-city/new-facility/media-owned teams in baseball began to monopolize the post-season landscape. During the present off-season, many non-advantaged teams have publicly waved the handkerchief before the season has begun. Owners such as Carl Pohlad of the Minnesota Twins, whose net worth is $1.3 billion, according to *Forbes*, have decided that maintaining a payroll in the $25 million–$45 million range won't allow them to win their divisions. So their profit-maximizing strategy has become to minimize their payrolls down to $10 million–$15 million. Pohlad follows the ignominious example set the previous year of his fellow owner Wayne Huizenga, each attempting to punish his fans for not supporting the team by building a new stadium with public funds.

By most reckonings, the NFL, the NHL and the NBA have all avoided the pitfall of advantaged-team domination. The NFL formula is simple: extensive revenue sharing among the owners, reverse-order draft, unbalanced schedule, prohibition against corporate ownership and a fungible salary cap set at 62 percent of league defined gross revenues. [**Note:** *The cap has since been raised to 65.5 percent of defined gross revenues. For the 2005 NFL season, the cap, including benefits, was $103.4 million per team.*] The NHL formula entails curtailing unrestricted free agency until a player reaches thirty-one years of age, limitations on sales of players, and a reverse-order draft. The NBA, albeit dominated in recent years by the big-city Chicago Bulls, owes the strength of many of its small-city teams, such as the Utah Jazz, to the Larry Bird exception to its salary cap. The Bird exception allows a team to resign its own player and go over the salary cap. Thus, star players are much more likely to stay with their original teams. Seven of the eleven top-paid players in the NBA are with their original teams. The player's original team is determined in a reverse-order draft. That is, if Michael Jordan had been drafted initially by the Milwaukee Bucks, the odds are strong that he still would have been playing with them last year.

If and when competitive-balance problems manifest themselves in other sports, as they appear to be doing in baseball, affected leagues would do well to study the NFL example of revenue sharing. By dividing equally all revenue from the national television contract ($2.2 billion a year) and national licensing, splitting the gate 60–40, as well as sharing other revenue sources, the NFL has attained unprecedented balance. (Though arguably, the NFL's system should be modified because the league offers owners little or no profit incentive to win.)

The NBA's response to revenue inequality among its teams has been to attempt to lower the players' share in league revenue (which was already several percentage points below that in other leagues) and to turn the soft cap into a hard cap. That is, the NBA has tried to make the players bear the burden of a problem (revenue inequality) among the owners. Baseball owners attempted to do the same thing in 1994–95. In both cases, the outcome was predictable: a lengthy work stoppage. At the very least, the burden of dealing with the problem needs to be shared. Players should accept some additional restraints, but owners need to do additional revenue sharing. Baseball tried to do this in its last collective-bargaining agreement, but its revenue-sharing plan does not seem to have gone far enough (next year, the top-revenue team, at around $160 million, will transfer $13 million to the bottom-revenue team, at around $40 million).

Of course, it is far from a simple matter to convince advantaged owners voluntarily to tax themselves. They argue that they paid more for their advantaged franchise, and additional taxation amounts to a form of asset confiscation. Unbalanced competition and work stoppages, however, will also lower the value of their asset—and possibly by more than will additional revenue sharing.

If this logic is unpersuasive to the owners, then it will be up to Washington politicians to awaken from their longstanding sports slumber. The natural economic solution is competition. With two leagues in each sport, monopoly teams in big cities will soon find another team from the competing league in their territory. The artificial shortage of teams will evaporate, and deserving cities will no longer have to compete against each other through public subsidies to get teams. This will erode the competitive-imbalance problems from new facilities.

The public-policy solution is simple: Pass legislation that will break each league up into competing business entities.

Selig, Players Both Err Early Regarding Competitive Balance

Still salivating from the hardening of the NBA salary cap, MLB Commissioner Bud Selig set up a "Blue Ribbon" panel last month to study baseball's growing competitive imbalance. The committee includes an economist who did a good job controlling the growth of the money supply between 1979 and 1987, a former senator from Maine, several team owners, and a few others. To conclude that this committee is by, for, and of owners is a no-brainer.

The problem is that any prospective resolution or amelioration of the competitive balance problem is 90 percent political and 10 percent technical, and at least half of the political issue is between the owners and the players. The absence of union representatives on this committee, therefore, is foreboding. The owners will debate the matter and come up with their solution. Having invested their time and energy in the subject and convinced each other of the wisdom of their ways, their position will be hardened. Come 2002, they will present the plan to the players, and baseball will be back where it was in 1994.

Thus, the commissioner has taken an initial misstep, but so has Gene Orza of the players' association in pronouncing competitive balance to be a nonissue. As far as Orza is concerned, there has always been competitive imbalance, and whenever the owners raise it, it is no more than a fig leaf for a salary-cap drive.

In a sense, Orza is correct. There always has been competitive imbalance in baseball. It was worse before free agency came along in 1977. Under the reserve clause, rich owners bought good players from poor owners. The money went to the owner, not the player. With free agency, it became more difficult to hold a winning team together, and weak teams became more able to improve themselves rapidly in the free-agency market. The era of team dynasties seemed forever gone, and MLB's 1990 economic study committee found there to be only a slight correlation between city size and team performance.

Then came the 1990s. At first, the news was good. Baseball signed a new national television contract with CBS and ESPN for 1990–93 that, together with growing central licensing, superstation, and Copyright Royalty Tribunal revenues, meant that each and every team received some $19 million a year from baseball's central coffers. In 1990, this was almost 40 percent of average team revenues.

But in 1994, baseball's new national television contract fell by more than 60 percent. Exacerbating matters, certain big market teams, such as the Yankees, were earning more than $40 million a year in unshared local media revenues, and the era of the new, big-revenue-generating stadiums was ushered in by Camden Yards in 1992. With centrally distributed monies below $10 million per team, big-market and new-stadium teams found themselves with a rapidly growing revenue advantage.

While the revenue disparity between the richest and poorest team was around $30 million in 1985, by 1998 it was close to $110 million. To this volatile mixture add the presence of new franchise owners who also own international communications networks and who value their ballplayers not only by what they do on the field but what they do for their networks. Further, baseball's expansion by four teams in the 1990s, while adding excitement to the game, makes the star players stand out more and thereby makes it easier to buy a winning team.

Baseball tried to deal with these inequalities in the last collective-bargaining agreement. It is now clear that the revenue-sharing plan across the teams (wherein the top-revenue team will transfer approximately $13 million to the bottom team in 1999) and the luxury payroll tax (wherein the top five payroll teams in 1999 will pay a 34 percent tax on that portion of team salaries above approximately $76 million) do not go nearly far enough toward leveling the imbalances.

Consider these statistics. In 1998, of the eight teams that made the playoffs, all were among the top twelve teams in payroll. Further, of these top twelve teams, all had winning percentages above .500, save the Baltimore Orioles, who finished at .488. Of the bottom eighteen teams in payroll, only two teams finished above .500. Of the bottom ten teams in payroll, none finished above .475.

Some of these results, no doubt, are from poor management or owner machinations. To wit, Huizenga's fire sale in Miami, which the Padres seem to be emulating this year now that they have won a referendum for a new stadium, and other teams, such as Minnesota, are doing reasonable facsimiles thereof at a lower level.

But some of this behavior results from baseball's increasingly convoluted incentive structure. What will fan attendance be this year for the bottom eighteen payroll teams?

Something needs to be done, whether or not Orza buries his head in the sand. The options include different and deeper revenue-sharing schemes among the owners; tighter artificial restraints on salaries; freer team movement; and public policy forcing divestiture of MLB into two competing business entities. These issues are all intensely political, and Bud Selig should know that. Selig, then, would have done better to establish a bilateral, not a unilateral, committee to study competitive balance.

Talent Decompression and Competitive Balance in Major League Baseball

Sixteen perfect games have been pitched in ninety-six years of modern baseball, but two of those were in the past fourteen months. Sixty home runs stands up for thirty-four years; sixty-one stands up for thirty-seven more, and then two players hit sixty-six and seventy in one year. If Mark McGwire's record is due to a lively ball, lower mound, smaller strike zone, or the prohormone andro, how come pitchers are also setting records? Part of the answer lies in MLB's expansion by four teams in the 1990s. The good news is that, thanks to talent decompression, records once again are being challenged and broken. The bad news is that talent decompression presents some new problems for baseball's growing competitive imbalance.

Ever wonder why almost all of baseball's personal-achievement records were set between 1910 and 1930? Hornsby batted .424 in 1924; Wilson knocked in 190 runs in 1930; Webb whacked 67 doubles in 1931; Ruth scored 177 runs in 1921; and Leonard had a 1.01 earned-run average in 1914. Many seem to believe that the reason is players in the good old days were better. Not so. Baseball stats are the product of competing forces and reveal little about the absolute quality of the players. (Too bad for me: I batted .714 in a Northampton league a few years back and never got a call from the Yankees.)

The reason in large measure has to do with relative degrees of talent compression. The distribution of baseball skills in the population follow a standard normal distribution (like a bell-shaped curve). For any curve, the larger the number of people selected to play major-league baseball, the greater will be the difference between the best and the worst players in the league. If the population grows and the number of baseball teams does not, then the proportion of the population playing falls and the distribution of talent becomes more compressed. This is what happened in MLB between 1903 and 1960, with the population growing from 80 million to 181 million and the number of teams remaining constant at sixteen.

Moreover, in the late 1940s, baseball began to accept black players and recruit Latin and other international players in greater numbers. This accentuated the compression, while better nurturance of baseball skills and physical abilities in general offset the growing appeal of football and basketball to American youth.

With talent increasingly compressed, the difference in skills between the best and worst players grew narrower, and it became more difficult for the best players to stand out as much. Hence, records ceased being broken, or even approached (save the asterisked performance by Roger Maris in 1961, the first year of MLB expansion).

Thus, it makes little sense to argue that Babe Ruth hit more home runs per season than Harmon Killebrew because he was stronger or had superior baseball skills. It makes more sense to suspect that Ruth played during a time when talent was more dispersed, so he faced many superb pitchers, but he also faced a much larger number of weak pitchers than did Killebrew. Similarly, Dutch Leonard or Walter Johnson (earned-run average of 1.09 in 1913) faced some spectacular hitters, but they also faced a much larger number of weak hitters than did Sandy Koufax, Ron Guidry, or Roger Clemens.

The ratio of the U.S. population to the number of major-league players rose from 250,000 to 1 in 1903 to 307,500 to 1 in 1930 and to 452,500 to 1 in 1960. Thereafter, it fell gradually to 385,000 to 1 in 1990 and to 360,000 to 1 in 1998, after MLB's second expansion by two teams in the 1990s. Thus, talent decompression gradually set in after 1960, and by 1998 the ratio had almost fallen back to the level in 1930.

So in the late 1990s, the McGwires, Sosas, Ramirezes, Wellses, and Cones can more easily excel. Equally important, when the better players can more reliably outperform the others, it becomes easier to buy a winning team. It is one thing for the Yankees to generate $170 million in revenue while the Expos generate $40 million. If George Steinbrenner and Brian Cashman spend their budget on underperforming, overpaid players, then the Yankees will squander their revenue advantage. Yet the more certain players stand out, the more difficult it is for inept management to squander a revenue advantage.

When the latter phenomenon is combined with sharply growing revenue disparities among teams and the presence of media-conglomerate ownership, baseball's delicate competitive balance becomes more problematic. Sure, rich teams are not guaranteed to finish first, and poor teams can still finish first. The problem is that the historical probabilities shift against poor teams. The question is how far can these probabilities fall for poor teams before their fan bases lose interest. Baseball's future success hinges critically on the answer.

Minor-League Basketball: There's a Right Way and a Wrong Way

Isiah Thomas has a dream. He wants to corner all professional basketball below the NBA and launch an NBA minor league under his control. Two months ago, he bought the Continental Basketball Association (CBA) for $10 million, and it is reported that he is now negotiating to purchase another league, the International Basketball Association.

To realize his dream, Thomas needs the blessing of both David Stern and Billy Hunter, the head of the players' association. The NBA owners need to design a player-development system, including promotion and demotion procedures, and to take on a hefty financial responsibility to support a new minor league. In baseball, each major-league team pays out close to an average of $10 million annually in support of its player-development program. In basketball currently, the NBA pays out a diminutive subsidy to the CBA that averages less than $100,000 per team. Each team spends a slightly larger sum on scouting. Taking on a minor league is a significant financial commitment.

The NBA owners also need the players' association, the NBPA, to accede to any minor league because it will have implications for job stability and salary for the union's membership. Before consenting, the union will want an elaborate system to protect today's and tomorrow's NBA players from repeated demotions and attendant salary cuts.

The union will also want assurances that the minor league is not a back door for Stern to impose age limitations on NBA players. Stern has made it clear that he would like to see a minimum age of twenty for the NBA. The union wants players who are good enough to be in the NBA to be able to play at the top level. Why should a Kobe Bryant be forced to wallow in a minor-league system for two years, earning a shadow of what he is worth in the open marketplace, if he is ready to play in the NBA at eighteen?

The union is also likely to ask: With three new independent leagues attempting to form that could serve as a minor league for the NBA (National Rookie League, International Basketball League, Collegiate Professional Basketball League), why should the NBA work with Isiah Thomas? Thomas plans to reorganize his CBA as a single entity, which among other things means that there will be no competition for players among teams. He also wants random drug testing.

The union will want a league that safeguards the players' economic and civic interests. They are unlikely to trust Thomas to provide these safeguards. After serving as union president during his playing years, Thomas became a team owner and was an active union basher during the 1998–99 owners' lockout. Since the minor-league players are unlikely to unionize, many of the necessary safeguards will have to be built into the initial structure through a give-and-take between the NBA owners and the union.

If the deal cannot be struck with Thomas, one hopes that an NBA minor league will materialize in another form. It is a historical accident that U.S. universities serve free of charge as the NBA's player-development system. To do this, U.S. universities pay a price. First, most college basketball programs run in deficit. Second, it is commonplace for upward of 80 percent of the players on NCAA Division I teams to be "special admits." That is, the school admits players who are not academically qualified and, more often than not, have no academic interest. They are in school to be trained and get exposure for the NBA. They spend the lion's share of their waking hours playing basketball and doing weight training. Their coaches steer them to a select group of athlete-friendly, often vacuous classes, and a team of tutors tries to ensure that they pass, sometimes resorting to writing papers for the athlete when necessary. In the end, despite this academic charade, only 41 percent of Division I basketball players graduate from college in six years.

This system is certainly not a good one for the basketball players. They don't get paid a cash income. Their jerseys are sold at retail outlets, and the school collects the licensing revenue. They are not allowed to use their basketball skills to earn summer income. They are forced to live a lie and endure the institutional cheating that maintains their basketball eligibility. Some apologists call this giving poor kids an opportunity. In fact, the present system degrades the athletes and undermines their self-esteem.

How about an honest opportunity? That's what minor-league basketball could mean to high-school star players without academic inclination. College is not and should not be for everyone.

The Commissioner's New Clothes

At their meetings last month, Major League Baseball's owners gave Commissioner Bud Selig unprecedented formal power. Given the historical disagreements among the owners and the game's absence of effective leadership, it is hard to quarrel with the effort to strengthen the commissioner's office.

One significant measure granted Selig the authority to do whatever is necessary to insure competitive balance in the game. A magnanimous gesture, and who could argue with its goal? The problem comes in implementation.

If we take MLB's press releases at their word, then George Steinbrenner, Rupert Murdoch, and Peter Angelos, among others, will sit idly by if Bud Selig decides that all local media money will be distributed equally among the clubs. Maybe so, but I think I'd bet on John Rocker playing shortstop for the Yankees first.

More likely, Steinbrenner, who already sued baseball once on antitrust grounds so he could pursue his sponsorship deal with Adidas, would take MLB to court, claiming that a significant portion of his property is in effect being confiscated. Presumably, Selig knows this and would act only with consensus among the owners.

Selig must also know that any initiative by him to redistribute the game's riches will smack of a conflict of interest. Even though his ownership interest in the Brewers is in a blind trust during his term as commissioner, when he leaves the job, the value of his team to him and his family will be much greater. Is Bud Selig really the man to lead this charge?

Furthermore, even if Steinbrenner did put Rocker at shortstop and offer to share his local television money, what would Selig do about Donald Fehr and the MLB Players Association? Revenue sharing is subject to collective bargaining, and with good reason. The more revenue that gets shared, the lower the payoff to having a successful team and the less a player is worth to an individual owner. After all, it is largely for this reason that the NFL, which generates significantly more revenue and higher franchise values than the other sports, has the lowest salaries. The average NFL salary is $1.07 million, compared with $1.19 million in the NHL, $1.72 in MLB, and $3.52 million in the NBA (according to *Sports Business Journal*, January 31–February 6, 2000). And the highest individual salary in the NFL this year was $5.87 million, compared with $10.36 million in the NHL, $11.95 million in MLB and $20.17 million in the NBA.

Thus, any changes in baseball's revenue-sharing rules will have to be collectively bargained with the players. While the players accepted the additional revenue sharing that was added in the 1995 collective-bargaining agreement (which next year will amount to a total of $140 million going from the top to bottom teams), it is likely that they will want concessions in exchange for further revenue sharing.

The players will also want a say in how the revenue sharing is done. If it is done out of a team's actual revenues, then the team will have less incentive to pay a player his full value (because some of that value is shared with other teams who do not hire the player). If, however, the sharing is out of projected or forecast revenues (based on the size of the local market and stadium conditions), then teams will have a greater incentive to win and pay players top dollar. All this has to be bargained and cannot be decided unilaterally by the commissioner's office.

Another vote the owners took at the winter meetings declared that in the future teams will pool their separate Internet businesses. (Judge John R. Padova's decision in *Piazza et al. v. Major League Baseball* notwithstanding, it is a lucky thing for baseball that most still presume the industry is protected by a blanket antitrust exemption.) Once MLB's contract with SportsLine.com ends after the 2001 season, baseball's central office will be able to contract with national advertisers and sponsors for its newly controlled website. It is possible, but not inevitable, that this will generate more revenue than would thirty separate websites. The central site will lose local advertisers.

What is positive, however, is that the Internet money will be shared equally among the clubs. But how much money will there be? Today, the most successful team sites generate a gross of around $1 million. If more companies advertise on websites, won't there be less demand for advertising at the ballpark and on television? Similarly, if more goods sell on the websites, won't fewer goods be sold via other channels? At the end of the day, there are a finite number of fans with finite income.

The Internet accord also raises the question about what happens when broadband technology begins to accommodate effectively both Internet and television data. Does this accord mean that the Yankees have already signed on to centralizing their local television money?

There is nothing wrong with these owners' initiatives. At the very least, they signal an emerging consensus among the owners that is positive. The issue is that these initiatives are being trumpeted as solutions, and they are not. They raise more questions than they answer. Stay tuned.

Baseball's Competitive Balance and the Amateur Draft

The 2000 baseball season has begun. And what a beginning! First, 5 A.M. (EST) games from Japan; then Western Hemisphere opening night coinciding with the college men's hoops championship game.

But we should take what we can get. If the players don't opt to extend the collective-bargaining contract for another year after this season, we might not get any baseball in 2001. If they do extend, we might not get baseball in 2002.

Labor and management have a lot to talk about, and one would hope that they begin their collaborative process sooner rather than later. One of the central topics will be the player draft. The reverse-order amateur draft in baseball was introduced in 1965. Almost overnight, the (old) Yankee dynasty was ended, and baseball entered an era of unprecedented competitive balance that lasted until the mid-1990s.

The selection of amateur players through the draft was an important leveler. In the 1990s, however, the selection of amateurs began to favor the high-revenue teams, contributing to a greater imbalance on the playing field. Why?

For starters, revenue disparities across the teams exploded. In 1985, the top-revenue team earned approximately $30 million more than the bottom team, while in 1999 this disparity approached $160 million (narrowed to around $125 million by baseball's revenue-sharing system). These inequalities were then reflected in vastly different player-development budgets across the teams. Last year, for instance, the Yankees spent more than $20 million on their player-development system, while the Oakland Athletics invested less than $6 million. This means that the Yankees, by offering far more handsome signing bonuses, have greater success in signing foreign players who come to the United States as free agents.

Only U.S. residents and Puerto Ricans (and foreigners enrolled at U.S. universities) are subject to the reverse-order amateur draft. All other foreign ballplayers come to the United States as free agents. Today, foreign-born players represent more than one-fifth of all major leaguers.

After the collapse of the former Soviet trade bloc and the ensuing meltdown of the Cuban economy, the supply of ball-playing Cuban defectors began to expand. Agents such as Joe Cubas exploited the opportunities and inspired still more defections. More or less simultaneously, free-agency rules in Japanese baseball along with government conscription regulations in Korea were liberalized, and many Asian ballplayers tested their market value in this country.

Sports Business Journal, April 17–23, 2000

As the foreign free-agent market developed, agents sought out players throughout the Caribbean and elsewhere. Agents staged foreign player workouts for prospectively interested teams. At first, these workouts were attended by scouts from most teams, but as the signing bonuses grew, the number of represented teams diminished. Low-revenue teams gave up ahead of time.

Complicating matters, as the signing bonuses for foreign free agents increased, U.S. amateurs, comparing their potential to that of the foreign players, demanded and often received higher bonuses. On occasion when the player didn't get the bonus he sought, he would refuse to sign, and the drafting team in essence would lose a draft pick. Rather than lose draft picks, low-revenue teams began to skip over the top prospects, anticipating that they wouldn't be able to sign them. The high-revenue teams, though lower in the drafting order, started to get better talent. Thus, the process of signing new talent, which had promoted competitive balance since 1965, today seems to be exacerbating the imbalance in baseball.

The solution? It would appear that making the amateur draft a worldwide, rather than strictly U.S., phenomenon would be a productive first step. The players' association, however, is likely to resist, arguing that the solution to the exploitation of U.S. ballplayers (by allowing the drafting team to have monopoly bargaining rights over the player for a year) is not to extend this exploitation to foreign players. Instead, the players' association will seek a modification in the draft process in exchange for internationalizing the draft. It might, for instance, demand that two teams be allowed to draft each player, so that there would be some competitive pressure in determining the player's signing bonus without forcing the player to sit out a year.

Why does the players' union get to bargain over baseball's draft rules? After all, minor leaguers are not part of the union. The union won an arbitration ruling back in 1992 that made the draft a subject of mandatory bargaining on the grounds that free-agent signings were compensated by draft picks. Thus, an element affecting the demand for free agents was connected to the draft process.

Since the system of free-agent compensation was originally sought by the owners as a way both to lower demand for free agents and support greater balance on the field, it is possible that the owners could now seek to remove the compensation rules. Without such rules, in turn, draft procedures might no longer be a mandatory bargaining subject.

Alternatively, the owners may seek another concession from the players. If two teams can draft one player, why not give the drafting teams permanent signing rights? The player will have an initial choice with whom to sign, but he will not be able to reenter the draft after one year and be selected by different teams. Such a rule should improve the chances that lower-revenue teams could actually sign the players they draft.

Finally, in the name of competitive balance, why not give each team two or three picks in each of the first two rounds of the draft? This would give a further advantage to teams that finished low in the standings the previous year.

Complicated stuff. Yet productive compromises seem available. They will not, however, emerge spontaneously, and they will not be made in isolation of compromises around revenue sharing or new mechanisms to restrain salary growth.

Soon Commissioner Selig's Blue Ribbon Panel will release its report on the economics of the game. If previous reports of this ilk are any guide, it will advance baseball no closer to a new labor agreement. But with the report out of the way, let's hope that the real bargaining can begin.

Baseball's Blue Ribbon Panel: Good News and Bad News

Baseball's hired geniuses—George Will, George Mitchell, Paul Volcker, and Richard Levin—should have done better after eighteen months of work. Their Blue Ribbon report is marred by superficial and wrongheaded analysis at points, but much of its message is sound, and some of its prescriptions are worth considering. The danger is that the report will be dismissed for its weaknesses, and its strengths will be overlooked.

This is precisely what the *Forbes* magazine writers Michael Ozanian and Kurt Badenhausen did in their *Wall Street Journal* op-ed on July 27. Ozanian and Badenhausen denounced the report as a "charade" because its authors uncritically accepted MLB's claim that only three teams made money between 1995 and 1999. To be sure, this claim is not credible. Baseball accounting provides all sorts of ways to hide profitability, as MLB President Paul Beeston instructed us several years ago: "Under generally accepted accounting principles, I can turn a $4 million profit into a $2 million loss, and I can get every national accounting firm to agree with me."

Ozanian and Badenhausen base their argument on their own estimates of MLB franchise values, which reveal substantial appreciation over the last two decades. They reason that franchise values would not rise if the industry were not profitable. They are half right.

First, their data show appreciation over a longer time span than the period considered by the Blue Ribbon report. Second, franchise values properly reflect expected future profits, not recent profits. Third, there are multiple ways that an owner can receive a return on his investment in a baseball team besides financial profits. Others include related-party transactions between the team and other businesses that belong to the same owner, synergies between the team and these businesses, greater access to politicians and ability to shape legislation, enjoyment of the power and perquisites of ownership, tax sheltering, and so on. The value of a franchise will reflect all these sources of investment return, not just financial profitability.

That said, it is likely that reality lies somewhere in between: Many teams in MLB do have financial difficulty, and many do not. The Blue Ribbon report unquestionably loses some credibility by uncritically regurgitating owners' claims of ubiquitous financial woes. Similarly, the report loses credibility when it incorrectly states that NCAA rules strip a college basketball player of eligibility once he enters the NBA draft and when it asserts that higher salaries cause escalation of ticket prices.

These and other shortcomings, however, have little to do with the main thrust of the report's analysis. The great bulk of the eighty-seven–page report concerns baseball's growing competitive imbalance and what to do about it.

After presenting compelling evidence of growing imbalance, the Blue Ribbon Panel makes several recommendations. First, tax between 40 percent and 50 percent of a club's net local revenues, put the money into a central pool, and then distribute one-thirtieth of the pool to each club. The 1999 revenue-sharing plan had each club (excluding Tampa Bay and Arizona) contribute roughly 17 percent of its net local revenue to such a pool. Distributions from the pool were then made equally to twenty-eight clubs, with some modest additional distributions to the bottom-revenue teams. In the 1999 plan, the Yankees contributed a net amount of $18 million.

In the Blue Ribbon Panel's plan, the Yankees' contribution would rise to approximately $21 million (using 1999 figures and assuming the tax is set at 50 percent, Yankee Stadium expenses are $20 million, and total MLB stadium expenses are $500 million). That is, the Blue Ribbon plan would increase the net Yankee contribution only by some $3 million—not much for George Steinbrenner to squawk about.

But the real impact comes from the incentive effect of this local revenue tax. Again, assuming the tax is set at 50 percent, then each increment to a team's net local revenue is reduced by 48.3 percent. This is because half is taken away by the tax and 1.67 percent is returned by the subsequent equal distribution from the pool to each club. Hence only suppose Steinbrenner is contemplating the signing of Manny Ramirez during the off-season and estimates that with Ramirez in the Yankee outfield, the team will generate an additional $14 million in annual local revenue. Without the local revenue tax, Steinbrenner should be willing to offer Ramirez any salary up to $14 million. With the tax, he should be willing to offer Ramirez any salary up to $7.24 million ($14 million × [1 − .483])!

Thus, the revenue-redistributive impact of this provision is likely to be considerably weaker than its salary restraint impact. Perhaps this observation helps to explain why the Blue Ribbon panelists avoided recommending a salary cap and why the players' association may be less than enthusiastic about this method of revenue sharing.

The panel's second recommendation—for an additional 50 percent tax on team payroll's above a fixed $84 million threshold—would create a further impediment to the upward drift of salaries. What is notable here is not the $84 million threshold (which is close to the threshold of the last year of the luxury tax in 1999) but the suggestion that it be fixed, even as MLB's revenues continue to grow—again cause for the players' association to balk. Of course, it is possible that with the 50 percent local revenue tax, the $84 million payroll would never be reached.

The third recommendation is also controversial. The commissioner would be able to use any increase in central-fund distributions above the $13 million per club in 1999 to make unequal distributions to assist low-revenue clubs. Since the new ESPN contract has grown severalfold, and the new network contracts are expected to grow by 100 percent or more, the central-fund payouts are likely to more than double in the coming years. This puts a very significant sum at the discretion of Commissioner Selig and may be resisted by high-revenue clubs. An interesting feature of this recommendation is the panel's suggestion that only clubs meeting a $40 million payroll would be entitled to receive these extra distributions from the commissioner—throwing a bone to the players' association.

The panel's recommendations end with suggested modifications in draft procedures and more lenient policies toward club relocations. None of the recommendations is without contentious elements, and none uses numbers that could not be altered. The panel's conceptualization of baseball's competitive-balance problem, however, is useful, and some of its ideas for reform can serve as a productive basis to initiate the coming round of collective bargaining. Now all we need is a Blue Ribbon Panel on how to engender a spirit of open-mindedness and compromise on each side.

NFL's Revenue Sharing Saps Will to Win?

Ask baseball fans outside New York City and they are likely to tell you that they have had enough of $100 million payrolls and the Yankee dynasty. Baseball, they say, has become too imbalanced.

Is it possible that football suffers from the opposite problem: too much balance? Consider the following. NFL teams share 40 percent of gate revenues, including club-seat premiums and sales of personal seat licenses (PSLs) (when not used for stadium construction); 100 percent of national and international television, radio, and Internet rights fees (more than $75 million per team per year [**Note:** *In 2006, this sum will exceed $130 million per team.*]); and 100 percent of net licensing revenues. NFL teams play only eight regular-season home games per year, and the norm is to sell out, or nearly sell out, every game. Any extra income a team earns from post-season contests, including the Super Bowl, is largely offset by extra team travel, training, and entertainment expenses.

The New York Giants' co-owner Bob Tisch said that if his team wins, "You really don't get any extra revenue. ... You do it for the glory and honor of winning a Super Bowl. I would venture to say it'll cost us $1 million to be in the Super Bowl."

Meanwhile, the Green Bay Packers claim that they lost $1.5 million on their two Super Bowl trips in 1997 and 1998. The team's president, Bob Harlan, flatly states: "It wasn't an opportunity to add to the bottom line."

Do the math and you'll agree that there is no financial incentive to win in the NFL. That is, it doesn't pay to build a strong team through free-agent bidding, because the additional salary outlay is not matched by additional revenues to the team.

Many owners, however, have other businesses that can be directly or indirectly boosted by a successful football team. From the perspective of their entire investment portfolio, the return to winning may be positive for some owners who may be induced to bid aggressively for free agents.

To curtail this behavior, the NFL has another mechanism: the salary cap. The cap kicked in for the 1994 season at around 63 percent of defined revenues. In 2001, the team cap was $62.2 million, and although this figure can be surpassed in any given year through the use of amortized signing bonuses, eventually any overage will have to be made up.

The salary cap and extensive revenue sharing, together with policies such as the reverse-order draft and compensatory scheduling, are great equalizers in football. The era of NFL team dynasties, most recently with the Cowboys and the 49ers, died out in the early to mid-1990s.

Winning teams come and go, and well-rounded, excellent teams no longer seem to exist. Instead, the NFL now experiences a collective Florida Marlins effect: Teams go from prominence to oblivion in one year. And just about any team can win—even the New York Giants, who went from having the eleventh first-draft pick following the 1999–2000 season (which was squandered on Ron Dayne) to the Super Bowl in 2000–2001 despite having the NFL's third-lowest payroll.

To be sure, there is something appealing about the NFL's rare realization of the equal-opportunity principle. The problem is that football may have gone too far. The outcome of the championship season appears increasingly random to fans. The nonpareil announcer John Madden says the game is more exciting when there's a king of the hill to beat. And Fox's ratings for the NFC Championship Game two weeks ago were down 23 percent from last year, despite the fact that this year's game included teams from the first- and fourteenth-largest media markets, while last year's included only the fifteenth and twenty-first markets. Ratings for the 2000–2001 Super Bowl itself were down 6.7 percent from last year and were the fourth lowest since 1972.

The NFL's pattern of extreme equality is new, and its long-term effects are not yet apparent. Will fans accept as legitimate a championship season in which the teams do not openly compete financially for the best players and in which the eventual outcome may have more to do with chance and the cunning of coaches than it does with the quality of the players?

Even Commissioner Paul Tagliabue seems to think there is an issue here. Read his written testimony before the U.S. Senate Judiciary Committee on January 23, 1996: "To encourage local ties and operations, and in an effort to ensure the integrity of their competitive performances on the playing field, each NFL franchise is held by separate ownership." Where is the competitive integrity if private ownership does not have a financial incentive to win?

The league has a lot on its plate during this off-season—lurking (albeit limping) competition from the XFL, Al Davis's lawsuit against NFL Properties and the Commissioner's Office for alleged corruption, media attention to players' violence, among other things. The NFL would do well, however, to worry most about the quality of its product and the incentive system that produces it.

The Sports Industry during Recessions

Conventional wisdom has it that the sports industry is largely immune to economic downturns. While it is true that in previous recessions the sports industry fared better than manufacturing and most service sectors, it is prudent to recall that the U.S. economy has not experienced a recession since the first quarter of 1991 (and the recession before that was in 1982).

The nature of the sports industry and the structure of its revenues have changed dramatically over this time span. These changes make the industry more sensitive to macroeconomic conditions and more vulnerable to recessions than in the past.

Economics may be the dismal science, but it is too early to join the pessimists and assume that a downturn is around the corner. Virtually all economic forecasters are projecting slow, not zero or negative, growth for the balance of 2001, with accelerating growth for 2002. Forecasting models, however, while good at projecting the continuation of existing trends, are notoriously poor at predicting turnarounds.

The best gauge for turnarounds is the index of leading economic indicators. After falling mildly for three consecutive months, the index increased by a robust 0.8 percent in January, wiping out the decline in the previous two months.

Alan Greenspan's delay in cutting interest rates, though, is not encouraging. Nor is the 40 percent increase in the U.S. trade deficit last year, which averaged $1 billion a day in 2000. The trade deficit is financed by foreign investment in the United States. Foreigners hold 38 percent of all Treasury bonds and more than 40 percent of their investment in this country is in the high-tech sector—and much of this is investment they must now regret.

So if there is a recession here and foreign investors lose confidence, expect to see substantial capital flight, with attendant drops in the stock market and increases in the interest rate. These are the ingredients that can turn a small recession into a bigger one. And the extent of any prospective downturn will have a lot to do with how the sports industry fares.

In previous recessions, consumers tended to cling to sports for an extra fix of entertainment, distraction, and escapism. Yet ten years ago, it was not nearly so expensive to attend a live game. Average tickets prices were $8.64 in baseball, around $20 in hockey, $22.52 in basketball, and $25.21 in football. By 2000, these prices (which exclude the hefty amenities charges for club seats and luxury suites) had roughly doubled, to $16.65 in baseball, $47.69 in hockey, $48.97 in football, and $51.02 in basketball. Concessions, parking, and other prices have similarly increased.

Sports Business Journal, March 12–18, 2001

And, of course, ten years ago marked only the beginning of the modern sports facility, laden with premium seating, catering, signage, sponsorships, and so on. Post-1991 stadiums and arenas have added anywhere from $15 million to $60 million annually to a team's revenues, and most of this has come from corporate and high-income family spending. High-end incomes have benefited the most from the expansion of the past ten years; accordingly, spending for stadium amenities has flowed abundantly. A recession in 2001 may have a serious impact on this new, important source of team revenue.

Another argument about past recessions is that they sent fans from the ballpark to their television sets. Indeed, sports on television tended to substitute for any entertainment outside the home that cost money. Thus, even if a team's gate revenues faltered, TV ratings boosted advertising-spot prices and rights fees. While this same pattern would apply to some degree in 2001, it would likely be attenuated because much more of sports viewing today is via pay cable or satellite distribution. And while there may be more eyeballs glued to the TV set than before, consumers will have less income to purchase Bud Lite and Air Jordans.

To be sure, there are indications that the demand for TV advertising spots has already begun to slacken. For instance, Dan Rank, managing partner of the media buyer OMD, reported last week to *U.S.A. Today*: "We're seeing plenty of advertisers cutting back. They're deeper cuts than we've ever seen." Tim Spengler of Initiative Media predicted the first drop in a decade in TV's up-front market. And Toyota, Ford, and Chrysler put a scare into the minds of TV executives by announcing that they would not honor ad-rate increases in 2001. Not only are existing companies cutting back, but there are fewer dot-coms and other startups bidding for advertising space as TV spots, signage, or naming rights.

One effective countercyclical force is likely to be gambling. People tend to gamble more when they are financially challenged, and gambling in the United States has grown enormously in the past several decades. The Harvard Law Professor Paul Weiler estimates that the amount U.S. citizens spent on legal gambling alone increased from $2 billion a year in the early 1960s to $18 billion annually in the mid 1970s and to $640 billion a year in the late 1990s. Not a trivial share of this in on sporting events. The more folks gamble, the more they watch the games—on the networks, on NHL's Center Ice or NFL's Sunday Ticket, or at the sports bars.

There's also a silver lining in the clouds of economic downturn. The sports marketplace has become much more crowded in recent years. Several quarters of falling gross domestic product is likely to help clear the deck, reducing the number of bidders for the sports dollar.

On balance, however, the scales of recession tip against the sports industry. And the deeper the recession, the deeper the hit. The sports industry was never recession-proof, but it was at least recession-resistant—a quality that has diminished as the industry has grown. If I were Mark Cuban, I'd be hoping that the index of leading economic indicators keeps going up.

On Contraction, Selig Should Change His Mind Again

Last month MLB Commissioner Bud Selig told the media that he is no longer opposed to contraction—that is, a reduction in the number of teams. It is encouraging to see that the commissioner is willing to change his stance on an issue. Next time let's hope he changes it in the right direction.

Why did Selig have a sudden change of heart on contraction? Likely he would adduce two key factors. First, it will improve the absolute quality of play. He's correct here. The only problem is that the difference (the number of major-league ballplayers will decline from 2.6 per million of U.S. population to 2.3 per million) won't be perceptible to the naked eye.

More important, MLB's expansion by four teams in the 1990s was great for the game, bringing live baseball to Denver, South Florida, Tampa Bay, and Phoenix, and adding twenty pitchers to each league, which has made it easier for Mark McGwire and Sammy Sosa to supply their power-hitting heroics. With improvements in physical conditioning and baseball-specific training, along with population growth and internationalization, baseball could expand by another ten teams and still have the absolute level of play be better than it was in the 1950s or 1960s. If Selig wants to maximize the absolute quality of play, there is a simple solution: Contract to two teams—an all-star team in each league.

Second, Selig would say, competitive imbalance has grown so severe because there are two too many cities unable to support a top-quality team. Or, put less cryptically, since Montreal and Minneapolis refuse to use public funds to build new baseball stadiums, let's eliminate them. But this is like having gangrene on your whole leg and amputating your foot.

The unspoken motivations for Selig's change of heart are different. He wants to bolster his bargaining leverage vis-à-vis the players' union and baseball's recalcitrant host cities. Put the fear of God into Jesse Ventura and his legions, into San Diego, Oakland, Miami, Kansas City, and others, and maybe they'll change their tune and build a new ballpark.

For their part, the players don't want the number of union members diminished by eighty. Two fewer teams also means lower demand for players with supply staying the same. Although Montreal and Minnesota currently do not sign big-ticket players (and hence, demand for stars should not be affected in the short run), they do sign midlevel players and thereby help to sustain midrange salaries. So, Selig probably figures, make the contraction threat and use it as a bargaining chip in the upcoming negotiations.

Sports Business Journal, April 2–8, 2001

The only problem is that it is a hollow threat, and Don Fehr knows it. First, baseball cannot afford to leave two of its current markets vacant, especially when other attractive markets beckon (e.g., Washington, D.C., Sacramento, Portland, New Orleans, Raleigh-Durham, Nashville, Las Vegas, Monterrey). That's the formula for provoking a rival league. It's also a formula for reducing national television audience and thereby decreasing future rights fees, licensing and sponsorship income, and naming-rights deals.

Second, MLB is a monopoly. As such, it reduces its output below competitive levels and charges a higher price. One form this takes in sports leagues is that the number of franchises is reduced below the number that would prevail in competitive markets. While this practice helps to increase public subsidies and to raise franchise values, it diminishes consumer welfare.

A good reason why baseball should be loathe to reduce the number of its teams is that such an action will provoke Congress and other entities to look into MLB's presumed antitrust exemption—an inquiry that baseball wants to avoid. Without its exemption, labor-market restraints in its minor leagues and its amateur draft, among other things, would become vulnerable.

Third, baseball, like most businesses, is trying to grow its operations. It has been seeking new markets in which to sell its products and will continue to do so. It has even entertained the idea of beginning play in Mexico.

Eliminating two of its franchises—one of which is in the nation's fourteenth-largest media market—would be admitting defeat. It would make more sense for MLB to continue to expand the number of teams and deal with its competitive-balance problem through other means.

In short, contraction is bad for fans because it will make the game less exciting (fewer record-breaking performances) and less accessible (fewer cities with teams).

Moreover, the public-relations value of contraction does not live up to its billing. This is because the gambit of threatening contraction will not work with the players, and it is unnecessary for dealing with baseball's host metropolises. If Selig needs a sword to brandish at the cities, he already has one: team relocation.

It's time for Bud to change his mind again on contraction.

Un-Fair Ball

Allen Barra's April 13, 2001, piece in the *Wall Street Journal* invokes Disraeli's famous remark: "There are three kinds of lies: lies, damn lies, and statistics." By observing that no Major League Baseball team in 2000 had a win percentage above .600 or below .400, Barra purports to resolve the dispute about whether there is competitive imbalance in baseball. He doesn't.

One should begin by asking why Barra, seemingly like just about everyone else who has joined this debate, insists on hyperbole. Either baseball has never been better or it is on the edge of a precipice, with all fans in small markets about to turn off their TV sets.

Any clear and open-minded consideration of the evidence reveals that (1) there is imbalance, and it grew more problematic during the 1990s; and (2) MLB is not about to self-destruct. Further, it is precisely the extreme dichotomous view that baseball does not need right now as it prepares to negotiate a new collective-bargaining agreement and revenue-sharing agreement.

Now let's consider Barra's statistical legerdemain. First, other than being round numbers, are the cutoffs of .400 and .600 more telling than those, say, of .394 and .406—or, for that matter, any other two thresholds? They are not. In 1999, for instance, there were three teams below .400, but they were all between .394 and .400. Only one win separates these two percentages.

Second, if Barra is correct that there is a clear trend toward more balance, then why was the spread between the highest and lowest win percentage in 1998 the highest it has been in at least twenty years, and at .370 this spread was 63 points above the next highest spread (in 1988)? And why, if one uses a more common measure of disparity—standard deviation—was there less or equal disparity to 2000 ten times between 1983 and 1999?

Third, do baseball fans really care about win-percentage spreads? Does a Milwaukee fan care if the Brewers win an additional one to five games per year? Or does he want to believe that his team has a chance to play in the post-season and World Series?

In any event, team owners do not try to assemble a team that maximizes the number of wins per season. Such an effort would break the bank account of any franchise. Rather, owners who believe their team has a chance attempt to hire enough players to put them over the top. Top teams, in fact, would prefer winning a tight pennant race to running away from the pack. Hence, Barra's premise that the win spread rather than, say, post-season success is the appropriate measure of competitive balance makes little sense.

Fourth, the remarkable concentration of post-season success since 1995 (only 3 out of 189 playoff games have been won by teams in the bottom half of payrolls) is compounded by the sharp correlation between success and team payrolls (and signing bonuses). It is becoming more and more apparent that the best-performing teams are buying their success. And since payrolls correlate with team revenues, there has been little turnover at the top. Not surprisingly, fans view baseball's emerging caste system as unfair.

What MLB needs most at the moment is an attitude of pragmatism and compromise. The growth in the national media contract and the new stadiums in Milwaukee and Pittsburgh will help to right a small part of the imbalance problem, but baseball also needs more revenue sharing, a stiffer luxury tax on the top team payrolls, and a modification in its drafting rules.

Neither the high-revenue team owners nor the players will abide by radical changes overnight. If such changes are pushed forward, another work stoppage seems inevitable. But a modest expansion in revenue sharing that removes the incentive for teams to bottom feed, along with other reforms, is within grasp as long as the rhetoric of cataclysm can be avoided and the voices of moderation prevail.

Competitive Balance Is a Problem

With the Minnesota Twins and their $25 million payroll jumping out of the gate to take a one-game lead over the Cleveland Indians after fifty games, it seems that baseball's journalistic Pollyannas are coming out of the closet. Allen Barra (*Wall Street Journal*, April 13, 2001) discovered that the spread of win percentages in Major League Baseball has been narrowing over the decades. Now Leonard Koppett (*New York Times*, May 20, 2001) reveals that the share of World Series participants coming from baseball's largest markets has fallen over time. The conclusion of both authors is that there has always been an imbalance in team strength, and rather than getting worse, the problem is getting better. The policy implication is clear: Do nothing.

The problems with this logic are profound. First, the argument that MLB has always had competitive imbalance and that there is therefore nothing to worry about makes no more sense than the claim that the United States should cease to worry about environmental degradation because there has always been pollution. Acute imbalance has never been productive for the baseball industry. The last Yankee dynasty, from 1949 to 1964, for instance, was marked by virtually stagnant attendance (it grew by less than 3 percent over the entire period) even though real ticket prices scarcely changed while real disposable income in the country increased by 74 percent.

Second, while it is true that by various measures competitive balance has grown more equal over the long haul, this trend reversed itself in 1995 and appears now in a more pernicious form. The reduced spread in win percentages resulted from secular talent compression, the introduction of the reverse-order draft in 1965, and the advent of free agency in 1977. The latter point calls for an explanation.

Franchise owners who believe that their team has a reasonable chance to go to the World Series endeavor to assemble a team that will outperform its competitors. Their profit-maximizing strategy is to win a tight pennant race, not to run away from their league or division. As players' salaries skyrocketed following the introduction of free agency, the cost of raising a team's win percentage to the next level also skyrocketed. Rational owners became more conscious of assembling a team that would win by a small margin.

Third, competitive balance is only important insofar as it affects fan behavior. If fans are indifferent to rooting for a lousy team, then competitive balance is irrelevant. Competitive balance, however, becomes more important when fans have higher expectations for their team's performance. Prior to the 1960s, baseball stood alone on the sports pedestal. Today, it has growing competition from other leagues and new technologies. Fans have more choices and hence are more demanding.

Further, fans' expectations have been changed by the structure of post-season competition. Until 1961, two teams out of sixteen (12.5 percent) made it to the post-season; today, eight teams out of thirty (26.7 percent) make it. The odds are better than doubled, and fans expect more. Moreover, the combined effects of the reverse-order draft and free agency produced three decades of improving balance, further fueling fan expectations. Yet between 1995 and 2000, only three out of 189 post-season games have been won by teams in the bottom half of payrolls. (Contrast that with Koppett's own figures showing that between 1921 and 1993, approximately 23 percent of World Series teams came from baseball's smallest markets.)

What happened in the 1990s to reverse the equalizing trend is quite clear. The spread in team revenues grew from some $30 million in 1989 to around $160 million in 2000. Together with the perverse incentives in MLB's 1996 revenue-sharing system, which rewarded teams for performing poorly, and relative talent decompression, a sharp correlation between team payroll and team performance has emerged for the first time in baseball's free-agency era. (Until 1995, the correlation between payroll and performance was never statistically significant at the 1 percent level, but since 1995 it has been significant at this level every year.) The actual and perceived ability of teams to buy their way into the World Series is not likely to energize MLB's fan base.

Of course, spending big money does not guarantee success—management prowess matters. Nor does impecuniousness guarantee failure. The point is that the probability of success rises sharply for high-revenue teams.

So baseball does have a real competitive-balance problem that has taken on new dimensions in the past five years. Part of the problem will be ameliorated by the growth in the national TV contract and the construction of new stadiums in the industry's smaller markets, such as Milwaukee, Pittsburgh, Cincinnati, and San Diego. But modest increments in TV money and new facilities will not suffice to balance the scales.

More needs to be done. How much more is something only the fans can tell us. In any event, the George Steinbrenners and Rupert Murdochs of the baseball world will not sit by idly if MLB attempts to raise local revenue taxes abruptly. And since increased revenue sharing, in most forms, diminishes the financial incentive to win, it usually lowers the value (and hence, the salaries) of players. The players' union, then, is likely to resist abrupt changes, as well.

Thus, the only sensible and politically practicable plan is to do what Alan Greenspan did with monetary policy and the unemployment rate: change them gradually and observe their impact on inflation before proceeding further.

In this spirit, one approach might be to raise baseball's net local revenue tax in steps up from the current 20 percent to 30 percent and mandate a minimum team payroll of $40 million (average over three years) to qualify for revenue-sharing transfers. Or, better yet, tax teams based on the size of their local market rather than their success in generating revenue. In the meantime, I'll take any bets that the Phillies and Twins won't meet in the 2001 World Series.

How to Reform the NHL's Economic System

In the October 1–7 issue of *Sports Business Journal*, Andy Bernstein wrote a provocative and thoughtful piece that suggested a new economic system for the NHL. Bernstein touted his plan this way: "Imagine an NHL in which every team has an equal chance to be competitive even without a salary cap or artificial restraint on player salaries." He also promised "no revenue sharing" and "no luxury taxes."

The NHL's collective-bargaining agreement expires after the 2003–2004 season. Judging by early pronouncements, the owners are looking for major concessions from the union. Claims that salaries have gone haywire and that more than half the teams are losing money are commonplace. So if Bernstein's plan can do everything he says it can, then he should bottle it and sell shares.

Let's start with a question about Bernstein's goal to give "every team an equal chance to be competitive." Actually, his plan does not do this, and that is a good thing. A profit-maximizing league would prefer to engineer a league in which every team had a chance to win, but big-city teams had a somewhat higher chance. After all, when big-city teams win, more fans are pleased than when small-city teams win. Consumer welfare is higher, and so are league revenues.

Bernstein's plan has three elements. First, all teams must have payrolls within a certain percent of the league average payroll (he suggests a range of between 5 percent and 15 percent of the average). Second, teams are assessed an annual franchise fee based on the size of their market (defined by population and local per capita income). Third, all players become free agents after their initial rookie contracts, and to encourage stability on the roster, if a player re-signs with his original team, then a league fund (from the fee assessment) subsidizes 15 percent of his salary.

There are some original and clever ideas here, but there are also some problems. The average payroll plan is indeed more flexible than a conventional salary cap. But guess what: The Bernstein plan is also a salary cap. Suppose the average team payroll in 2000–2001 was $40 million and this year's payrolls must fall within 10 percent of this figure (i.e., $36 million–$44 million). The cap is $44 million.

The only advantage of the Bernstein plan is that his cap is not linked directly to revenue. As such, it appears to avoid the knotty issue of having to define team revenues, and in concept it gives team payrolls more room to maneuver.

But it is still a cap. The players' association will resist it, like any other cap, if it is set too low—or in this case, if the range of variability around the average is set too low. For instance, Bob Goodenow, executive director of the NHLPA, may be able to live with the plan if the range is set at last year's average payroll plus or minus 50 percent, but may be unable to do so if the range is set at plus or minus 10 percent. Team owners, in contrast, will want to see a smaller range.

Goodenow will also seek a mechanism to insure that payrolls will grow over time to at least keep up with the growth in team revenues. Part of this mechanism can be provided by the upper permissible end of the payroll range. If average team revenues grow by 20 percent and payrolls are allowed to vary by plus or minus 20 percent, then it is likely that more teams will spend above last year's average payroll than below it. Indeed, many teams will go up to the maximum of 20 percent above the previous year's average. But some teams will not go to the maximum, and hence, average payrolls will not grow as rapidly as average revenues. This problem will occur whenever league revenues grow near or above the top of the payroll-variability range. And, of course, finding a mechanism to insure that payroll growth at least keeps up with revenue growth means that we have to worry again about measuring revenue.

Bernstein's second element, the franchise fee, is a superior idea to revenue sharing. Revenue sharing always has the disadvantage of reducing a team's incentive to market itself successfully and to win (though the disincentive is not as strong as Bernstein represents). Revenue sharing also reduces the net value a player contributes to a team's revenues and, hence, puts downward pressure on salaries—a feature that players would obviously dislike and owners would embrace.

Bernstein's franchise fee essentially taxes potential, not actual, revenue and contains no performance disincentive. The fee is fixed (based on market size) and does not vary if the team succeeds or founders. That is, any additional revenues coming from a team's competitive success are fully retained by the team's owner. Here I'd only suggest that Bernstein might consider adding some other important elements to potential revenue, such as the number of local corporations with more than 500 employees and the age and lease terms of its facility. Naturally, Bernstein's plan, similar to revenue sharing, will encounter political resistance from owners of big-city teams.

Bernstein's third element, the league payroll subsidy, is also novel. In my view, however, it is of dubious merit. It is premised on the assumption that more stability on the roster is always better. Why? Are Washington Capitals fans less appreciative of Jaromir Jagr in the aggregate than Pittsburgh Penguins fans? I doubt it.

Certainly in the early days of free agency, many fans reacted negatively to the movement of star players. This reaction itself was curious because it was not clear that star players were moving more than they had been under the reserve system. The difference was that they were now moving because they chose to move (and usually for higher salaries) rather than because the owners chose to move them.

Free-agent movement today, however, has become a part of sport culture and is fully accepted by most fans. Indeed, most fans find players' movement to be an exciting part of the game. The problem is not players' movement in the abstract; it is disproportionate players' movement to high-revenue teams (and this was always a part of the game).

Aspects of Bernstein's plan may eventually find their way into the NHL's collective-bargaining mix. In the meantime, fans have three years of work-stoppage–free hockey to enjoy, and Gary Bettman and Bob Goodenow have three years to find a meeting of their minds.

MLS Remains Minor League, World Cup Notwithstanding

Major League Soccer Commissioner Don Garber could barely contain himself. The success of the U.S. team in the 2002 World Cup was going to legitimize soccer in this country and catapult MLS into the ranks of our most popular professional sports.

Writing in the June 30 issue of the *New York Times*, Garber gushed: "The success of America's team has led to increased visibility and credibility for our sport, our leagues and our players. ... [B]y any measure soccer has arrived. It has established its rightful place in the new America and will continue to spread its influence in the years to come."

Of course, many expressed similar words of optimism during and following the 1994 World Cup, hosted by the United States, in which the U.S. team also reached the final sixteen.

When, on the heels of the successful 1994 World Cup games, MLS began to play in 1996, it seemed that professional soccer in the United States had indeed come of age. Average attendance at MLS games that year was 17,406. People expected that number only to grow as MLS began to receive media coverage and the league matured.

Yet the opposite occurred. Average attendance steadily trailed off to 14,616 in 1997, 14,312 in 1998, 14,282 in 1999, and 13,756 in 2000, before modestly recovering to 14,961 in 2001. The recovery in 2001 seems to be primarily due to a schedule shift toward more weekend games and more doubleheaders with exhibition matches between leading international teams. Nonetheless, average attendance in 2001 was 2,445 below where it had been five seasons earlier, a drop of 14 percent.

Average attendance in 2002 has shot up again. Through July 14, the average was 16,081—up 1,120 above 2001, but still 1,325 below the level of 1996. One prominent reason behind the attendance uptick this year is that MLS eliminated its two weakest franchises, in Tampa Bay and Miami, after the 2001 season.

MLS would have us believe that the success of the U.S. World Cup team provided the attendance boost. If so, someone forgot to tell MLS fans. Average attendance at MLS games during the World Cup month of June 2002 was 13,011, and since July 4 it has been 13,678.

What's the problem? Soccer itself is the most popular youth-participation sport in the United States, so it's not the game. The problem is that soccer has not caught on as a spectator sport in the United States. This takes time. Some would say a generation or two.

Sports Business Journal, July 22–28, 2002

But why has average attendance at MLS actually fallen off since 1996? Most soccer fans will tell you the same thing. MLS soccer is not major-league quality. Knowledgeable fans believe they are watching minor-league soccer, and their attendance level matches this perception.

The world's top soccer stars sign multimillion-dollar contracts to play in Europe. In contrast, MLS salaries are tightly controlled. All players are hired out of the central office, where they are allocated across the teams.

Without competition among the teams for the players, salaries are strikingly low. The minimum salary is $24,000, the statutory maximum is $256,750, and the average is around $70,000. The world's best players generally opt to play in England's Premier League, Germany's Bundesliga, Italy's Serie A, or Spain's La Liga.

Of the twenty-three members of the U.S. World Cup team, only eleven play in MLS. Twelve play in Europe. Two members of the U.S. team made the FIFA (Fédération Internationale de Football Association) All-Star Squad: Carlos Reyna and Landon Donovan. The team's outstanding goalie, Brad Friedel, plays for the Blackburn Rovers in England's Premier League. Reyna plays for Sunderland in the Premier League.

Donovan currently plays for MLS, but he is on loan. In fact, he launched his pro career in the Bundesliga as a teenager and was expected to return to the Bayer Leverkusen team in that league after the World Cup.

Contrast this with the European World Cup squads, where the members all play in Europe, and most play in their home country. Of the twenty-three players on the Spanish team, twenty-two played in Spain's La Liga, and one played in Itlay. Of the twenty-three on England's team, twenty-two played in England's Premier League, and one played in the Bundesliga. And on the German team, twenty of the twenty-three played in the Bundesliga, with two in the Premier League and one in France.

Over time U.S. players will become stronger and stronger. But as long as professional soccer in the United States continues to pay the top players roughly one-tenth as much as they can earn on the free market, the country's leading players won't be accessible to U.S. fans. The U.S. team will continue to have success, but MLS will continue to be minor league, and its attendance will reflect as much.

Beantown's New Brain Trust Touches All the Fans' Bases

Now that baseball fans have the trauma of the 2002 near-strike behind us, it is time to reflect on and appreciate some of the good things that we have. One of the notable trends over the past decade in baseball is the improved quality of team-management staffs and ownership. The number of intelligent and experienced people running the front offices today is impressive. Whatever else the game's problems, it is always helpful to have better executives managing the show.

One significant upgrade has taken place in Boston. John Henry, Larry Lucchino, Tom Werner, and partners bought the Boston Red Sox in January 2002. The three are not only excellent baseball people, but they are sharp businessmen. Under Werner's initiative, the group put aside the longstanding plans of John Harrington to mothball Fenway Park. Instead, they realized that Fenway is an incomparable gem, so they set out to study whether the park is structurally viable and, if it is, how it can be improved for fan comfort and revenue enhancement. They hired the design genius behind Camden Yards, Janet-Marie Smith, who has been turning out multiple upgrade ideas. It is still not clear where it will all lead, but the Henry ownership group deserves mountains of credit for trying to preserve Fenway before playing the public-subsidy–extortion game, as did its predecessor.

Henry and partners, under the ingenious guidance of their public-relations guru Charles Steinberg, have engaged in several other initiatives to build stronger team–community bonds, and they have done so by adding an important personal touch. Henry, as do many owners today, watches many of the team's home games from his field box next to the Sox dugout. Security is such that fans can walk over to his seat and chat. My fellow resident of Northampton, Massachusetts, Ed Driscoll, took his son Ryan with him to the Tigers–Sox game on July 7 at Fenway. They went on the annual field trip of the Northampton Recreation Department. Their seats were in the lower–left-field grandstands. After a few innings, Ed and his son decided to wonder around the park. They paused for a few moments on the concourse behind home plate.

While there, they were approached by a family from Kentucky making their first visit to Fenway. The family was looking for a men's restroom. Moments later, they were approached by a slender man in khaki pants and button-down shirt. The man asked how they were doing and whether they were enjoying the game. After a few more questions, the man said that he would like it if Ed and his son would sit in his box for the rest of the game. Ed said he couldn't do that, but the man insisted.

At this point, Ed thought he recognized the man to be John Henry. He asked, and Henry confirmed with a simple "yes." He then called over an usher and asked that he lead Ed and Ryan to his box and get them any refreshments they desired. Henry then disappeared. When Ed and Ryan got to their new seats, they found the Kentucky family sitting in the box next to them.

A few weeks ago, I saw John Henry at Fenway and asked him about the incident. He didn't remember it. But we continued a conversation over e-mail, and I was able to extract the following perspective about Henry's approach to ownership. I hope that he will not mind my quoting one of his e-mails at some length:

> Suffice to say that owning a team here gives us unending opportunities to make a difference within the community. When I kicked off the Ted Williams tribute evening at one point I correctly said, "Everyone of us here tonight will, for the rest of our lives, remember this evening." Just creating opportunities for allowing people the ability to walk on the grass or play catch at Fenway creates a lasting memory for parents, grandparents, and kids.
>
> It's the little things you do every day that define your life and character. The little things have the greatest impact on your fans and let them know that you actually care about them. The Red Sox owners are detail-oriented. That can be a problem for the people you work with sometimes, but not here. In baseball I believe it happens to be a blessing. Not many items are too small for us because we know the responsibility we have. I think that's true at many levels of our organization.
>
> We are outsiders who have been adopted by New Englanders because they learned very early on how much we had in common with them. Our passion for baseball, our passion for Fenway even down to the color and consistency of the dirt has been part of the bonding process. They know we are trying every day.
>
> The Red Sox are so much a part of the fabric of New England that for the sick, the old, the healthy, the young, the front office—well, everyone here— I think we all understand that wondrous events go by quickly and need to be appreciated, that we're all in this together. The baseball season in New England is much like an epic saga in which every day a new chapter is being written. The characters are not confined to the field. The protagonists sit in the stands every night. They call the radio stations, they read the books, the papers, they watch the games on TV, and they stay connected in this long-suffering determination, actually, crusade, to win a World Series at Fenway.
>
> I am a very fortunate man allowed to work with bright, committed people and be a part of an institution that I hope to play a positive part in passing it on eventually to the next stewards. One can generally only dream of being in the position I find myself today.

When owners mess up, the media and fans are sure to let them know about it. When owners do the right thing, it is usually taken for granted. It makes sense to take the time to notice.

The NFL's Report Card

Commissioner Paul Tagliabue gave his state-of-the-game speech before last week's Super Bowl. Here's my assessment of what's right and what's wrong with the business of the NFL.

The main story is a good one. The NFL is a well-managed league. Tagliabue is a sober, smart leader, and his union counterpart, Gene Upshaw, is the same. Together they have fashioned an owner–player partnership that is the envy of every U.S., and many a foreign, team-sports league.

The NFLPA has come under attack by some critics who claim that the union has not done enough to guarantee players' contracts and raise salaries. To be sure, the union wants to accomplish more in the area of contract guarantees, but the reality is not what the critics believe. First, contract guarantees are not negotiated by sports unions into their collective-bargaining agreements; they are negotiated by players and agents into individual contracts. The greater probability of serious injury in football has made it very difficult to convince owners to offer such guarantees. Many players, however, receive healthy signing bonuses, making almost one-half of all earned salary guaranteed.

Second, the union has put a lot of emphasis on the players' benefits package. This year, the owners contributed some $350 million to players' benefits, nearly $200,000 per player. Players who suffer disabilities from football are entitled to receive up to $235,000 per year for life. (They also are entitled to workmen's compensation payments, and if Dan Snyder knows what is good for his league, he will stop seeking to modify the system in the Virginia legislature rather than at the bargaining table.)

Third, while it is true that the average NFL salary, at $1.1 million, is lower than that in the NBA, the NHL, or MLB, it is also true that the NFL roster has fifty-three players. If one takes the top twenty-five–paid players on each team in the NFL, their average salary is $2.1 million, just below MLB's ($2.38 million) and well above the NHL's ($1.64 million) average salaries. The new collective-bargaining extension will see the nominal cap rise to 64 percent of defined gross revenues (or roughly 60 percent of all revenues—a level similar to that in the other leagues).

The real story about labor–management cooperation in the NFL is that it is good for the industry. Fans, corporate sponsors, and media companies basically don't have to worry about work stoppages. Removing this uncertainty and the negative publicity that surrounds it encourages the NFL's clients to spend money and invest in the sport. Franchise values and salaries both benefit.

Sports Business Journal, February 3–9, 2003

Another piece of good news is that the NFL has accepted some responsibility in helping to finance new football stadiums. Under the league's G3 policy, the NFL makes a "loan" to team owners of up to half of the private money committed to stadium construction. So, for example, if a new stadium is built for a large city's team that is projected to cost $500 million, and the team's owner offers to pay $250 million, the NFL will "loan" the owner $125 million. The owner pays this back over time without interest by sharing 34 percent of club-seat revenues with the league. However, the club-seat sharing takes place with or without such a construction "loan," so the "loan" really functions as a grant from the league. Now some may argue that the owner or the league should assume a still larger financing burden (and I wouldn't quarrel with such a position), but the NFL has taken a positive step—not taken by the other leagues—with its G3 policy.

What about the bad news? First, back to the stadium issue: The NFL makes grandiose and unrealistic claims about the economic impact of the Super Bowl and its teams on a local economy. The league claimed that last week's Super Bowl in San Diego would bring the city $250 million–$300 million in economic impact. Don't count on it.

Existing scholarship suggests that the football fans largely replace tourists and business travelers when the Super Bowl is held in cities with warm climates. Hotel occupancy does not reliably increase, although room rates might rise (a good chunk of this extra cash may go to the home office of hotel chains). During the Super Bowl week, hotels often require that reservations be made for a minimum of five to seven days. Fans and media personnel oblige, but they may only stay for two or three days, meaning that less money is spent on per diems than when tourists and business travelers book the rooms and actually stay in the city for the entire time. Further, the host city must carry a substantial part of the cost to put on the game: security (estimated at $9 million this year), sanitation, setup, and infrastructure.

The 2003 Super Bowl was also affected by the country's economic doldrums and concern about an impending war. Corporate spending on lavish parties and sponsorships was off; average hotel-room prices were 20 percent below their 1998 level (the last time the Super Bowl was in San Diego); and room-occupancy rates were down 7 percentage points. If San Diego was expecting a financial bonanza, it is likely to be disappointed.

One of the reasons the NFL hypes the supposed economic benefits of the Super Bowl is that the league uses the game as a carrot to get cities to invest in new stadiums. Without a new stadium for the Chargers, the NFL will not give you another Super Bowl, Tagliabue told San Diego last week. And remember, says the commissioner, the team itself generates hundreds of millions of dollars for your local economy.

Again, dispassionate scholarship on this question suggests nothing of the sort. Tagliabue says he looks forward to his retirement when he will do his own study and prove all the academic economists who have studied the economic-impact issue to be wrong. Stockholm is hereby notified to hold the Nobel Prize in economics for this pathbreaking research.

Then there is the question of whether the Super Bowl might be more aptly dubbed the Mediocre Bowl. These days, one scarcely has a clue when the season begins which teams will make it to the championship game. This year, the biggest story seems to have been Coach Jon Gruden, not the players. If the rosters are even enough, then the coaches or the referees may provide the crucial margin of victory. The NFL may have gone too far in promoting parity and stripping away any owner's financial incentive or ability to field a winning team. But that's a long and complex story.

For now, the NFL news is mostly good, and its report card shows a solid B-plus.

Trading Deadline Activity Raises Issue of Baseball's Competitive Integrity

Baseball's July 31 trading deadline came and went, but it left behind some questions about the sport's competitive integrity. Consider what happened with the Cincinnati Reds and how it was handled by Commissioner Bud Selig.

The Cincinnati Reds' owner, Carl Lindner, said that his team needed a new stadium so it could be competitive again. Hamilton County obliged him, building a $330 million facility on the river. The Great American Ballpark opened this year. The Reds were ten games under .500 at the trading deadline.

Baseball's new revenue-sharing system also kicked in this year. The Reds stand to receive some $16 million in transfers from the other twenty-nine teams. Lindner is on baseball's version of welfare.

Yet after the late-July moves by the team, Reds fans must be wondering what went wrong. Lindner began the week by firing the team's field manager, Bob Boone, and its general manager, Jim Bowden. He then traded away four of the team's star players. By doing so, Lindner lowered his team's payroll by more than $9 million. He also received nearly $3 million in cash as part of the player transactions.

Baseball owners used to tell Congress not to worry about the game's special exemption from the nation's antitrust laws because the game's "independent" commissioner would protect the consumer from the potential abuses of monopoly. Then the owner of the Milwaukee Brewers was appointed commissioner. The veil of independence was removed.

Historically, one of the commissioner's main roles was to preserve the competitive integrity of the game. The founder of the National League, William Hulbert, routed out player corruption in the late 1870s through consistent and strict enforcement of a propriety code. Kenesaw Mountain Landis enforced honest behavior by imposing severe punishment in the Black Sox trial of 1921. In 1976, Bowie Kuhn attempted to strengthen the game's competitive integrity by limiting cash transfers between teams to $400,000 per trade.

Since Kuhn's ruling in 1976, baseball has followed the practice of not allowing more than $1 million (level adjusted in early 1990s) to change hands between teams as part of any trade. Two weeks ago, Commissioner Bud Selig forced the Yankees to restructure the trade of their star triple-A pitching prospect Brandon Claussen and $2 million in cash to the Reds for the third baseman Aaron Boone. Selig was quoted as saying, "There's no way that they're [the Yankees] are going to exceed the $1 million limit." Selig did allow the Yankees to transfer $1 million to the Reds along with Claussen and Charles Manning, another left-handed pitching prospect. He also allowed the Yankees to transfer $400,000 or a player to be named later to the Reds in a separate deal to obtain the relief pitcher Gabe White.

Selig, however, let the Red Sox trade a single-A pitcher of questionable talent (Phil Dumatrait, with an earned-run average of 3.02, a win–loss record of 7 and 5, 74 strikeouts, and 59 walks in 104 innings), a player to be named later, and $1.2 million in exchange for the Reds' star reliever Scott Williamson. Many analysts questioned whether the Reds got anywhere close to equal value in this trade. The transaction had the markings of a cash transfer—precisely what Kuhn was trying to avoid—rather than an exchange of commensurate player talent. (It is also not uncommon for the "player to be named later" to become cash if the two sides cannot agree on the player.)

So why did Commissioner Selig allow the Red Sox, but not the Yankees, to surpass the $1 million threshold even though the Yankees were giving up a highly coveted pitching prospect? MLB Vice President Sandy Alderson explained: "The commissioner has the discretion to look at situations on a case-by-case basis, and he has exercised some flexibility in the past as he did in this particular case." Does this mean now that only the Yankees cannot exceed the $1 million limit?

There was still another curious set of transactions involving the Red Sox and Pirates before the trade deadline. The Sox first obtained the prized left-handed reliever Scott Sauerbeck and the minor-league pitcher Mike Gonzalez for Brandon Lyon and Anastasio Martinez. The Pirates complained that Lyon, who immediately went on the disabled list with a strained elbow, was damaged goods.

Rather than have the Sox send the Pirates another player, the two teams made a new trade: the Pirates' superlative starter Jeff Suppan for the Sox minor-league infield prospect Freddy Sanchez and cash. And, oh yes, the Sox also got back Brandon Lyon and Anastasio Martinez (and returned Gonzalez). Do all the math and it appears that the Pirates may have received no players in return for Sauerbeck—another possible cash transaction.

Now there are plenty of baseball fans who would love to see the Red Sox beat out the Yankees in the American League East this year. But there are even more fans who want to see a fair competitive process. If the Yankees have an unfair revenue advantage, the way to balance the league is through a more efficient and effective revenue-sharing system. (This year, the Yankees will pay around $56 million into this system.) It is not through arbitrary and inconsistent interventions from a compromised commissioner. Every team should play by the same rules.

One may have thought that baseball already learned this lesson back in 1939, when, after the Yankees won their fourth consecutive World Series, the owners of American League clubs passed a rule intended to break the Yankees' victory string. The rule barred each year's pennant winner from buying, selling, or trading any player within the league during the following season. The Tigers edged out the Bronx Bombers for the 1940 pennant, and the owners repealed the rule, only to see the Yankees storm back with a vengeance to win the next three pennants in a row.

To be sure, the Red Sox and General Manager Theo Epstein did nothing wrong at the trading deadline. They were making the best deals available and doing so with great acumen. But it is the commissioner's job to insure that the playing field is level for all teams.

The commissioner also seems to have turned his head on the principle behind baseball's new revenue-sharing system: to create more balanced competition across all teams. Last year, when the system was introduced, I, and others, argued that the system's incentives were improperly structured and would not encourage the low-revenue teams to spend their transfers on improving their teams. Selig responded that he would police these teams: "The money must be spent on their franchise and on players, and it's going to be enforced and it's going to be enforced by me."

Yet the Reds are dumping salaries and star players in exchange for cash and dubious prospects. The Pirates (who are also playing in a new publicly funded stadium and traded away Kenny Lofton to the Cubs and the all-star pitcher Mike Williams to the Phillies in addition to Sauerbeck and Suppan) seem to be doing the same, despite receiving an estimated $8 million from MLB's revenue-sharing system this year, a sum that uncannily only increases as the team gets worse.

Let me be clear. There is nothing wrong when a team trades a player to rebuild. The problem is when the player imbalance in each transaction is made up for by cash (and sometimes not even then) and when the cash transfers are being made to teams that are already receiving $10 million–$20 million on the baseball dole—not to mention hundreds of millions in subsidies for public facilities.

The Gold in Baseball's Diamond

As the 2003 season drew to a close, remarkably half of baseball's teams had a chance to make the playoffs. Has Major League Baseball's year-old collective-bargaining agreement, with its revenue-sharing plan and luxury tax, leveled the playing field? Not exactly.

The tight races were chance occurrences, the result of a muddle of mediocrity at the top of the American League's Central Division and in the battle for the National League's wild-card slot. They had nothing to do with greater parity among the teams.

If the changes in the collective-bargaining agreement were having their intended effect, the payrolls of the top teams would be falling, and those for the bottom teams would be rising. But this isn't happening. The standard deviation, or the dispersion, of opening-day payrolls actually rose to $27.3 million in 2003 from $24.7 million in 2002, an increase of 10.5 percent.

Viewed differently, of the fifteen teams in contention in mid-September, ten were among the top twelve teams in payroll. Only two (the Oakland Athletics and the Kansas City Royals) came from the bottom ten teams in payroll.

So why is the new-collective bargaining agreement not working? Put simply, the agreement taxes increased earnings of low-revenue clubs at around 45 percent. Every time a relatively poor team such as the Milwaukee Brewers increases its revenues by a dollar, the league gives the club 45 cents less in revenue-sharing money. The team thus has little incentive to use its revenue-sharing money to buy better players and improve itself.

But wait, you say: Doesn't the new agreement require teams that receive revenue-sharing money to meet a minimum payroll standard? No. Rather, it sets out a vague criterion: A team must use its transfers "to improve its performance on the field." According to this standard, then, Bud Selig, the MLB commissioner and the person charged with enforcing this provision, could conclude that a team that pays off its debt or increases executive pay is taking steps to improve itself. In fact, almost any action could be justified as potentially improving the team.

Interestingly, the team owned by Selig's family, the Brewers, is faring pretty well under the new system. According to league estimates, the Brewers will receive a larger increase in revenue-sharing money than any other team, with receipts growing to an estimated $8.2 million in 2003 from roughly $1.2 million in 2001. (This is because Selig insisted on a revenue-sharing system that taxed the top teams most heavily and benefited the lower-middle, rather than the bottom, teams the most.)

New York Times, September 30, 2003

But are the Brewers improving themselves by signing better players? Well, the team's opening-day payroll fell to $40.6 million this year from $50.3 million last year.

Of course, the Brewers are not alone. Other teams benefited from increased revenue sharing—and cut their payrolls. Transfers for the Tampa Bay Devil Rays, for example, grew by $5.1 million, yet the team's opening-day payroll fell to $19.6 million this year from $34.4 million in 2002.

Baseball's competitive-balance problem is mostly a problem of bottom-dwelling teams performing poorly year after year. If these teams don't have the economic incentive or the statutory compulsion to raise their payrolls or invest more in their farm systems, then they will remain uncompetitive. The game will go on—but nothing will change.

What Went Wrong with WUSA?

Had he stuck around ESPN a bit longer, Rush Limbaugh might have opined: "The only reason anyone ever paid any attention to WUSA [the Women's United Soccer Association] is because people want to see women succeed in sports." Okay, maybe he wouldn't have said it, but more than one sportswriter has questioned the financial viability of women's professional sports in the last few weeks. Did they ever hear of Annika Sorenstam or Serena Williams? Have they observed the fan fervor and electricity of the Women's World Cup competition?

In fact, the suspension of WUSA has nothing to do with the viability of women's professional sports. Rather, it is the result of a misguided business plan that was poorly implemented, along with an inauspicious macroenvironment.

Let us begin with the obvious. WUSA started competitive play in 2001, the year the country's economy entered the economic doldrums after a decade-long boom. The U.S. economy remained weak for WUSA's three years, and the advertising market is just now beginning to show some signs of possible life. At the same time, corporate-management scandals have yielded a more cautious approach to sponsorship deals.

WUSA's timing was also unfortunate in coinciding with the eruption of digital cable, the explosion of new channels carrying niche sports, and the maturation of the Internet revolution.

The largest problem, however, resides in WUSA's strategy. The league's media-company investors committed $40 million and expected to see profits after several years. Yet anyone who has reflected for a moment on the experience of fledgling sports leagues knows that they do not become successful overnight. Our most popular league, the NFL, began operations in 1920 but did not capture the national imagination until the sudden-death–overtime championship game between the Giants and the Colts in 1958. The men's league, MLS, has been playing since 1996, and it still is not profitable.

Starting a new league requires deep pockets and a lot of patience. It also helps to have passionate, committed individuals rather than calculating corporations seeking to pad the bottom line.

A second problem with WUSA's plan lay in its single-entity structure. Single-entity sports leagues make little sense. MLS has struggled with it. So did the WNBA until it saw the light and allowed individual team ownership last year.

In single-entity leagues, investors together own all of the teams, and the key league decisions are made out of the central office—including the allocation of players. This robs fans of the opportunity to root for the team in the off-season by following trades, player development, and free-agent signings.

Intense sports fans need to be fed year-round. It is their energy that helps to spread enthusiasm to new fans.

Moreover, teams are better operated by local owners who understand, and have the incentive to cater to, the local market. Developing markets for new products is never easy. Investors need to be directly rewarded for the risk they undertake. The centralized management structure of single-entity leagues curtails the needed local initiative and thereby undermines the development of regional fan bases.

WUSA also made some fundamental management missteps. It took its games off TNT after the first year, where they were averaging a viewership of 425,000 households, and put them on the lesser-known PAX network, where they averaged 100,000 households.

Despite having reduced its media-market exposure to less than one-fourth its prior level, WUSA did not lower its $2.5 million a year price for major corporate sponsorships and found itself able to sell only two of the projected eight deals. Sound management would have responded to the market conditions and adjusted price to demand.

Similarly, initial ticket prices were too high. Scheduling was poor, often conflicting with MLS games. Promotion was inadequate, especially to new, potential fan bases. Stadium choices was often curious.

Women's professional sports do have some unique challenges. Probably foremost among them is identifying a distinct advertising-market target. Advertisers who want to reach women buy spots on daytime soaps and evening series. They don't need women's sports leagues to reach their female target audience.

Advertisers who want to reach men find that men's sports is the best way to do it. Thus, women's sports leagues face a more competitive advertising market and have a tougher time generating the advertising money that drives television-rights fees. The WUSA strategy to cultivate soccer moms should have been complemented by a strategy to cultivate soccer dads.

Of course, if the next women's soccer league gets it right, the real payoff will not come in five or ten years. It will come when this generation of soccer-playing youth take their daughters and sons to watch the next generation's Mia Hamms, Brandi Christains, and Julie Foudys.

Money Game:
Baseball's Short-Lived Rally

Judging by the healthy increases in television ratings for MLB's 2003 post-season games, it might seem that baseball is reasserting itself as our national pastime. The felicitous combination of avoiding a work stoppage in 2002; more competitive divisional and wild-card races; the unusual appearance of the Cubs, Sox, and Marlins in the League Championship series; and the emergence of exciting young stars has allowed MLB to decisively reverse a long-standing downward trend in its post-season television viewership.

This is good news for baseball fans like me, and some of it is due to better management of the game. One has to hope, however, that the present gloating of baseball executives does not distract attention from some of the sport's longstanding problems.

One such problem is the continued dominance of high-payroll teams. As of July 15, the Yankees' payroll for a forty-man roster was tops at $180.3 million, almost six times higher than the lowly Devil Rays' at $31.6 million and 2.25 times the average team payroll of $80 million. Consider this: Of the fifteen teams in playoff contention on September 15 of this year, ten came from the twelve highest-payroll teams, while only two came from the ten lowest-payroll teams. Of the final four teams, three came from the twelve top-payroll teams, and none came from the bottom ten teams.

High payroll, of course, does not guarantee a good team—just ask Fred Wilpon. Nor does low payroll guarantee a poor team. But there is a strong statistical correlation between team payroll and win percentage. Thus, spending more on players' salaries greatly increases a team's chance of being successful.

In his bestselling book *Moneyball*, Michael Lewis is right about one thing: Winning requires smart management. But he is wrong to suggest that smart management and state-of-the-art statistical analysis alone are sufficient to build a winning team.

Indeed, according to Lewis, the most important statistical insight applied by Billy Beane's Oakland Athletics is that a player's on-base percentage is far more significant than his batting average. Yet this year's As team ranked tenth out of fourteen American League teams in on-base percentage. Nonetheless, the As won the American League West.

So why did the team win? For the same reason that it has been successful each of the past four years: Good, old-fashioned scouting along with some good fortune landed the team a corps of top-flight starting pitchers. If the As continue to be parsimonious with payroll, their partial success will be short-lived.

Baseball's new revenue-sharing and luxury-tax system were supposed to solve the competitive-imbalance problem. So far there is little evidence to suggest that it will make a difference. There is no minimum payroll that revenue-receiving teams must meet, and the marginal tax rate on these teams is around 45 percent. Every time their revenues grow by $1, MLB gives them 45 cents less in revenue transfers. This leaves no compulsion and little incentive for the poor teams to use their transfers productively.

A related problem for baseball has been falling attendance. In 2002, attendance fell by 6 percent. This year, despite a late-season recovery, attendance fell again by 0.5 percent. Baseball cannot count on so many teams vying for post-season berths at the end of every season to drive attendance.

Rather, it must design sensible long-run strategies to build the game. Artificial and illogical gambits—such as granting World Series home-field advantage to the team from the league that wins the All-Star Game—both are unlikely to succeed in the short run (the All-Star Game's ratings this year did not improve) and send the wrong signal to the fans.

Baseball's largest challenge is to attract new young fans. Ratings among the under-eighteen male demographic are troubling, and Little League participation is falling, even as the population grows. Baseball needs to take concrete steps to appeal to youth, such as World Series games that start before 8:20 P.M. EST; opening ballparks early enough before games so that fans can watch the home team take batting practice and have players sign autographs; sponsor family days where children's tickets are heavily discounted; and so on.

But perhaps most crucial is for major-league baseball to be played in more of the nation's top cities. There is no better way to turn on the youth than to give them an opportunity to go to the ballpark and watch the Barry Bondses, Pedro Martinezes, and Derek Jeterses perform in person. The eighth-largest media market in the country, Washington, D.C., doesn't have a team; nor do Portland, Oregon, Sacramento, California, or Riverside/San Bernardino, California, all in the top-thirty media markets and growing rapidly.

Baseball, as a legal monopoly, is holding out for a fat stadium deal from one of these areas. If it doesn't get one, it even threatens to reduce the number of teams.

If baseball's barons continue to prioritize short-run profit over growing the sport in the long run, the game will suffer, and consumer welfare will not be served. One hopes that the success of this post-season will not make the barons take their eyes off the ball.

No Reason to Break Up the Yankees

Ever since the Yankees landed A-Rod, the mercury on Yankee hatred seems to have busted through the thermometer. Peter Gammons had one of the better quips: "The Beatles just got Elvis."

The analogy is apt in more ways than one. The Beatles had trouble getting along with each other. Add Elvis and his self-aggrandizing manager, Colonel Tom Parker, to the mix, and who knows what kind of noxious chemistry would have resulted.

Never mind that the Yankees basically will pay A-Rod's 2004 salary by unloading the salaries of Drew Henson, Aaron Boone, and Alfonso Soriano, and with subsidies from the Rangers' owner, Tom Hicks. Calls to break up the Yankees are being heard with increasing frequency and vehemence.

Baseball singled out the Yankees once before for prejudicial treatment. After the Yankees won their fourth consecutive World Series in 1939, the owners of American League clubs passed a rule intended to break the team's victory string. The rule barred each year's pennant winner from buying, selling, or trading any player within the league during the following season. The Tigers edged out the Yankees for the 1940 pennant, and the owners repealed the rule, only to see the Bronx Bombers rebound with a vengeance to win the next three pennants in a row. Maybe the rule worked!

Of course, baseball already has various rules that are intended to blunt the Yankees' competitive edge. For instance, the Yankees' forty-man payroll this year is likely to end up at about $190 million. As second-time "violators" of the luxury-tax threshold, George Steinbrenner will pay a 30 percent tax on the portion of his payroll above $120.5 million—or roughly $21 million. Steinbrenner will also contribute about $55 million net to MLB's revenue-sharing system. Effectively, the Yanks will be transferring $75 million-plus to help baseball's low-revenue teams.

According to baseball's collective-bargaining agreement, the low-revenue teams are supposed to be using these transfers to improve their competitive performance—that is, by raising their payroll and player-development expenditures. The two problems with this lovely plan are (1) the low-revenue teams face marginal tax rates of more than 45 percent on new revenues, stripping them of any incentive to increase payrolls; and (2) the plan is supposed to be enforced by an owner of a low-revenue team, Commissioner Selig.

His own team, the Brewers, has experienced larger increases in revenue sharing transfers than any other team (in July, the Brewers projected their 2003 net receipts to be $18 million), yet the Brewers have lowered payroll from above $50 million to close to $30 million over the last two years.

Sports Business Journal, April 5–11, 2004

Selig himself waxes Pollyannaish about how the new system has worked wonders for competitive balance. He told *Sports Illustrated*'s Tom Verducci, "Last September 1, 17 or 18 teams were still in playoff contention. ... That couldn't have happened seven or eight or nine or ten years ago." Actually, on September 1, 2003, there were seventeen teams within four games of their division lead or wild card. But go back eight years to 1995, as Selig suggests, and on September 1, there were eighteen clubs within four games.

The proper system would not rely on Selig's, or any other commissioner's, discretion to implement. It would be a system that had the right incentives built in. The clear way to do this is to base the revenue-sharing tax on the revenue-generating capacity of a team's market (e.g., metropolitan statistical area population, stadium characteristics) rather than on a team's success.

The present system penalizes success. Why should the Red Sox, in the sixth-largest media market, pay almost $40 million in revenue-sharing taxes (the second-highest amount in 2003) while the Phillies, in the fourth-largest market, have been revenue recipients? The Sox are being penalized for succeeding, and the Phillies are being rewarded for failing.

The Red Sox's tax should be set according to the Boston market and Fenway. If the team does well on the field and in marketing itself, and revenues go up, the team should not pay a higher tax. Conversely, if the team does poorly, it should not pay a lower tax.

Same for the Yankees. Steinbrenner should not be penalized for investing in his team. Isn't this what all fans want their owners to do?

According to Selig's Blue Ribbon Panel, competitive balance means that all well-managed teams should have a regularly recurring chance of making it to the post-season. The Yankees are not keeping the Devil Rays, the Tigers, the Brewers, the Pirates, or the Reds from making it to the playoffs. But baseball's incentive system is.

Most people either love or hate the Yankees. Passion is good for the game. It is also good for the game to have teams in the larger media markets win more often.

In recent years, team payroll accounts for only 20 percent to 40 percent of the variation in a team's win percentage. That means 60 percent to 80 percent is determined by proficient management, effective player development, positive chemistry, and good luck. The Yankees haven't won the World Series for the past three years, and a reasonable statistical assessment would put their odds no higher than 15 percent to win it this year.

Baseball doesn't need to break up the Yankees. It needs to manage itself properly.

So everybody, repeat after me: Thank you, Mr. Steinbrenner.

More Financial Smoke and Mirrors from MLB

After years of gloomy proclamations about the state of baseball's financial condition, the commissioner's office is beginning to sound surprisingly upbeat. Average players' salaries in 2004 are $2.49 million, down 2.7 percent from 2003. That might not seem like much, but it is a big turnaround from the 11.5 percent annual growth rate in salaries from 1995 through 2003.

So there's some cause for optimism at 245 Park Avenue, but MLB's chief financial officer, Jonathan Mariner, made an eye-popping claim to *Sports Business Journal*'s Dan Kaplan last week: Only five MLB teams are in danger of not meeting the league's pending debt restrictions.

Baseball's new debt restrictions were collectively bargained in the 2002 agreement. In brief, they state the following: Each club may have a total debt (including future payment obligations to players) equal to ten times (or fifteen times if it has a new stadium) the club's average EBITDA over the preceding three seasons.

EBITDA stands for earnings before interest, taxes, depreciation, and amortization and is a rough measure of operating income. The new debt rule also allows a $25 million exclusion, so that teams with negative average EBITDAs may still hold $25 million in debt.

This rule is not scheduled to be fully applied until after the 2005 season. This means that the relevant measure in its first year will be a team's average EBITDA during the 2003, 2004, and 2005 seasons. (For purposes of the debt rule, EBITDA is computed before revenue-sharing payments and receipts.)

It is apparent that, for a team to meet the new debt-rule obligations, either it will have to have debt below $25 million or it will have to be operating with a profit. Average team debt in 2004 is between $100 million and $133 million, and this excludes long-term obligations for players' salaries, according to MLB's figures.

Thus, even without long-term player obligations, the typical team would have to experience an average operating profit between $10 million and $13.3 million during 2003–2005. This is a tall order given the data that MLB and its teams have been putting out.

Remember that back in 2001, Selig went to Congress and proclaimed that MLB teams had a joint operating loss of $232 million. In 2002, MLB claimed that the teams' operating losses had risen to around $500 million.

Last year couldn't have been much better. Salaries were up, and attendance was down. This year's prospects are a bit brighter, but consider some spotty data that have been released for individual teams.

The Mets projected an operating loss of $15 million–$20 million in 2003. The Diamondbacks projected losses of $40 million–$50 million in 2002. The Giants expected a loss of $15 million in 2003 and a similar result in 2004. The Blue Jays reported an operating loss of $10 million–$12 million in 2003, with smaller losses in 2004. The Dodgers reported a negative EBITDA of $42.98 million in 2003 and hoped to cut this number by roughly $15 million a year in the next two years. Michael Ozanian at *Forbes* magazine, who is generally more sanguine about MLB's finances than baseball executives, estimated that half of the teams had operating losses in 2003.

Given that the EBITDA standard will average the results for the 2003, 2004, and 2005 seasons, it strains credulity to imagine that all but five teams will have operating profits in the eight digits. The only other possibilities are (1) that teams will lower their debt loads below $25 million, requiring significant (and unlikely) new equity contributions; or (2) that the economic figures MLB has been dishing out substantially understate the financial strength of the franchises.

Of course, MLB has played fast and loose with its debt rule in the past. The owners introduced their 60–40 rule in 1982, which stated that a club had to maintain a ratio between assets and liabilities of at least 60 to 40. In March 2002, Selig announced that he was going to begin enforcing the rule again. Then, on January 16, 2004, a week before MLB approved Murdoch's sale of the Dodgers to the Boston developer Frank McCourt for $430 million, Selig told the Associated Press: "Rules are rules, and there are no exceptions. We have very stringent ownership rules, guidelines that we follow fastidiously."

Well, if Selig followed his 60–40 rule fastidiously, McCourt would have been able to borrow only $172 million, tops. Yet according to Kaplan, McCourt borrowed more than $400 million.

The lesson here is clear. When MLB says its finances are in bad shape, take it with a grain of salt. When MLB says that only five teams are in danger of being in violation of its new debt rule, put your hands in your pockets.

Enough Already:
Time to Award D.C. a Franchise

Some day soon, we are told once again, MLB will let us know whether the nation's capital is deserving of a baseball team. Washington, D.C., ranks eighth nationally in the size of its media market (with 2.5 times the number of television households as Milwaukee) and fourth in the number of companies with more than 100 employees.

Its median family income in 2000 was $84,800. This is well above the level in the other cities in contention: $65,800 in Portland, Oregon; $55,200 in Norfolk, Virginia; $54,700 in Las Vegas; and $50,500 in San Antonio, Texas. And it is well above that in many existing baseball markets: $68,000 in Denver; $66,700 in Kansas City; $63,900 in St. Louis; $62,600 in Milwaukee; $59,900 in San Diego; $54,100 in Pittsburgh; and $49,700 in Tampa, to name a few.

So what gives? Why can't MLB just proclaim that D.C. gets a team? Let us count the ways.

First, there is the stadium issue. MLB wants a well-located, well-appointed, publicly funded stadium. The more money that the team's new owner has to put into the stadium, the less money he or she will be willing to pay MLB for the Expos. MLB's clear strategy has been to draw as many cities as possible into the bidding for the Expos until it gets a stadium offer to its liking. Mayor Anthony Williams, after holding out for more than a year, told MLB in April that he would support a fully publicly funded facility costing about $400 million. That's a step in the right direction, but Williams needs to bring along at least the City Council. Northern Virginia is behind D.C. in this regard.

Second, there is the matter of an ownership group. MLB wants a group that is well funded, with a managing partner whom Selig can trust. It would not hurt if the individual had good political and business connections. It would be even better if he or she belongs to an ethnic minority.

Third, MLB is waiting for the arbitrator's decision in the fraud grievance brought by the Expos' former minority partners. After the fraud claim is settled, a civil racketeering charge remains that needs to be adjudicated in federal court. Currently, there is an injunction that requires MLB to give the plaintiffs a ninety-day notice before it moves the Expos from Montreal, so that the plaintiffs have time to do discovery and bring motions. I don't have any idea how all this will play out, but for the time being it is another obstacle to be hurdled.

Fourth, there is Peter Angelos, owner of the Baltimore Orioles. Angelos claims that if a team goes to D.C., then his Orioles will become a noncompetitive, perhaps failing, franchise. To be sure, a team in D.C. would have a negative impact on attendance and TV ratings for the Orioles, but diminution in the team's revenue is not likely to be more than 10–20 percent.

There is, of course, also the possibility than an interesting rivalry could develop between the D.C. and Baltimore franchises, boosting the financial fortunes of each. More important, however, is that there is no reason why both D.C. and Baltimore should not have franchises. The Baltimore media market is just slightly smaller than that of St. Louis and larger than that of San Diego, Kansas City, Cincinnati, and Milwaukee. The Orioles also have an excellent stadium deal. Both cities should have teams.

A number of news articles have reported that Selig told Angelos during the All-Star Game break: "I will not do anything that makes Peter Angelos unhappy." Reportedly, Selig also repeated the comment to baseball's bankers.

Why would Selig say this? Angelos has no legal rights here. Baseball grants territorial monopolies to its teams that are defined by counties. The Orioles' counties do not include D.C. or Virginia.

It is true that D.C. is part of the Orioles' television reach, but television territory is fully allocated across the country. If it were inviolable, then there could never be a relocated or expansion team—not now, not in twenty years.

Some have suggested that Selig meant that, if he were to decide to put the Expos in D.C., he would provide compensation to Angelos. Angelos himself rejected the idea, stating that taking money but killing his franchise is not a deal he'd want to make.

This could be a bargaining posture, but why would Selig compensate Angelos anyway? If Selig is to keep Angelos from becoming unhappy, he'd undoubtedly have to offer him a healthy sum. Not only would that reduce the payout to the other owners from selling the Expos; it would set a precedent for the future. Would Nintendo be compensated if a team eventually went to Portland? Would Moreno and McCourt be paid off if a team went to Vegas?

Angelos will be able to comfort himself with the increased revenue sharing he'll get if a team moves to D.C. That, along with some good management, can keep the Orioles competitive.

Anybody know what the average attendance was in Montreal in 1994 before the strike?

Tweaking the NFL Juggernaut

So, what else is new? The 2004 NFL season is upon us, and the Patriots opened with a victory over the Colts, thanks in no small part to the steady foot of the placekicker Adam Vinatieri.

Another thing that is not new this year is that NFL clubs will, once again, be massively profitable. According to the estimates of Michael Ozanian at *Forbes* magazine, in 2003 only one of the NFL's thirty-two teams, the Arizona Cardinals, failed to make a profit. The NFL's worst stadium deal, a lousy team, and a less than effective front office left the franchise with an estimated $4.9 million loss. (According to *Forbes*, the Cardinals were actually profitable in the two previous years. In any event, the Cardinals will have a new, state-of-the-art stadium in Glendale in two years, so there's no need to create a new subsidy program on their behalf.)

All of the other NFL teams were in the black in 2003, with team profits rising as high as $69.6 million for the Redskins (despite having a poor team) and average profits of $27.6 million. In addition to their yearly financial returns, owners reap handsome capital gains, benefits to their other businesses, tax-sheltering opportunities, and a plethora of perks.

The players aren't doing too badly, either. The team payroll cap in 2004 is $80.5 million, and that is routinely exceeded via amortized signing bonuses. On top of that, each team pays roughly $15 million for player benefits.

So when you read that the NFL has created a revenue-sharing–study committee, that it is beginning to negotiate an extension to its labor deal with the players' association, or that it is in discussions with the networks over a new television contract, there is no cause for alarm. The NFL is simply tweaking its economic juggernaut. It is as if you owned a new Lexus and got a note from the dealer reminding you to bring in your car for its first 2,000 mile lube.

Nonetheless, the NFL does have some interesting issues to tackle. Despite sharing more than 70 percent of its revenues, stadium economics have propelled growing inequalities in team revenues. Dan Snyder's Redskins are expecting to earn $75 million in premium seating alone and another $50 million from local sponsorship and marketing this year. Overall, the Redskins' revenues will likely exceed $250 million in 2004, while that of the Cardinals will be around $140 million. This constitutes a ratio of top to bottom team revenue of 1.8 to 1.

This ratio might seem high to NFL egalitarians, but consider that the post–revenue-sharing ratio in baseball is higher than 3 to 1. MLB Commissioner Bud Selig has said that the current system in baseball is working just fine. Why does the NFL need to worry about a 1.8-to-1 ratio, especially when virtually all teams are profitable and the bottom teams are getting new stadiums?

Good question. Doesn't some inequality preserve the incentive to innovate, to grow the product, develop the local market, hire the best players, and so on? Some say that the greater equality is needed to preserve competitive balance, but the NFL should also be concerned about encouraging mediocrity. Moreover, together with the existing revenue sharing, the league's salary cap, reverse-order draft, and unbalanced scheduling combine to give the NFL unparalleled competitive balance.

Oddly, the players' association is also in favor of more revenue sharing. In general, more revenue sharing means that each player's value to a particular team is reduced, because whatever revenue his talent produces has to be shared with other teams. This, in turn, reduces players' salaries. In the NFL, however, the salary-cap system pretty much sets the aggregate salary level, and revenue sharing has little impact in this regard.

But the players' association is interested in something else this time. Because stadium-related revenues have been growing so rapidly, the union wants all of these revenues included in the base for the salary cap. The sports consultant Marc Ganis was quoted in the September 6–12, 2004, issue of *Sports Business Journal* as saying that this union proposal was "unfair." Ganis's idea is that local revenue growth often comes along with substantial team investment in a new stadium. If the team had known that it would have to share the fruits of its investment, then it might not have made it or might have made it under different terms.

Ganis's position seems confused. First, one could also argue that it is unfair to owners to have to share more revenue with other owners on the same grounds. Second, under the present collective-bargaining agreement, teams already share stadium revenues, since around half of them are included in the salary-cap base (defined gross revenue). So if the union proposal is unfair, then the present system is also unfair.

Third, most team owners received substantial public funding to construct new facilities (the average public share is around 70 percent), and most received NFL G3 loans (which are really grants) for most of the rest. Of course, many also paid for the "private" portion by selling naming rights or PSLs. For the truly private share of construction costs, it would make sense to arrange for a revenue-sharing credit.

Fourth, the NFL model is built on the notion of a partnership between the owners and players. Why should part of the revenue that the players help to generate be excluded from this partnership?

Even with $15 million per team for player benefits, players' health benefits still leave something to be desired. To entertain us, players put their limbs (and sometimes lives) at constant risk. Virtually all players sustain an injury to the body that affects them long after they retire. Yet health benefits are covered only for five years after retirement.

The moral is this: There is no good case that owners should be sharing more revenue with each other. There is a good case, however, to share more with the players.

Single Entity, Though Alluring, Won't Solve Hockey's Problems

[**Note:** *This piece appeared during the 2004–2005 owners' lockout in the NHL that caused the entire season to be lost.*]

Two weeks ago. Bain Capital (BC) and Game Plan International (GPI) made a bold and tempting offer to the NHL: They would buy the entire league, all thirty teams, for $3.5 billion. The implied average franchise value is $116.7 million, but BC and GPI said they had a formula to pay high-revenue, large-market teams more than the average and low-revenue, small-market teams less than the average.

BC is run by Steven Pagliuca, co-owner of the Boston Celtics, and GPI is run by the sports-financing veterans Bob Caporale and Randy Vataha. Following the old adage "Buy low, sell dear," they saw an opportunity to snatch up future asset value at a bargain price. Before this year's lockout, *Forbes* magazine estimated that the average NHL franchise was worth $163 million. But one week before the offer, Disney's Anaheim Mighty Ducks sold for only $75 million, and that price included a training facility valued at $15 million.

There are doubtless many NHL owners who found the BC–GPI offer enticing. To be able to undo themselves of a depreciating asset in a league with no viable economic system in sight and a despoiled brand at an average price more than $100 million must have had several owners salivating.

Most owners of large-market teams, however, could not have been very tempted. The potential value of their teams would be substantially above the BC–GPI offer. Moreover, many of these franchises are owned by individuals or companies that use the hockey team to support other assets in their portfolio (such as television stations, regional sports networks , arenas, or concession companies).

Presumably, what tempted BC and GPI was the opportunity to turn the league around and realize potential value. Any reasonable analysis of hockey's economic system would conclude that two things needed fixing.

First, the league expanded willy-nilly in the 1990s to new and dubious markets, at $70 million-plus a pop, without introducing any revenue-sharing system to support these and other weak franchises. Because the NHL commands only a diminutive national TV rights fee and because it does not share any local revenue, the expansion by nine teams in the 1990s without a new sharing plan was imprudent in the extreme. In fact, it smacked of a short-term money grab without regard to the long-term consequences.

Second, whether one believes that the share of players' salaries in league revenues is 75 percent, as the league claims, or closer to 68–70 percent, as some union estimates would suggest, either share is unsustainable. The pre-lockout average team revenues of approximately $70 million were simply too low to support a salary share above 60 percent. *[**Note:** As part of the 2005 collective-bargaining agreement that introduces a salary cap based on revenues, the league agreed to count an additional $100 million–$150 million in revenues. This acknowledgment of revenues is consistent with the union's previous contention about the true salary share.]*

BC and GPI had a plan to deal with both problems: create a single-entity league. That is, create a league whose teams all belong to the same company under the same ownership. This way, revenues could be shared as equally as desired without risking the opposition of big-city owners.

Further, if all the teams were owned by the same entity, then they would not compete against each other in the market for players. Theoretically, players' salaries could be controlled as needed.

Theory and practice, however, diverge. The first problem is that the NHLPA is no more likely to accept dealing with a single entity than it was willing to accept NHL Commissioner Gary Bettman's team salary cap at $42.5 million.

The union could decertify as a collective-bargaining unit and sue the league's owners on antitrust grounds. The legal victory of Major League Soccer over its players in its single-entity suit might not help the new league, because in that instance a new league was being created rather than being converted from one with a competitive labor market to one without competition. The new ownership would have to argue that it is enhancing competition by preserving professional hockey in North America. But that would be declaring a premature death for the NHL.

Even without decertification, the new league and the union would have to agree on a contract. This would be no easy matter. The players could also pursue the alternative of a new league.

Beyond the labor conundrum, there is a more fundamental question about the viability of the single-entity model. The WNBA started with this model and abandoned it. MLS retains it, but the league has underperformed expectations. One element of this underperformance is that local teams do not have sufficient incentive and freedom to market themselves locally.

Another element is that without an open, competitive players' market, fans are deprived of one of the most exciting aspects of being a fan. Spectator-sports culture in North America seeks the ability to root for a team year-round. If player assignment is done out of a central office rather than by local general managers, this feature is at least vitiated, if not eliminated.

Sitting at the lunch table discussing what trades or free-agent signings one's team should undertake fuels the hot-stove league. Fan intensity is thereby promoted. This intensity, in turn, radiates out into the community to create more fans.

In the end, single-entity structures seem like a simple solution to a complex, intractable problem. The real solution, however, lies in strong, intelligent, forward-looking leadership.

British Soccer Fans, Kicked Again

Last week, globalization hit Manchester, England. Specifically, an American businessman who owns the Tampa Bay Buccaneers bought Manchester United, the world's most famous and richest soccer club. Malcolm Glazer has no known interest in either the city or the sport (his son Joel is said to be a soccer fan but is not known ever to have attended a game). Tampa Bay is 4,300 miles from Manchester, and it seems unlikely that the new owners will be spending much time in the clubhouse.

Most observers reckon that Glazer's interest is purely financial. The franchise he bought was not "sweating its assets" properly: ticket prices were too low, promotion was too weak, and not enough income was being extracted from broadcasters. Any NFL owner could draw up a plan in an afternoon that would raise income 20–30 percent in the short term. And then there's the potential of the global brand. Manchester United, England's most popular team, is big in China, Japan, and the rest of the Far East. With proper marketing, Glazer could be sitting on a gold mine. He's already planning a casino-hotel complex across from the stadium.

Amid all this beamish marketing talk, it may be easy for you to miss the look on the faces of the local Manchester fans. Glazer may have paid $1.47 billion for the team, but they think he robbed them of their rightful heritage. To understand why they feel this way, you have to understand a little bit about soccer culture, English style.

Soccer—"football" in England and in most of the world, of course—was born in England in the middle of the nineteenth century, the product of a leisured upper class, and spread rapidly abroad. It was loved precisely for the gentlemanly virtues of teamwork and fair play that its founders espoused. Unlike cricket and baseball, both of which carry an overbearing national identity, soccer was embraced wholeheartedly almost everywhere it was played. In the early twentieth century, a global governing body emerged, empowered to spread soccer to every corner of the globe using funds generated by international competition. Even the heathen United States was brought into the fold in 1994.

Today, virtually every conflict known to man or woman is played out on the soccer field. Catholic versus Protestant, fascist versus communist, aristocrat versus the working man, town versus country, east side versus west. For any given feud there is a soccer rivalry to match. Soccer hooliganism is often presented as an aberration on the face of the beautiful game, but in fact it is merely the dark side of the intense rivalry soccer inspires everywhere.

Washington Post, May 22, 2005 (co-authored with Stefan Szymanski)

Such strong emotions do not make for serene enjoyment, and the tormented life of an English soccer fan is vividly depicted in Nick Hornby's autobiographical 1992 novel *Fever Pitch*. Hornby managed to explain just how difficult it is to support a team—the sheer volume of unhappiness one has to go through to experience the buzz from winning. Now consider that Hornby is lucky to support Arsenal, which, like Man U, is one of the few successful English clubs. The peculiar misery of most English fans arises from the fact that for most teams, the prospect of ever winning a championship is remote. That's because there is an extreme playing-field imbalance built into English soccer, and it creates a defeatist mind set that few Americans—except, perhaps, Cubs fans—are likely to understand.

Think of it this way: American sports, not unreasonably, are built around the concept that spectators want to be entertained. Since they are largely entertained by winning, American leagues routinely redistribute resources, impose salary caps, implement reverse-order drafts, and the like to maintain some kind of competitive balance. That doesn't happen here. There is almost no revenue redistribution in the soccer world; therefore, big-city teams dominate perpetually. When the Yankees won three World Series in a row at the end of the twentieth century, many fans were outraged, and the baseball establishment expressed dismay. When Manchester United won eight out of the first eleven championships of the Premier League (1993–2003), no one batted an eyelid.

Of course, even a losing team can console its fans with good food, drink, and the razzmatazz of going to the game. Not so in English soccer. Part of the misery evoked by Hornby involves the antiquated stadiums, the lousy food (generally a lukewarm meat pie of dubious provenance and a cup of the beef-extract brew known as Bovril), and the long lines, which mean that if you do opt to buy something during the fifteen-minute half-time break, you are almost guaranteed to miss the first five minutes of the second half. No scantily clothed cheerleaders, no cartoonish mascots, no wacky races. And by the way, it's illegal to drink beer anywhere in view of a professional soccer match in the United Kingdom—in a so-called luxury suite.

So if it's all so miserable, why do the English care so much? Many outsiders attribute their passion to a specific brand of masochism. But there must always be hope. And while English soccer doesn't redistribute money, it does dangle in front of every fan, no matter how lowly his team or humble the league in which it plays, the maddening possibility of a better future. This comes through the "promotion and relegation system," whereby the two or three teams finishing at the bottom of one league are demoted to a lower league the next season, and the two or three teams at the top of the lower league are promoted to the higher rank. Lowly teams really do rise to the top. This month Wigan, a smokestack town of 300,000 in northern England, saw its team promoted to the Premier League (first in a hierarchy of five professional English leagues) after twenty-seven years of fighting its way up from the equivalent of single-A baseball. Such a possibility breeds resilience.

But it also works the other way. This season, Nottingham Forest, once champion of Europe, was relegated to the equivalent of the minor leagues. Given the scale of the drama, you, too, might find it hard to worry about the quality of the food.

In case you're wondering, that law against beer was introduced in the 1980s to deal with the hooliganism problem. Until recently, the misery of the soccer experience was compounded by a high probability of being close to some kind of violence. In the 1970s many fans abandoned the game entirely because of hooliganism, and attendance fell to an all-time low in 1986.

Gentrification reversed this trend. For most of the past century, English soccer fans came mostly from the working class. One reason they were so badly treated was that they had no money to spend on revenue-generating frills. Until the 1960s, the working class put up with this peacefully, but as traditional soccer authority broke down, the game attracted the kind of young thugs more likely to be found in inner-city gangs in the United States. Eventually, under Prime Minister Margaret Thatcher, the British government stepped in and imposed draconian policing and new laws to stop the violence. Since the 1990s, English hooligans have had to go abroad to find the kind of opportunities to fight that they once enjoyed at home.

Once English soccer became safe again, it became fashionable. Hornby himself played a role by raising the misery of the soccer fan to the status of art. Recognizing a lucrative audience, broadcasters started to pay huge sums to show live games, giving clubs the resources to attract star players from abroad and to fund a massive investment in new stadiums. At this point, business saw an opportunity to make serious money in soccer. Clubs raised equity, issued IPOs, and moved from the back pages to the financial pages.

The new guys in suits set about finding a way to maximize soccer's value. Higher prices brought in a new kind of clientele, more hedonistic and less fatalistic. But the old guard still has the biggest voice in the game, and it is not happy. Roy Keane, the iconic captain of Manchester United, derisively referred to the newcomers as the "prawn sandwich brigade" and blamed them for the declining volume of cheers at the club's stadium.

The old fans are not happy that their story of true grit is being sanitized. They don't want pizza and hot dogs at the stadium. They don't want fair-weather fans who pay fancy prices for executive boxes. They don't want Americans and American accents, and most of all they don't want an American businessman who's only in it for the money.

In England, the vast majority of soccer clubs have never made a profit. Emulating the U.S. model and uniting Europe's top clubs into a single, closed league would be a sure-fire way to make more money. Not only would it add to the value of broadcast rights; it would create a system for controlling costs and raising revenue.

Some might have said that Roman Abramovitch, the Russian billionaire who bought the Chelsea soccer club and invested $400 million to make the team champions this season, brought globalism to English soccer. But he borders on being acceptable because he loves the game. Glazer doesn't.

Hornby's *Fever Pitch* was recently released as a film, in what you might call the American translation, as the rather more upbeat story of a Red Sox fan. If Malcolm Glazer is trying to rewrite downbeat English football as upbeat American soccer in Manchester, he is going to have to overcome the English taste for misery.

It's one thing for the British to buy Chinese-made shirts or Chilean fruit. There's no cultural subversion there. But sporting passions are another matter. The implicit ethos of globalization that one size fits all just might meet its match as American capital invades the playing fields of England.

McClatchy Is Barking Up the Wrong Tree

Kevin McClatchy would like to turn baseball into a welfare state. This year, baseball's top-revenue franchises will transfer nearly $300 million to its bottom-revenue teams. Of this, McClatchy's Pirates are projected to receive more than $20 million.

McClatchy's also been getting some welfare from the state and county. Pennsylvania and Allegheny County put up $239 million toward the construction of PNC Park in 2001.

The total development cost of the stadium was approximately $260 million, so the team put up less than 10 percent. The team keeps all baseball revenues generated at the stadium, including parking, and pays only $100,000 a year in rent.

McClatchy bought the team with his partners in 1996 for $90 million. Today it is worth upward of $220 million.

All this welfare, and McClatchy's Pirates still had the second-lowest opening-day payroll in baseball in 2005, at $33.6 million. Earlier this year, the Pirates traded Matt Lawton ($7.5 million salary) for Jody Gerut ($360,000 salary), and the team's payroll dropped further.

When he bought the team, McClatchy repeated the oft-heard refrain: "We need a new stadium to build a competitive team."

In fact, McClatchy's team has not had a winning record in the ten years of his ownership, and things just keep getting worse.

Between 1996 and 2000, the Pirates won an average of 73.6 games per season. As I write, the 2005 Pirates have a record of 57 victories and 85 losses, 33 games out of first place. This projects to 65 wins at season's end.

Using this projected total, the Pirates will have won an average of 69.2 games per season for the five years playing in their new ballpark. That is, PNC Park, despite being one of the top three new stadiums in the country, has witnessed a decrease of 4.4 victories per season on average.

All this losing and public support have generated a lot of negative public relations for McClatchy. No matter, McClatchy is making out like a bandit.

With a diminutive payroll, $20 million-plus in transfers from MLB, and a new stadium, McClatchy's profits this year are estimated by the *Pittsburgh Post-Gazette* to be $12.8 million—not bad for a perennially losing club in a relatively small market.

And McClatchy takes no responsibility. He blames the team's poor performance over the past decade on MLB's economic system. The revenue-sharing total of nearly $300 million is not enough, he says.

But the real problem is not that baseball's level of revenue sharing is inadequate. It is, in part, that the underlying incentive system does not encourage the recipient teams to spend their transfers on improving themselves.

Rather, when a recipient team improves its performance and revenues rise, it must give back more than 45 percent of the new revenues in the form of reduced transfer payments from MLB.

Thus, even though the collective-bargaining agreement states that the revenue transfers are supposed to be spent on improving on-field performance, the system's incentives militate against it.

The only line of defense is the commissioner's office, which has been loath to tell the low-revenue teams to increase their payrolls. The consequence is that most recipient teams have not increased their payrolls, and some have even reduced them.

A better system is easy to identify. Teams should be taxed according to the inherent advantages of their market, not according to their actual revenue.

If ownership in a medium-size market runs an efficient operation, fields a competitive team, and promotes itself well in its local market, it should not be penalized with higher taxes.

Similarly, if ownership of a team in a large market runs an ineffective operation, fields a losing team, and does weak promotion, it should not be rewarded with higher transfers. The Phillies, in the nation's fourth-largest media market and largest unshared market, received close to $10 million a year in transfers in 2002 and 2003.

Why should the Boston Red Sox be paying the second-highest revenue-sharing taxes in MLB? The Sox are in baseball's sixth-largest media market and twentieth-largest television market, according to MLB's allocation of television territory. The present owners have hired a topnotch front office that has performed marketing miracles in New England, refurbished and expanded Fenway Park with superlative taste and private funds, and fielded a world-championship team.

Their reward is a revenue-sharing bill approaching $50 million—more than the Mets in New York, the Cubs and White Sox in Chicago, the Dodgers and Angels in Los Angeles and Orange counties, and the Phillies in Philadelphia.

Good management matters, and small-market teams can win, as the As, Twins, and Indians, among others, have demonstrated. McClatchy's front office put Bronson Arroyo on waivers after the 2002 season. And it wasn't deep pockets that enabled the Red Sox to sign the free agent David Ortiz for $1.2 million three years ago.

Baseball needs a system that encourages initiative and good management. It doesn't need to throw more good money into a bad system.

McClatchy didn't need a new ballpark, and he doesn't need more revenue sharing. He needs a rescue effort from FEMA. On second thought ...

III

Stadiums: Financing, Mega-Events, and Economic Development

Fan Freedom and Community Protection Act of 1996

The NFL, NBA, NHL, and MLB are monopolies. For public-relations purposes, these leagues will contend that they are not monopolies but, instead, just competitors in a large entertainment industry. They are part of the entertainment industry just as my socks, shirt, and jacket are part of the garment industry. They all keep me warm. The real question from an economic point of view is whether there is meaningful price competition among these various entertainment forms. If the San Francisco 49ers raise their average ticket prices from $40 to $42, will fewer people attend their games and more attend the games of the Golden State Warriors? If the New York Knicks raise their average ticket prices from $40 to $44, will fewer people attend their games and more go to plays on Broadway? Not likely. There is no direct competition, and to use economists' jargon, the cross-elasticity of demand is close to zero. Each major sports league is effectively in a league of its own.

As monopolies, the sports leagues restrict the supply of franchises below the demand for franchises from economically viable cities, thrusting cities into competition with each other to procure or retain teams. The outcome is that some cities lose teams and others spend hundreds of millions of dollars to build new facilities for prospective teams. The new facilities enable the generation of anywhere from $10 million to $50 million in additional revenues, which go into the already deep pockets of the owners and the players. It is an income transfer from the average citizen to some of the wealthiest citizens, and it is often done in the name of promoting economic development in a metropolitan area.

Since sports play such a prodigious role in a city's culture, it is sometimes difficult to come to grips with the reality that sports teams have a diminutive impact on a city's economy. First, the average NFL team in 1994 grossed $65 million. Compare that with the 1993 effective buying income (EBI) for the metropolitan limits of St. Louis of $21.1 billion. The gross of an average NFL team, then, would account for 0.3 percent of St. Louis's EBI. Or it would account for 0.6 percent of the EBI of Jacksonville, Florida, or just 0.05 percent of the EBI of the metropolitan limits of New York City. Before the 1994–95 work stoppage, the average Major League Baseball franchise also had gross revenues of about $65 million, while the average revenues in the NBA were approximately $50 million, and those in the NHL were closer to $35 million.

Oral Testimony before the Committee on Commerce, Subcommittee on Commerce, Trade, and Hazardous Materials, on H.R. 2740, "Fan Freedom and Community Protection Act of 1996," May 16, 1996

In terms of permanent local employees, sports teams employ between 40 and 120 full-time workers, along with several hundred low-skill and low-wage, part-time and temporary stadium or arena personnel.

Second, economic studies have shown that most public stadiums and arenas do not cover their own fixed and operating costs. Indeed, using available data for twenty-five publicly owned stadiums and arenas for 1989, James Quirk and Rodney Fort, authors of the 1997 book *Pay Dirt: The Business of Professional Team Sports*, estimated an average public-stadium subsidy (net fiscal cost) of $6.8 million and conservatively projected in excess of $500 million in government subsidies to all professional sports teams in the same year. Operating and debt-service deficits mean that city or state governments will have to levy additional taxes. Higher taxes, in turn, discourage business in the area and reduce consumer expenditures, setting off a negative multiplier effect.

Third, virtually all independent economic research has confirmed a diminutive or negligible economic effect from the relocation of a sports team to a city. Promotional studies, done under contract with interested parties, produce dozens of glossy charts and computer printouts and purport to demonstrate an impending economic boom if construction is undertaken. Invariably, these studies have deep methodological problems: They are based on unrealistic assumptions; they conflate gross and net spending; they use sales rather than income multipliers; they use fixed input coefficients; and they ignore the powerful negative multiplier effect from higher taxes.

However, even accepting the excessively inflated claims of these studies, it is apparent that building stadiums is not a good economic investment for a city. Consider, for instance, two recent promotional studies on the economic impact of Camden Yards in Baltimore—one by the State of Maryland's Department of Business and Economic Development and the other by the Department of Fiscal Services. The former estimated benefits at $110.6 million, with 1,394 jobs created, and the latter at $33 million, with 534 jobs created. Using a modest project-cost estimate of $177 million, the cost per job created is $127,000 in the first study and $331,000 in the second. These estimates, though based on excessively optimistic assumptions, should be contrasted with the cost per job created of the state economic-development program of $6,250 per job, a typical spending-to-job ratio for urban-development expenditures. Further, Camden Yards benefited from being part of the harbor redevelopment, from absorbing Washington, D.C. (the seventh-largest media market in the United States by its location off the interstate in south Baltimore), from being the first example of its architectural genre, from the novelty effect of the park itself, and from housing a successful ball club.

The proper inference from this analysis is not that cities should not try to attract sports teams, or that they should never invest public funds for this purpose. Rather, the proper inference is twofold. First, if a city is going to spend public monies, it should be done with the understanding that it is an investment in the city's cultural life for the enjoyment of its citizens and the possible generation of civic pride. Second, to avoid fiscal distress and possibly intensifying social tensions, it is imperative that the financing package and the lease for any future stadium or arena be fiscally prudent from the city's point of view. The only way to achieve this outcome is for the playing field to be leveled. This is what H.R. 2740 (the Hoke bill) attempts to do.

To be sure, there are imperfections in the bill. First, there is absolutely no justification for excluding Major League Baseball from the protection provisions in this bill. If Congress interprets present case law to mean that there is a blanket exemption for MLB, then excluding baseball from the provisions of this bill constitutes a legislative endorsement of this anomalous exemption. Legislators might want to review the August 1993 opinion of District Court Judge John Padova in *Piazza et al. v. Major League Baseball*, wherein Padova interprets the 1972 Supreme Court in *Flood v. Kuhn* to limit baseball's exemption to the reserve clause. Moreover, several host cities in baseball are currently being threatened with the exodus of their team, and in the case of New York, there is discussion about investing $1 billion for a new stadium for the Yankees at the West Side Railyards in Manhattan. Host cities in baseball need the protection of the Hoke bill as much as those in the other sports.

Second, Section 4(a) of H.R. 2740 sets a price for a city's franchise recovery to be equal to the price of the last league expansion team. The difficulty here is that virtually all expansion sites have new facilities with high revenue-generation potential. A new facility makes it possible for the owner to meet the league's exacting expansion franchise fee. A team in an existing city will not generally be worth nearly as much as the expansion team, because the existing host city will not have a new facility. This will be true almost by definition, since it is almost certainly the reason why the owner wanted to move the ball club in the first place. Thus, for the bereaved host city to find an investor willing to pay an expansion-fee price, the city will have to provide a new facility. A superior protective mechanism would provide for the recovery price to be set by an arbitration procedure that determines the value of a franchise in that city under existing conditions.

Third, since the bill provides for the possibility of city, county, or state ownership of sports teams, Section 8 should be modified to allow for the amendment of the National Labor Relations Act to cover collective bargaining for employees of public employers in sports leagues.

These weaknesses notwithstanding, H.R. 2740 is worthy of your support. After years of neglect and even passing legislation that strengthens the monopoly power of the sports leagues, it is time for Congress to act responsibly and farsightedly to curb the blackmailing of American cities.

What's BOB Really Worth to Phoenix?

The finance department of the city of Phoenix, Arizona, published a study last month on the local economy during the first six months of 1998. The numbers are impressive: Sales revenue in the downtown area where the new Bank One Ballpark (BOB) is located went up 34.1 percent compared with the same period during 1997, and sales revenue for the whole city was up 7 percent. The city did not waste a moment trumpeting these results to the media, and the media (*Sports Business Journal* included) dutifully regurgitated these numbers to the public. The message: The dismal economists are wrong. There is a positive economic impact from sports facilities, after all.

To be sure, the study comes at an auspicious time for the promoters of publicly funded ballparks. Over the past year, voters have rejected subsidized stadiums in Pittsburgh, Minnesota, and North Carolina. The citizens of South Boston took to the streets to prevent some of their land from being used for a new Patriots stadium. The people of Cincinnati have forced a referendum on the siting and terms for a new ballpark for the Reds. And the private component of stadium financing has been steadily on the rise throughout the country.

Supporters of a new stadium in San Diego for the Padres have been quick to exploit the Phoenix study. The president of San Diego's Center City Development Corporation gleamed, "This is great ammunition. It's another argument we can make—that there's increased spending when there are increased opportunities." San Diego voters will decide in a November referendum whether to finance a new park for the Padres.

The problem with the Phoenix study is that it tells us little about BOB's impact in the broader metropolitan economy. The lion's share of the money being spent at BOB is coming from the suburbs and other areas in the city. The transfer of dollars may well promote sales in the downtown area, but it does so at the expense of sales in other areas of the local economy. If it is an explicit policy goal to promote the urban core, then this tradeoff may be welcome.

To the extent that some of the money spent at BOB comes from people who live in other areas of Arizona or out of state, then there is net new spending in the metropolitan economy, and there may be some small, positive effect on the local economy. Two additional factors, however, must be analyzed. First, where does the money spent at BOB go? Primarily to Jerry Colangelo, Eddie Lynch, Billy Crystal, various corporate owners, and the Diamondbacks players. These recipients all have astronomical incomes, save high proportions of their earnings, and spend large shares of their money out of state.

If Phoenicians did not spend their money at BOB, it would be spent at other local entertainment venues, owned most likely by local proprietors with more normal incomes. Much more of the money spent at a local bowling alley would be recirculated in the greater Phoenix metropolitan economy than the money spent at BOB.

Second, of the $354 million it cost to build BOB, at least $253 million was from public funds. These funds must be paid eventually out of higher taxes or lower services, either of which would cause a drag on the local economy. Further, the terms of BOB's lease are highly favorable to the Diamondbacks, and it is likely that the stadium authority's operational costs and the city's and county's infrastructural, environmental, sanitation, and security costs will bring on yearly operating deficits. These, too, would cause a drag on the local economy.

A closer look at the Phoenix study suggests that there is already a spending-substitution effect. The study finds that sales revenue in downtown Phoenix was $71.1 million during January–June 1997 and $95.3 million during January–June 1998—that is, it rose by $24.2 million in 1998 after BOB opened.

Now consider the Diamondbacks' revenue projections for 1998, which were made public as part of their bond offering. The team projects that its stadium-related income for the entire 1998 baseball season (April–September) will be $97.3 million. Half of the season falls in the January–June period analyzed in the Phoenix report, so approximately $48.7 million of sales occurred at BOB during the first half of 1998. Since BOB is in downtown Phoenix, it contributed $48.7 million to sales downtown, while total sales downtown rose by $24.2 million during this period. This implies that downtown sales at venues other than BOB experienced a drop of $24.5 million.

Analyzing economic impact is more complicated than citing sales increases in a particular part of a city. It is also necessary to control for other factors that affect the area's growth and to assess whether the higher growth in one part of a metropolitan area comes at the cost of lower growth in another part. Further, it is important to decide whether it is total area income or income per capita or some other measure that is of interest. The effect of the stadium's construction and operational costs on the city's fiscal health and public services, such as education, will also influence its eventual impact on the region's economy.

In the end, the real story of a baseball team's impact is not economic at all. It is cultural, and citizens should decide on this basis how much, if at all, they wish to subsidize a team's owners and players as compared with spending public funds on education, parks, the arts, and so on, or to lowering taxes.

Football Stadium Folly

Talk about an offer you can't refuse. The one that Governor John Rowland of Connecticut made to the owner of the New England Patriots to lure the football team to Hartford was so generous and encompassing that it put the recent sports giveaways in Tampa, Baltimore, St. Louis, and Cleveland to shame.

The deal, which the State Legislature will consider on December 15 after a hearing next Wednesday, includes, at Connecticut's expense, a riverfront stadium for at least $280 million, $70 million to acquire and improve the site, $25 million–$100 million for environmental cleanup, land for a pavilion and hotel, a $15 million practice site, 26,000 parking spaces, $170 million in a fund for future improvements, and assorted state guarantees. Plus, of course, cost overruns, which can easily add 20 percent or more to the final bill.

In return, Robert Kraft, the team's owner, would pay no rent for the thirty-year life of the deal and keep all revenue from ticket sales, luxury suites, parking, concessions, and so on. All told, Kraft's stadium income could be $100 million a year. The state would get only a 10 percent ticket tax.

With such an alluring offer, one might think that Kraft needed enticement. Far from it. The team's current home in Foxboro, Massachusetts, is nearly an hour from Boston and fed by only one inadequate access road. The 1971 stadium has virtually none of the amenities or revenue-generating accouterments of new parks. And Massachusetts and Boston have done little to try to keep the team.

So why did Governor Rowland have to cut the worst deal in the history of the NFL? He didn't. But it is easy for small cities like Hartford to lapse into a bidding-war mentality where NFL franchises are concerned for two reasons.

First, far more than in other sports, the NFL has extensive revenue sharing among its teams. Teams split all regular and post-season television revenue equally, as well as all licensing and sponsorship income. They also split 40 percent of net gate sales. As a result, the top revenue-making team in the NFL might earn 50 percent more than the bottom team, while in baseball the top team earns more than three times as much as the lowest.

Second, an NFL team plays only eight regular-season home games a year. The Patriots in Hartford would have to sell only 680,000 seats (counting two exhibition games) a year; a baseball team would have to sell about 4 million seats to sell out.

Thus, the NFL has dozens more cities ready to bid for its teams than other sports have, and it capitalizes on that dynamic. Public subsidies tend to be much larger in the NFL than in other sports.

New York Times, December 5, 1998

There is an argument for some public subsidies of stadiums. If nothing else, a sports team can build community pride.

If Connecticut believes that such benefits, largely intangible, warrant the spending of $35 million–$65 million a year on debt service and other costs, then it should support Rowland. (The 10 percent ticket tax would generate $5 million–$7 million a year, but much of that would only replace sales-tax money lost elsewhere in the state. The deal is decidedly not revenue-neutral, despite claims by Rowland and a new study by the consulting firm KPMG.)

Connecticut, however, should not support the plan if it expects the Patriots to create jobs or raise per capita income. All experience with new stadiums and new teams suggests that the Patriots would not have a significant impact on Connecticut's economy. Indeed, Rowland's largesse portends either higher taxes or reduced services.

Hartford might enjoy a bit of a revitalization. But this would largely consist of shifting economic output toward Hartford and away from other parts of the state. In any case, if Hartford's welfare truly concerns the governor, things like tax incentives for industry and increased spending on education would provide more bang for the buck.

If Connecticut legislators are determined to have a football team, they would do well to try to modify Rowland's deal. There is, for instance, no reason the state should guarantee $17.5 million of premium seat revenue annually. In other NFL leases, any such guarantees are usually arranged through business associations, not through the local government.

That some legislators have begun to ask questions is a good sign. Connecticut has more leverage than Rowland thinks and should use it.

When Teams Move, Protecting Both Fans and Owners Is Tricky

Suppose you're a football fan and you are lucky enough to live in one of the twenty-nine metropolitan areas that hosts an NFL team. The team's owner is a long-time resident in your city and publicly declares that he has nothing but scorn for owners who move their teams and that he would never do such a thing. The next year, you buy two season tickets with the understanding that you will have a right of first refusal to continue to buy those seats for each subsequent season unless you did not exercise this right in the prior year. That is, when you purchase your season tickets, the price you pay includes not only this year's tickets but a right to purchase the same seats in subsequent years.

Now suppose that during the year, the team's owner has a change of heart and decides to move the team for the following season. The new town is hundreds of miles away, and the owner does not offer you the opportunity to buy seats at the stadium in the new city. Indeed, he sells permanent seat licenses (PSLs) for the right to buy season tickets at the new stadium, generating about $70 million to help defray team expenses. Your right of first refusal is thereby confiscated without your consent.

A class-action suit filed on behalf of some 15,000 season-ticket holders for the erstwhile Cleveland Browns claiming all of the above was filed in November 1995. It was subsequently dismissed in the state's Court of Common Pleas, but it was recently reinstated by an Ohio State Appeals Court. The case raises some interesting questions about consumer rights in professional sports.

Should sports teams be allowed to move from one city to another in search of ever larger public stadium subsidies? The NFL sometimes allows teams to move; sometimes it does not. When the league has said no, it has often been sued on the grounds that the league is interfering with the owners' property rights and with free commerce. MLB has not allowed teams to move since 1972, but it has allowed teams to threaten to move and extort large stadium subventions.

In this environment, how can the rights of the team's owner, the city, and the consumer be protected at the same time? Short of breaking the leagues up into competing business entities, there is no easy answer, but the plaintiffs in this case believe that matters can be ameliorated if false advertising is punished.

According to the plaintiffs, the 1995 Cleveland Brown season ticket was promoted in written advertisements pledging that all season-ticket holders would have a right of first refusal on tickets for the next year. In the mid-1990s, the Browns did not have a strong team, and this right to buy tickets in subsequent years was an essential inducement for many consumers.

Since the ticket holder presumably could renew this right each year by buying a season ticket, it would, like baseball's old reserve clause, be valid in perpetuity (unless explicitly limited to the individual consumer as opposed to his or her family). As such, the value of this right can be approximated by the value of a PSL, the owner of which has the right to purchase season tickets over a lengthy period of time.

Since the Browns did not sell PSLs at the old Municipal Stadium, it is reasonable to look at their value in Baltimore as a proxy. The difficulty is that the supply-and-demand conditions are different in the two cities. The value of a PSL is directly proportional to the excess demand for season tickets at a given ticket price. Thus, estimates of this excess demand would need to be made with appropriate adjustments in the proxy. Alternatively, PSL sales for the new Browns could be used, but here, too, adjustments need to made for the different number and price of seats.

The greatest challenge for consumers in the sale of PSLs is not the critique that fans have to pay twice—once for the ticket and once for the right to buy the ticket. Rational consumers will simply treat the (amortized value of the) PSL as part of the ticket price. Rather, the challenge is that owners receive up front a good portion of the ticket value over a twenty- or thirty-year period. With a substantial share of their ticket revenue guaranteed, the owners have less incentive to bid competitively for top players to put a winning team on the field. The consumers, then, pay before they know the quality of the product they are buying (or, at least, the owner's effort to produce a quality product).

For this reason, PSLs are another way to lower consumer welfare, but unlike the allegations in the case of the Browns, they do not involve false advertising.

*[**Note:** A settlement in this case was reached in favor of the former Cleveland Browns season-ticket holders.]*

Now You See the Patriots, Now You Don't: NFL Musical Chairs

Why did Robert Kraft, owner of the New England Patriots, walk away from the most lucrative stadium deal in NFL history? Oddly enough, the "new" deal in Massachusetts was essentially what Kraft had already been offered before his cat-and-mouse game in Connecticut—$70 million in state money for infrastructure, $250 million in private money for the stadium in Foxboro.

Massachusetts House Speaker Thomas Finneran was excoriated in the Boston press for playing hardball with Kraft and seemingly losing the Patriots. Now the Pats are back on Finneran's terms, and Kraft, doing his best imitation of the Oakland Raiders' owner, Al Davis, is declared the hero.

Finneran's success in standing up to the NFL stadium-extortion game is a byproduct of the NFL's peculiar economics that allows cities of 100,000 population such as Green Bay to survive and thrive. The league's extensive revenue sharing and gargantuan national television contract ($17.6 billion over eight years), together with the growing importance of stadium revenues, has led to Los Angeles's losing two teams in the past four years, as well as to Cleveland's and Houston's losing their teams, all to smaller cities. The Bears have been threatening to bolt Chicago, and greater Boston (the sixth-largest media market in the United States) was about to lose the Patriots to Hartford.

From the NFL's perspective, there are two major problems with this trend. One, teams were migrating from the country's major media centers, threatening the league's television ratings and future rights fees. Two, when Cleveland lost the Browns (a.k.a. Ravens), the city prepared an antitrust suit against the league. Rather than face the consequences of the suit, the NFL decided to expand back into Cleveland, just as it is now doing in Los Angeles. That is, when teams leave the large media markets, the league ultimately will be compelled to expand.

But the NFL wants to control expansion and thereby grow the value of its scarce franchises. So at the owners' meeting in March, the NFL initiated a new protect-the-big-city policy. Hereafter, when a team from one of the six largest media markets (the cutoff of six was set by the owners' Finance Committee, chaired by Robert Kraft) pledges some of its funds to help build a new stadium, the NFL will lend the team up to 50 percent of the private share of financing. Not only is the loan interest-free, but the principal is paid back out of premium seat and PSL money that otherwise would be shared with the visiting team. In

Sports Business Journal, May 16–23, 1999

other words, if Kraft spends $250 million on a remake of Foxboro Stadium, the NFL will pay $125 million. This is the first reason Kraft changed his mind.

The second reason is that Commissioner Paul Tagliabue undoubtedly reminded Kraft of the teams being restored to Los Angeles and Cleveland. All Massachusetts had to do was bring an antitrust suit against the league and Boston would end up with New England's second team to compete with the Hartford Patriots.

The third reason is that Kraft owns Foxboro Stadium and the MLS team New England Revolution. The Revolution plays at Foxboro, and any revenue-enhancing improvements to the facility would benefit the soccer team along with all other events at the venue.

The fourth reason is that Governor Rowland still hadn't resolved the site issues in Hartford. Environmental cleanup costs appeared to be well in excess of $100 million. Cleanup studies were still going on, and the resulting delays meant the new stadium would not be ready until the 2002 season, at the earliest. Kraft was facing three years or more as a lame duck in Foxboro.

Sports Illustrated believes that Kraft decided to return because he is a loyal Bostonian. That's good fantasy that fails to explain how Kraft could have been lured to Connecticut in the first place. But the sports world flourishes on such fantasy, and many have already anointed Kraft Massachusetts's favorite son. Somehow such accolades eluded Al Davis when he returned to Oakland.

The real lesson here, however, is not about Kraft, Rowland, or Finneran. It is about the unsavory competition between two neighboring states over a football team. As a monopolist, the NFL successfully limits the number of its franchises below the demand for the same by U.S. cities. States are forced into competition, and the federal government subsidizes this with municipal-bond–interest exemptions. The NFL's new stadium-financing plan is actually a step in the right direction. A larger step is being proposed in a bill recently introduced by Senator Arlen Specter that calls for the NFL and MLB to contribute up to half of all financing for new stadiums. The trick will be for Specter to find significant support for his bill apart from Senators Joe Lieberman and Chris Dodd of Connecticut.

Flawed Specter Bill Gets an A for Effort

On May 4, Senator Arlen Specter of Pennsylvania introduced the Stadium Financing and Franchise Relocation Act of 1999. The senator's own state is committed to spending approximately $1 billion on four stadiums over the next several years. His bill would require the NFL and MLB to set aside 10 percent of their national-television–contract revenues each year to create a stadium-construction fund. This fund would then provide up to 50 percent of the construction costs of new facilities. If the leagues did not comply, they would be penalized by the removal of their broadcasting antitrust exemption, which allows them to enter leaguewide network-television contracts.

The senator's goal is admirable. Specter also suggested in his floor state-ment that, of the remaining 50 percent, half should be public money and half should come from the team's owner.

I am supportive of the senator's ends but a bit skeptical of his means. Let me explain. First, specifying a single formula for distinct situations, especially when the lease terms for the new facility have not been spelled out, is prob-lematic. Second, the present size of MLB's network contract renders it insuf-ficient to meet the financing expectations of the bill.

Third, while the geographic stability of franchises has its virtues, in the pres-ent context, extending the NFL an antitrust exemption with regard to franchise relocation is potentially perilous. If the NFL is allowed to decide when teams move, then it also is allowed to prevent two or more teams that seek to move to the same city from competing with each other. Such competition would give the city a modicum of bargaining leverage in setting the financing arrange-ments and lease terms for the new stadium. Moreover, although it might limit the actual frequency of team relocations, it would not prevent teams from threatening their host city. No baseball team has relocated since 1972, but many franchises have threatened to move and thereby obtained tens or hundreds of millions of dollars in public subsidies. While it is probable that granting the NFL this exemption would reduce the amount of litigation against the league, and this is certainly desirable, it is simply too dangerous to grant a monopoly league still greater economic power.

Fourth, the senator's bill mandates that any monies put into the stadium trust fund will be excluded from the NFL's defined gross revenue (DGR) and hence not subjected to the 63 percent sharing with the players implied by the league's salary cap. While there is a reasonable logic behind this provision, it is inappro-priate for the U.S. Congress to insert itself into the collective-bargaining relationship between the owners and players. It would be equally inappropriate, for instance, for the bill to require the abolition of the NFL's salary cap as a means to bypass its automatic sharing provisions and to encourage players' contributions to stadium construction. In fact, the NFLPA recognizes the value to the players from new facilities and already has, on its own accord, entered into agreements with the owners that allow the exclusion of certain league financing of stadium construction from DGR. This is not an area where the NFL and NFLPA have failed. It would set a destructive precedent if Congress were to mandate a particular collective-bargaining outcome, especially on a subject where the league and players have accomplished much the same on their own.

Fifth, Senator Specter's bill proposes to punish a league's failure to establish a stadium trust fund by removing its member teams' ability to join together to sign a leaguewide network-television contract. The NFL derived its ability to do this in the 1961 Sports Broadcasting Act. MLB claims to have derived its ability from its presumed blanket exemption from the nation's antitrust laws granted by the Supreme Court in 1922, but MLB is also covered by the Sports Broadcasting Act. But if Congress proscribes leaguewide television deals, yet continues to allow the NFL and MLB to function as monopolies in other regards, it is courting disarray. Revenue from network television is shared equally among all the teams. If each NFL team signed its own television deal, then the annual average of $73 million per team under the current contract would disappear. Certain popular big-city franchises such as the New York Giants and Dallas Cowboys might earn larger contracts, but the Charlotte Panthers and Jacksonville Jaguars might find themselves $60 million–$70 million in the hole. Financial stability in the league would disappear, and competitive balance might be undermined. Less dramatically, a similar pattern would affect baseball. Thus, the punishment for noncompliance is too draconian and certainly would not be in the fans' interests.

Further, the punishment does not fit the crime. It is a bit like punishing a child who steals candy by not letting her go to school. Noncompliance in stadium finance would more appropriately be sanctioned by removing the opportunities for federal financing of stadium construction—that is, not allowing the interest on municipal stadium-construction bonds to be exempt from federal income taxation.

The NFL, in an effort to maximize its long-term television revenues, has passed a policy providing league support for financing new facility construction. In the case of the six largest NFL markets, the league will provide an interest-free loan to a team owner for up to half of the owner's commitment to stadium financing (with smaller proportions of support for teams' smaller markets). The loan is repaid by monies that the owner otherwise would have to share with the league. Since large cities have more bargaining leverage around stadium issues, they are likely to extract a larger component of financing from the team owner. This policy is a step in the right direction, but it does not go far enough and provides too little support for the twenty-five smallest markets in the league. MLB has no policy at all that provides league-financing support of facility construction.

Thus, more needs to be done to bring sports-industry welfare under control. Senator Specter's effort is to be commended. The task now is to make appropriate refinements to the bill and to overcome the ever so effective lobbying of the NFL and MLB by enlisting support for the measure among members of Congress from outside the few cities and states currently being extorted for large public stadium subsidies.

*[**Note:** As I explain in "More Benevolence in Stadium Games" in this volume, since 2002 MLB also has had a leaguewide program to support stadium construction.]*

A Tale of Facilities in Two Cities: Boston and Green Bay

Teams seeking public funds to help finance new facilities are fond of making three claims. First, the facility will generate thousands of jobs and promote local economic development. Second, the new facility will help team finances, enable the team to purchase higher-priced free agents, and make the team more competitive. Third, most teams claim that they are offering a fair deal in helping to finance construction.

The first claim is false. All independent research on the subject has found that there is no boost to area employment and income from a new facility. And no new income means no new tax revenue for local government.

The second claim is basically true for baseball and false for football. In baseball, a new facility increases the revenue-generating potential of the team. (The Red Sox estimate that a new park would raise team revenues by $45 million a year.) In today's Fenway, Pedro Martinez draws 34,000 to the game and fills forty-two luxury suites. Put him in a new park and he will draw 44,000 and fill 100 suites. And, of course, ticket prices, concessions and catering, signage, and other revenues will all be higher in a new park. So Pedro would produce more value in a new park, and the Sox could afford to offer him or other free agents a higher salary. Hence, other things equal, the Sox should be able to build a relatively stronger club.

Football is different primarily because of its salary cap, set at 62 percent of "defined gross revenue" during 1999–2000. Last year, the per team cap was $57.3 million, and all but six of the thirty-one teams had payrolls at or above the cap. Of the six below the cap, four were within $3 million of the cap, and the other two, the Washington Redskins (at $50.6 million) and the San Diego Chargers (at $47.7 million), were doing just fine financially, with revenues at approximately $170 million and $120 million, respectively. In fact, during the previous season, the Chargers had the second-highest payroll in the NFL at $66.9 million, and the Redskins had the sixth highest at $63.6 million.

The reason a team's payroll jumps up and down from one year to the next in the NFL is the use of prorated signing bonuses to get around the cap limits in a particular year. But when a team employs this loophole in one year, it implies that it will have to give it back with lower payrolls in subsequent years. The upshot is that team payrolls in the NFL tend to average out at the cap threshold over a series of years. That is, payrolls are virtually invariant to team revenue. Hence, new stadiums in the NFL have next to nothing to do with team quality.

So if the Packers' fans in Brown County, Wisconsin, think that a $295 million renovation of Lambeau Field will improve the team's performance, they should think again. Last year, the Packers' payroll was the second highest in the NFL at $76 million. In coming years, the Packers will have to reduce their payroll relative to the cap to make up for last year's signing-bonus excess—with or without a renovated stadium.

The third claim depends entirely on the circumstance and how one does the accounting. The Red Sox have presented a broad outline of a financing plan for a facility that is projected to cost $627 million, including $275 million in land acquisition and infrastructure costs. In the plan, the Sox have offered to pay for the $352 million stadium as well as cover any cost overruns on the construction. Thus, assuming proportionately equal cost overruns in the building, land, and infrastructure, the Sox are offering to pay 56.1 percent of the total projected cost. Given the average public subsidy component of roughly 70 percent for recent sports facilities, the Sox offer seems eminently reasonable.

Where's the rub? Though the Sox proportions are fair, the potential problems are threefold. First, the absolute amount of public monies is enormous, at $275 million ($140 million from the city and $135 million from the state). Second, this amount is based on estimates for land value and infrastructure. There may well be significant cost overruns, driving the public bill still higher. (The Sox plan calls for taking fourteen acres in high demand in the Fenway area by eminent domain. If such a taking is deemed legal, the price is likely to be challenged in court.) Third, Boston is the sixth-largest media market and an avid sports town. As the recent deal with the Patriots proved, the city has significant bargaining leverage, and unlike the Patriots, the Sox don't have a viable alternative location.

Add to this mixture the billions of dollars that have been wasted on Boston's Big Dig project and the resentment that residents of central and western Massachusetts have toward the sharply disproportionate share of the state's resources going to Boston, and you have a very hard political sell in the state's legislature. The only way out seems to be for a new round of negotiation around the state's share of parking revenues and the city's levy of a fee in lieu of property taxes, among other items. It will also make sense to revisit the viability of renovating Fenway as well as the attractiveness of alternative sites if a new park is to be built.

When the Sox are sold, reportedly 55 percent of the proceeds will go to Yawkey trusts and 60 percent of that will go to Boston-area charities. That is, roughly one-third of the public subsidies will come back to the public. It is in everyone's interest to work out a sensible compromise.

*[**Note:** The previous owners of the Red Sox claimed that one of the reasons the team needed a new facility was that the existing park, built in 1912, was structurally unsound. When John Henry and his partners bought the Sox in 2002, their engineering study found the park to be sound. Henry and partners proceeded with renovations to Fenway that cost more than $100 million and were privately financed.]*

Share of Ballpark: $16 a Year

Should Florida use public funds to help build a new stadium for the Florida Marlins? There's a proper way to focus on this question, and there's a misleading way.

Unfortunately, MLB Commissioner Bud Selig and Florida Senate President John McKay are making comments that distract from the real issue. Selig's letter to Senator Alex Villalobos threatens either the elimination or the relocation of the Marlins. Don't believe it. Selig has used the relocation threat on multiple occasions in the past. It hasn't happened. Before the Marlins are allowed to relocate, MLB would have to consider several teams in more desperate financial straights. Remember that MLB has not allowed a team to relocate since 1972. The main reason is that relocation creates political problems.

Elimination is less likely still. If MLB contracts by two teams, the Marlins are not likely to be one of them. But MLB won't contract. That would invite the U.S. Congress to reconsider the game's antitrust exemption; it would provoke litigation; and it would be strenuously resisted by the players' union.

Senator McKay states that a new stadium will not help the state economically. According to every academic study on the subject, this is the correct conclusion. Hence, any sales-tax rebates will be losses to the state treasury.

It is puzzling, however, that the issue of economic development and the sales-tax rebate are suddenly being joined. Hasn't the sales-tax rebate been used to fund a dozen or more major- and minor-league sports facilities throughout the state? The evidence will show that none of these facilities has promoted economic development.

So why is the issue being raised for the Marlins? Unquestionably, Wayne Huizenga's fire sale of the team following the 1997 miracle season ruptured the emerging bonds between the team and the community. John Henry probably made the problem worse by agreeing to a terrible stadium deal with Huizenga when he purchased the club and by announcing initially that he would fund a new stadium with private sources. Neither the team's competitive strength nor its bonds with the community has been recovered. Thus, political opposition to public financing comes easily.

This is not to say that opposing public financing is necessarily a mistake. I would only suggest that three questions be considered before taking a position.

First, does it make sense to have the bad-faith actions of the team's previous owner or the team's recent history determine the relationship of the team to the community for the next several decades?

Miami Herald, April 30, 2001

Second, MLB, like the NFL and the NBA, is a monopoly. As such, it restricts the number of its franchises below the demand for teams and forces cities into competition with each other. It is this circumstance that has compelled every host city, county, and state to pony up subsidies to build or renovate stadiums. Even the vaunted "privately financed" Pac Bell Park in San Francisco received more than $10 million in public support from land and infrastructure contributions. Since 1990, the average public contribution to ballpark financing is around 70 percent.

This is the reality of major league sports today. Would it be different in a more just world? Probably. But should public policy in Florida be based on current realities or a hypothetical just world?

Third, although no positive economic benefits should be anticipated from building a new stadium, there will be certain noneconomic benefits. These benefits will range from the increased convenience, comfort, and amenities of a new facility to the higher probability that the Marlins will field a competitive team. (If the team were eventually to relocate without a new facility, then an additional noneconomic benefit would be the enjoyment of retaining the team.)

A new stadium does not guarantee that the Marlins will generate more revenue. The new luxury boxes, club seats, catering and concessions options, and sponsorship and signage possibilities will be exploited only if the Marlins put a good product on the field. With a good product, the team's revenues may increase anywhere from $40 million to $60 million a year. Put differently, the value of a good player goes up because he can generate more revenue in a new park than he can in an old one. This fact will provide ownership with a strong incentive to build a winning team.

It is up to the people of Florida or their representatives to evaluate these potential benefits. And against these benefits they should put the costs.

Consider the following rough estimate. The new park is currently projected to cost $385 million. Assume that with cost overruns the bill will eventually rise to $450 million. In the present scheme, the team will contribute approximately $120 million via rental payments and ticket surcharges. Assume further that the team commits to paying 50 percent of the overruns of $65 million, or $32.5 million. That leaves the public bill at just under $300 million.

There are approximately 1.5 million television households in Florida's Dade and Broward counties. If all of the financing burden were assumed by these households, the public portion of the stadium bill would come to $200 per household. If the stadium bonds are retired over thirty years, then the price tag (annual amortization plus interest) would come to about $16 per household per year.

Hence, the question comes down to whether the noneconomic benefits are worth roughly $16 per household per year. Of course, the precise calculation will differ because there is substantial state financing, and part of the ticket surcharges may be passed on to the consumer, among other things. But these are details, and the financing package can be negotiated and tweaked.

I suspect that the 1997 championship team thrilled and uplifted a lot of people in Dade and Broward counties. A good team can bring significant enjoyment and community cohesion. Maybe it is time to rebuild the private–public partnership for baseball in South Florida.

Cards' Offer Is in the Ballpark

Two-thirds of Major League Baseball teams are currently playing in a stadium built since 1989 or are awaiting the completion of a stadium under construction. Another five teams are in advanced stages of negotiation for a new facility.

The Cardinals' Busch Stadium was built in 1966. As cookie-cutter–era stadiums go, Busch is one of the best. It still leaves a lot to be desired in terms of modern amenities, sight lines, fan proximity to the action, and revenue-generating features.

As I have written before, independent economic research finds that, on average, a new stadium does not raise an area's per capita income or employment level. Primarily, new sports facilities should be seen as consumption, not investment, goods.

This fact does not mean that the new stadium plan for St. Louis has no potential economic value. First, in the Cards' case, the team pays the highest ticket-tax rate in baseball at 12.6 percent. (The average is just over 5 percent.) Actually, the burden of this tax is shared by the team and the fans, since without the tax the Cards would be able to charge higher ticket prices. If the Cards were to move, say, to East St. Louis, the team's contribution via sales and income taxes of $18.5 million in 2000 would be lost to the St. Louis municipal and Missouri state budgets.

Second, the Cards are pledging substantial financing to develop a ballpark village. Total private financing for the village is projected at $300 million, and there are significant penalties for the Cards if this development is delayed. The team is in essence guaranteeing that the ballpark will generate commercial and residential activity, expand employment opportunities, and enrich cultural choices downtown.

Beyond these potential economic gains, the new stadium will improve the fans' experience, and it will offer an ensured minimum of 6,000 inexpensive seats per game and at least 100,000 free tickets per year to charitable and youth organizations. It will also generate an additional $40 million–$50 million of revenue for the Cards that will enable the team to field more competitive teams. Of course, along with the higher revenues, the value of the franchise will rise. Accordingly, the team owners have stated their willingness to negotiate a split of any future stadium-induced capital gains with the city.

The higher team revenues and ballpark-village development also mean increased tax revenues for the public coffers. Indeed, it is these incremental revenues that are slated to cover the annual service on the $210 million of public debt. If there is any shortfall, it will be made up by an insurance fund created out of the stadium-naming rights. Unlike most teams in new stadiums, the Cards are not laying claim to the naming-rights income, which can be appreciable. The average total value of naming-rights packages for new sports venues rose from $62 million in 1997 to $129 million in 1999. Baseball deals tend to be smaller than those in football, and the market is a bit weaker today than it was in 1999. Nonetheless, the Cards should be able to exceed comfortably the recent $52 million package signed for the new stadium in Cincinnati.

Further, the team has agreed to cover all cost overruns in construction. Since these overruns (resulting from adding new features, unanticipated expenses, and delays) frequently can vary anywhere from 20 percent to 60 percent above the initial projected cost, the team's commitment is of vital importance. The team has also agreed to be responsible for all maintenance, replacement, and capital-improvement expenses at the stadium.

The entire financing package proposed by the team meets the city and state more than halfway. Of the nearly $25 billion spent on the 100-odd professional sports facilities built since 1990, approximately 70 percent of the financing has come from public coffers. The public share for stadiums is considerably above this level (and below this for arenas). The Cards' proposal to contribute $135 million out of the total ballpark-project costs of $346 million represents a 39 percent share, leaving the public share at a well below average 61 percent. Further, by guaranteeing an additional $300 million in private financing for the ballpark village, the private share ($435 million) of the overall project ($646 million) rises to 67.3 percent. The public share falls to a modest 32.7 percent.

We are at the end of the post-1990 stadium cycle. A majority of the teams in the major pro sports leagues have new facilities. It seems reasonable that the remaining teams should also benefit from some public support in obtaining new facilities. The public-policy task for now is to make sure that the proposed financing and lease deals are equitable. The Cards' proposal appears to pass the equity test with flying colors.

New York City Can Do Better

The deals Rudy Giuliani struck with the Yankees and Mets on December 28 are the best argument in years for a new revision of the city charter. First consider the lease amendments. The city allows each team to deduct $5 million annually for five years from any rent due the city and to use the sum as the teams see fit to defray planning costs for the new stadiums. Total cost: $50 million. Bad deal. The right deal would spend less money, the costs would be shared 50–50, and the expenditures would be agreed on by both sides.

Rudy's deal also forgave the Mets for payments of 10 percent on certain stadium advertising and 10 percent of the Mets' share of national cable TV revenue.

Next, consider the provisional financing and lease deals for the new stadiums. These deals were touted as 50–50 arrangements: Each stadium would cost $800 million, and the team and the city would each pick up $400 million. There are several problems. First, the $800 million does not include infrastructure and parking-lot expenditures, which potentially will cost hundreds of millions of dollars extra. Second, the team's actual payments are $23 million a year for the first twenty years and then rise modestly. At any realistic interest rate, the teams are not picking up half the construction costs. Further, the teams' stadium costs are deductible from the Yanks' and Mets' revenue-sharing obligations to MLB. Third, the city is responsible for the costs of capital improvements and repairs.

The kicker, Rudy says, is that the city gets a great bargain on rent payments. The teams pay 4 percent of home gate receipts and 35 percent of net income from non-baseball events (the latter will amount to pittances). But under the current Yankees' and Mets' leases, the teams pay between 5 and 15 percent for gate receipts, as well as shares of parking, advertising, and local cable revenues. Under Rudy's deals, the teams get 100 percent of all stadium revenues, including parking and naming rights.

New York is the best baseball city in the world. It has much more leverage than was brought to the bargaining table.

The NFL and Los Angeles: Here We Go Again

Maybe the NFL and Los Angeles just weren't meant for each other. Signs that something was strange about the NFL–LA relationship first appeared in July 1972 when Carroll Rosenbloom traded his ownership of the Baltimore Colts for Bob Irsay's ownership of the Los Angeles Rams. Then came Al Davis's suit against the NFL to enable him to move his Oakland Raiders to Los Angeles. The courts said that the NFL's franchise relocation policy was too restrictive and that it was not acceptable to protect the Rams' monopoly over the Los Angeles market.

So Davis moved his team to Los Angeles in 1982. Then he moved his team back to Oakland in 1995 and is suing both the NFL and the City of Oakland for issues connected to that move. In the interim, Irsay moved the Colts to Indianapolis in 1984, and Rosenbloom's widow moved the Rams to St. Louis in 1994.

Los Angeles, the country's second-largest media market, has been without an NFL team since 1994. Over the past eight years, many would-be ownership groups have proposed, unsuccessfully, new and old sites for an NFL team in greater Los Angeles.

Recently, the Denver billionaire Philip Anschutz hatched a plan that appeared generous and workable—and, importantly, acceptable to the NFL. The Anschutz plan called for the construction of a $450 million stadium in downtown Los Angeles on land currently occupied primarily by parking lots and warehouses. The plan would require the city to float up to $100 million in low-interest municipal bonds to pay for the land on which the facility would be built. That money would be repaid, however, through ticket taxes as well as additional sales taxes and anticipated increases in real-estate taxes. The developers (Anschutz's group) would make up any shortfall.

This looked like a deal Los Angeles could not refuse: a privately funded stadium, and football fans in the city would get an NFL team back after an eight-, soon to be nine-, year hiatus. But the plan ran into an obstacle: Los Angeles politics. Anschutz, fed up with opposition to a plan he views as clearly in the city's best interests, last week decided to pull the plug on his project.

Much of the problem appears to have been the abiding resentment of some Los Angeles politicians that the NFL has repeatedly rejected a refurbished Coliseum or Rose Bowl as viable sites. Referring to Los Angeles's failed attempt to get the NFL's last expansion franchise, Pat Lynch, the Coliseum's general manager, asserted: "Not only are we viable, we were viable in 1999. If you don't believe me, talk to our leadership, the historical preservationists, the construction people, the architects and the Community Redevelopment Agency."

These politicians want to know why valuable real estate downtown should be used for a facility that will be played in fewer than twenty days a year when the city already has available stadiums that can be more than adequately renovated. Why should the NFL be able to dictate to the city what is in the city's best long-term development interests? Why should the city's existing assets lie idle?

The politicians might raise an additional question: When the city collects the ticket and sales taxes to pay for the debt service on its bonds, will it be collecting new tax revenues or simply relocating existing revenues? That is, suppose that a new NFL team in Los Angeles generates $40 million a year in ticket sales and there is a local ticket tax of 5 percent. The fans would pay out $40 million, and the city would collect $2 million in tax revenue. Now suppose that if there were no team in Los Angeles, the football fans would spend the same $42 million in other local entertainment venues. If these venues were also subject to a 5 percent tax, the city would still collect the $2 million.

The details of the Anschutz plan have not been fully laid out, but it refers to other additional sales-tax revenues to be collected by the city. The most popular sales taxes in recent years to finance stadium construction have been rental car and hotel taxes. Politicians somehow are able to convince local voters that these taxes fall on visitors, not local residents.

This is false for two reasons. First, higher rental-car and hotel taxes are likely to deter some people or companies from patronizing the city. Fewer tourists and business conventions will mean less revenue and lower taxes. Second, if it were possible to raise these taxes without affecting the behavior of visitors, then the city could raise the taxes and not spend the revenue on sports facilities. This would allow the city either to lower taxes on residents or to increase spending on education, roads, police, and so on.

All this said, Los Angeles's politicians would be well advised to be realistic. Certainly, the details of the Anschutz plan need to be scrutinized, and certainly it is irksome to have the NFL wield its monopoly power in ways that dilute the autonomy of Los Angeles's elected decision makers. Nonetheless, the Anschutz plan is considerably more generous than the NFL norm, even for large cities. It merits another look.

Meanwhile, the owners of the Chargers, Vikings, Saints, and Cardinals, who have been threatening to move if public money for new facilities is not forthcoming in their towns, now have one less arrow in their quivers. For the time being, the threat of an NFL team moving to Los Angeles is once again moot.

Live from New York City:
Inflation, Traffic—and the Olympics!

In the first round of the playoffs, New York City vanquished Houston and Washington, D.C. It went on to subdue San Francisco in the finals.

With all the exultation over the outcome, you'd have thought New York had won a Super Bowl title. In fact, the city had been picked by the U.S. Olympic Committee to be the U.S. entry in the contest to host the 2012 Olympics.

Up next is the three-year World Cup where New York, with its $13 million PR budget, will try to sway the International Olympic Committee judges enough to knock off Paris, Rome, Moscow, Istanbul, and Rio de Janeiro, among others, and grab the ultimate prize: the chance to host the games in Gotham for the first time. The competition for the competition is almost as good as the Olympics itself; one must be a deranged cynic not to buy into all the fun.

Yet, one is tempted to ask, what benefit—other than a lot of hype and further superfluous affirmation that the city is the world's cultural mecca—will the citizens of New York see for all this effort? Given the attacks of September 11, 2001, and the present economic doldrums, it's easy to welcome the idea of new construction in Manhattan and the surrounding boroughs as a lift to both the spirit of the city and its balance sheet. But what we really need to consider is what condition the city's soul and economy are likely to be in seven years from now, when construction for the games will have to begin.

If the local economy is once again strong, and the construction industry is fully employed, then the additional demand generated by building the hotels, stadiums, Olympic village, and infrastructure improvements needed for the games will push the price of labor and materials (and, hence, construction) upward in the greater metropolitan area. It will also require new workers to move into the area, many of whom will stay after the games are over, putting additional pressure on city services. Also staying will be the extra hotel capacity and the Olympic venues in Staten Island, Queens, Brooklyn, and midtown Manhattan.

The current urge to rebuild in Manhattan notwithstanding, the reality is that land in New York is scarce. Are dozens of acres of Olympic sporting facilities really the best long-term use of what real estate there is? Might there not be a higher return on investment by using the available land for commercial, residential, cultural, or other uses? More fundamentally, have these questions even been addressed by the games' boosters in government and elsewhere? Have the views of New Yorkers about this matter been solicited?

Wall Street Journal, November 14, 2002

Then there is the issue of how all this is going to be paid for. Current cost estimates are in the $5 billion–$6 billion range. But no one should be surprised if—with design elaborations, cost overruns, environmental remediation, etc.— the final cost were to exceed $10 billion.

We are told by Deputy Mayor Dan Doctoroff that a good chunk of this will be financed by corporate sponsorship and selling broadcast rights to television. But if corporations spend money on naming rights and sponsorships for the Olympics, they won't spend it on advertising for other products and support for other projects. The massive infrastructural improvements called for in the Olympic blueprint—the expansion of the Javits Center and Number 7 subway line and the construction of the huge concrete platform over the West Side Railyards on which to build the Olympic Stadium, among other things— will almost certainly be funded with public dollars. And once the facilities are built, New York will incur massive additional costs in insurance, sanitation, and security.

The city will be paying debt service on the Olympic bonds for decades. Mayor Michael Bloomberg hopes that most of this cost will be covered by tax-increment financing, but this will begin to happen only if property values rise and remain higher as a result of the Olympics.

In this regard, the budgetary experiences of other cities should be cause for caution. Barcelona, whose games cost $10.7 billion back in 1992, incurred $6.1 billion in public debt. Nagano's 1998 games engendered $11 billion in public debt (out of a total cost of $14 billion), even though the Olympic organizing committee claimed an $11 million profit. Atlanta (1996) and Sydney (2000), alas, report that they broke even.

Other than this uncertain budgetary outlook, New York City would get seventeen days of frenetic exuberance, guaranteed full occupancy of hotel space, busy restaurants, and bumper-to-bumper you know what. Who needs it? What makes New York great is that people around the world come to it for what is intrinsically New York—the museums, the theaters, the concert halls, the sports teams, the intellectual life, the parks, the restaurants, the cultural diversity. New York is already great. It doesn't need the Olympics to make it so.

Renovating the Stadiums:
The Real Economic Story

Residents of the greater Kansas City area are being asked to approve a bistate sales tax that is projected to raise $354 million to finance extensive renovation of the stadiums for the Chiefs and Royals and an additional $350 million for the metro-area arts programs. While there may be legitimate noneconomic reasons to support this bistate tax, voters should be aware that all of the independent, scholarly work on the subject has found that new sports facilities and teams do not contribute to an area's economic development. Voters should not expect the region's per capita income or employment level to be increased, and they should not expect any net positive budgetary outcomes for local or state government.

Most spending at ballparks substitutes for spending at other local entertainment venues. This is because households generally have a certain amount available to spend on leisure activities. If a father takes his family to the ballpark and spends $200, it is $200 that he does not have to spend at local restaurants, bowling alleys, golf courses, movie theaters, and so on. Spending the money at the ballpark does not promote the local economy. It just shifts money around within the greater metropolitan area.

Further, when money is spent at a Chiefs or Royals game, it is much more likely to leak out of the local economy than if the money is spent at, say, a local restaurant. Why? In both baseball and football, approximately 60 percent of team revenues go to the players, most of whom do not live in the area. Indeed, according to the economic-impact study done by Development Strategies for the Kansas City Chamber of Commerce, the teams' own figures show that only 27.7 percent of the Chiefs' wages and salaries and 16.9 percent of the Royals' were paid to Missouri residents. A good chunk of the rest goes to executives and owners who either don't live locally or have such high incomes that 40 percent goes to Uncle Sam, and a large part is saved (going into the world's money markets) or spent on trips out of the area.

Finally, if sales taxes go up to pay for the renovations to the facility, then consumers will have less money to spend on goods and services in general. This will have a retarding influence on local economic growth and will roughly offset any positive impact from the construction work undertaken. If stimulating the local economy were so simple, then every municipal government could do away with unemployment by raising taxes and using the funds to hire workers to dig a big hole and then hiring other workers to fill the hole.

There is also a distribution question. Sales taxes fall proportionately more heavily on low- and middle-income families. In the case of the two stadium renovations, most of the benefit would go to millionaires or billionaires (players and owners). The project represents a massive reverse–Robin Hood scheme.

In the proposed bistate tax for Kansas City, there is another issue at play. Roughly two-thirds of attendees at Chiefs' and Royals' games come from Missouri, with most of the rest coming from Kansas. If attendance at the Truman Sports Complex increases, or if ticket prices increase as a result of the renovations, then more people will be coming to the games (and spending more money) from Kansas. This means that spending Kansas residents otherwise would have done in Kansas will now be done in Missouri. Thus, although the economic activity and tax revenues in the greater metropolitan area as a whole will not be affected, it is probable that there will be some shifting of activity and revenue away from Kansas and toward Missouri. As such, it is difficult to see how a bistate tax is appropriate.

If the Kansas City area does decide to go ahead with the project, it will need to play close attention to the wording of the lease agreement. The proposal is for the teams to sign twenty-five–year leases. Kansas City will want a tight guarantee that the teams will stay put for the entire period, including protection against team contraction in baseball. If the teams stand by the bogus economic-impact estimates in the development-strategy report, then they should be willing to compensate the local governments hundreds of millions of dollars annually for any year they do not fulfill their lease. Would they agree to such terms? Don't count on it.

Foxboro's Gillette Stadium: A Model for Others to Ponder

Earlier this season, I made my first visit to Gillette Stadium in Foxboro, Massachusetts, home of the New England Patriots and the New England Revolution. From its stylistic touches to its seat backs with lumbar support, its two forty-two–foot video screens at each end of the stadium, and its spaciousness, this facility is a fan's delight.

Two characteristics in particular merit attention. First, 85 percent of the seats are on the sidelines, and all seats are angled toward the fifty-yard line. Second, the concourses are wide and open. All concessions and restrooms are against the back of the stadium, leaving open views to field from the concourses.

The biggest story, however, is how the Krafts built the stadium with private money. The construction of the stadium itself cost approximately $325 million. The land cost $30 million. Interest costs during the two years of construction were another $30 million. The Krafts also picked up the cost overruns on the infrastructural improvements—$70 million of which was initially paid by the state and about $4 million of which was overruns—and closed out the mortgage balance on the old Foxboro Stadium. Finally, the Krafts agreed to make annual payments to the state (as reimbursement for the infrastructural work) of roughly $1.5 million a year for twenty years, followed by ongoing annual payments of nearly $750,000.

Expenditures on the land and stadium alone came to more than $350 million, making it the most expensive privately funded stadium in the country. Privately funded PacBell (soon to be renamed), the magnificent new stadium for MLB's San Francisco Giants, cost $330 million and benefited from tens of millions of public-infrastructure work as well as a rezoning of the district that added tens of millions of dollars to the value of the land.

Moreover, Foxboro sits in open country, a forty-minute drive from downtown Boston. PacBell is a few blocks from the city's downtown and sits on the picturesque San Francisco Bay.

The Krafts eschewed selling PSLs, a financing vehicle employed by most new NFL stadiums over the past ten years, because they believed PSLs were not well received by fans. Instead, they arranged to purchase a triple-A debt rating through the Ambac Assurance Corporation and to float a twenty-seven–year bond for $312 million at around 8 percent.

They also benefited from the NFL's G3 loan program, obtaining $150 million. The G-3 money is paid back out of 34 percent of the revenues from club seats, money that would be shared with the other NFL teams in any event. In other words, the G3 money is essentially a grant from the league.

Sports Business Journal, December 8–14, 2003

(It is something for which the league deserves considerable credit. In essence, with the G3, the league and the players' association have taken on a substantial part of the cost of building new stadiums. None of the other leagues has done this.)

Debt-service payments on the bonds, along with the $1.5 million payment yearly to the state, and increased stadium operating expenses created an annual additional cost of around $33 million–$34 million for the Krafts. This financial nut was paid for by several new revenue sources.

First, CMGI bought stadium-naming rights for $114 million over fifteen years, or $7.6 million per year. This contract was taken over by Gillette at a small discount, with CMGI picking up the balance.

Second, Gillette Stadium currently has eighty luxury boxes that go for an average of $180,000 a year (compared with the NFL average of about $90,000). Gillette's luxury boxes average 1,250 square feet (compared with the NFL average of 700 square feet) and are finished in hard wood, with granite counters. Corporations that signed up for ten-year commitments have access to these boxes year-round for meetings and entertaining. Before catering revenues, suite rentals yield a nifty $14.4 million a year.

Third, Gillette has 6,000 club seats, which sell for an average $4,900, yielding $29.4 million in revenue. Club-seat holders also signed up for ten-year commitments and paid the first and last years up front. As with the luxury boxes, the club seats are fully sold and have a sizeable waiting list.

Fourth, the Krafts kept all catering and concessions (save McDonald's) in house, yielding greater flexibility in meeting customers' needs and significantly higher revenue streams.

Gillette is one of the largest stadiums in the NFL at 1.9 million square feet, but its capacity is a modest 60,000. Although the stadium is in the nation's sixth-largest media market, its capacity is below the NFL average. The choice here was deliberate. The Krafts opted for scarcity and for a high-quality experience—that is, fewer but better seats. The Krafts believe not only that this enhances the fans' experience but that it drives higher ticket prices and stronger sponsorship deals.

In the end, Gillette Stadium has produced a nice return for the Krafts, but it appears to be a lower return than that received by other team owners whose stadiums were paid for mostly or entirely with public funds and who received concessionary lease terms on the public stadiums. The Krafts chose to stay in the greater Boston market and to build a private stadium rather than move to Hartford into a 100 percent publicly funded stadium with myriad additional incentives. *[Note: See "Now You See the Patriots, Now You Don't" in this volume for a more complete discussion of the Krafts' motives in returning to Foxboro.]*

So the Kraft Gillette Stadium model might not be for every owner, but it stands as a monumental achievement.

Games People Play

Loathe as I am to question the authority of Joe Namath on the issue of stadiums and economic development, there are some issues I wish he would address in his next commercial.

First, documents obtained through the Freedom of Information Act suggest that the true public cost of Jets Stadium is more than $600 million. Not included in this sum, for instance, is the projected $55 million cost for a platform over West Street to connect the stadium to the waterfront. The Jets' plans call for extensive use of boat service across the Hudson River, and this platform is essential to the project. It is not clear whether the $55 million includes the cost of landscaping.

Also excluded from the $600 million is another $66 million budgeted for the park, stairs, elevators, and other improvements on the north side of the stadium over the Javits Center marshaling yards. In the Jets' images of the stadium, this area is described as the "Game Porch" and is one of the major entrances to the stadium. Nor does the $600 million include the allotted $30 million for the pedestrian tunnel linking the Javits Center to the stadium and the Number 7 train.

Second, Jets propaganda asserts that the team will be responsible for cost overruns on the stadium. However, the memorandum of understanding among the Empire State Development Corporation (ESDC), the Jets, and the Metropolitan Transit Authority (MTA) does not allude to cost overruns. The memorandum between New York State and New York City refers to overruns, but only with respect to the Jets' share of the stadium. That is, it appears that the city or the state may be responsible for overruns with respect to the platforms, the retractable roof and heating–cooling system, or the items mentioned earlier.

Third, in its successful response to the city's request for proposals, Citibank proposed a rather convoluted financing scheme for the project. The city would issue tax-exempt bonds to finance part of the Jets' $800 million contribution. The Jets in turn would make payments in lieu of taxes (PILOTS) to cover the city's debt service on these bonds. Because these PILOTS would be made in lieu of sales and property taxes, if the Citibank scheme is followed, the underlying financing should be considered part of the public, not the private, contribution.

Fourth, and related to one of the issues raised by City Comptroller William Thompson in an October 20, 2004, letter to Mayor Bloomberg, these PILOTS seem to be part of the mechanism that is being used to keep this project off-budget. As long as the project is not included in the city's capital budget, it can proceed forward without City Council approval. Not only is this a violation of democratic norms, it contravenes the 1998 City Council resolution that created NYC2012 as the entity that would pursue the possibility of hosting the Olympic Games.

Several years ago, former Mayor Rudy Giuliani was asked whether he would support a referendum on public financing for a new Yankee Stadium on the West Side. His answer was no. His reasoning was that, were it put to a referendum, the people would vote it down. Here, Mayor Bloomberg is doing Mayor Giuliani one better. He plans not only to avoid a popular vote but also to bypass a vote of the people's elected representatives on the City Council.

Fifth, Jay Cross has acknowledged that a football stadium alone would not provide economic-development benefits. For this reason, he initially sought to integrate the 300-plus events yearly of Madison Square Garden into his project. When Madison Square Garden turned him down, Cross decided that his facility could be yet another expansion on the Javits Center. He now claims that his stadium would host thirty conventions a year (though the city's Independent Budget Office estimates it would be only twenty conventions). While some believe that even the Independent Budget Office estimate is optimistic, even under the best circumstances it appears that the stadium facility would be in use less than one day in three during the year. Is this the best use that can be made of real estate in the center of Manhattan overlooking the Hudson River?

ESDC approval and an MTA air-rights agreement still need to be obtained before the stadium project can go forward. A proper process would also include budgetary sanction from the City Council and State Legislature.

If the economic benefits are as obvious as Joe Namath asserts, then the stadium's proponents should have no problem with standard democratic operating procedures.

[**Note:** *In July 2005, the International Olympic Committee voted to grant the 2012 Olympics to London. New York's bid finished in fourth place.*]

Straight Talk on Stadiums

Some issues just refuse to go away. The economic impact of sports facilities is one of them.

On November 2, there were eleven ballot initiatives on sports facilities across the country. Of these, two concerned the NFL, and one concerned MLB. Public funding for a new stadium for the Cowboys passed in Arlington, Texas, while an initiative for stadium funding for the Kansas City Royals and Chiefs failed. As I write, the financing fates of a new baseball stadium in Washington, D.C., and a new football and Olympic stadium on the West Side of Manhattan are being decided.

Each time a new stadium is proposed, the pattern is predictable. Each city reprises the old debates, rebuilds the predictable coalitions, and relives the accustomed acrimony.

Having worked in this area for many years, I'd like to suggest a synthesis of what we know that will probably please neither side in the great stadium debate. First, econometric studies all agree that a city cannot anticipate that a team or stadium by itself will contribute to the area's economic development. Second, a stadium may shift economic activity around locationally within a metropolitan area. Third, teams do offer noneconomic and intangible benefits to a community.

Consider the implications of each of these points. Econometric studies produce estimates that in effect are averages for all the data in the sample. If a variable is found to have no statistically significant impact on per capita income or employment, it means that over all the cases, on average, there is no impact. It does not mean that there can't be a positive (or negative) impact in a particular case. It only means that generally there is no impact, and it would be prudent not to anticipate a positive impact in a particular city.

Notice also that the statistical finding applies to a stadium or team by itself. If the stadium project is accompanied by a commitment also to invest in commercial, residential, or other development, it is certainly conceivable that the overall project will have a positive impact.

But stand-alone stadiums are used infrequently over the course of a year and by themselves won't induce significant collateral investment. In addition, if the goal is strictly economic development, building a stadium should always be compared with the best alternative use of the city's land and resources.

Next, because a stadium can shift around economic activity within a metro area, it may serve a productive purpose even if it does not raise employment or income. That is, a city's planners may consciously seek to relocate activity to generate a vibrant urban core or to promote a depressed area.

Relocation can also occur across tax jurisdictions. In the case of the proposed Washington, D.C., stadium, for instance, it is likely that a significant amount of leisure spending will be transferred from Virginia and Maryland into the district. Of course, not all spending by suburbanites at a D.C. stadium will be new to D.C. Some of it may substitute for spending at the Kennedy Center or a Georgetown restaurant. But some will be new and will have an incremental, positive effect on the D.C. budget. This will come at the expense of public treasuries in Virginia and Maryland.

(As an aside, it is also interesting that the D.C. financing plan leans significantly on user taxes at the new stadium. This is a step forward from a general sales-tax levy and the now common scheme of using tourist taxes. The latter are often claimed to be free revenues to the local population because only visitors use hotels and rent cars. This is fantasy. Either the higher taxes will reduce the number of visitors to the city or the collected monies could be used for other city needs or lowering other city taxes. Either way, tourist taxes are not free goods to the local population.)

Teams and stadiums produce a variety of unmeasured benefits to consumers. Economists have fancy terms for these: consumer surplus, externalities, and public goods. But we can all recognize that sports teams can provide a salutary cultural impact by enhancing community expression, excitement, and shared experience.

From the perspective of efficient resource allocation, these benefits would justify some degree of public support. This is not the support that comes from leagues' or owners' threatening to move the team, but the type of support that comes from public coffers to construct a public park or symphony hall.

Since with a sports team and stadium some of the benefits are privately appropriated, the issue of stadium-lease terms also becomes important. The real point, however, is that citizens and politicians should keep their eye on the ball. While subsidies cannot generally be justified on economic-development grounds, more modest subsidies may make sense on cultural grounds.

More Benevolence in Stadium Games

Baseball's stadium dramas have reappeared with a vengeance this year. First, there was the *pas de trois* with Mayor Anthony Williams of Washington, D.C., City Council Chair Linda Cropp, and MLB Chief Operating Officer Bob DuPuy. The rich stadium deal was on the table, off the table, and then on the table again. The public will fund about 80 percent of the roughly $550 million expense of the new stadium and grant all stadium revenues to the team in exchange for $5.5 million in annual rent. Score a victory for MLB.

Second, there was the drama in Minnesota, where after years of strong-arm tactics from MLB, including the threat of contraction, Hennepin County and the Twins finally agreed on a ballpark-financing plan. The park will cost nearly $500 million, with $125 million kicked in by the Twins. The public share will be funded with a sales tax increase of 0.15 percent that still must be approved by the state's legislature. Get ready to put another check in the MLB column.

Then there's the long-winded and tedious stadium battle in South Florida, a battle that was started by Wayne Huizenga in 1997 as his expansion team was on the way to a World Series triumph. Huizenga didn't get his way, so he unloaded all his best players, lowering the team payroll from $52.5 million in 1997 to $19.4 million in 1998.

Then he sold the team to John Henry. Henry at first offered to build a new facility with private funds but had second thoughts and called MLB to his aid. Commissioner Bud Selig obliged with an April 25, 2001, letter to Florida State Senator J. Alex Villalobos saying that, "unless [public stadium] funding was secured, the Marlins would be a prime candidate for contraction or relocation. Bluntly, the Marlins cannot and will not survive in South Florida without a new stadium."

Selig's admonition seemed to do more harm than good. Little progress was made until this year. The Marlins' current owner, Jeffrey Luria, reached a deal with Miami-Dade County commissioners for a $420 million stadium near the Orange Bowl. The deal included a $30 million sales-tax rebate from the state, something the state has regularly provided to sports teams in the past. Two weeks ago, however, the state's legislature rejected the rebate.

Miami-Dade County commissioners, Jeffrey Luria, and Bob DuPuy were not pleased. DuPuy sent a note asking for a new plan by June 9. Some read the note as an ultimatum, which DuPuy denied.

It also seems that the cost of land was underestimated so that the financial shortfall is now $45 million. Still, the deficit is a mere 10 percent of project costs. The Las Vegas alternative for the Marlins is possible but problematic. South Florida is the better baseball market today, and the sides are close enough to make this deal work.

Sometimes lost in all the stadium politics and power plays is the fact that MLB itself has begun to provide very significant subsidies for ballpark construction. Baseball's post-1996 revenue-sharing system is based on each team's "net local revenue," defined as local revenue minus stadium costs. Stadium costs include not only operating expenses, but also capital expenses. Capital expenses can either be the upfront financial contribution of a team to stadium renovation or construction amortized over a ten-year period or it can be the principal portion of annual debt-service payments on a construction bond. This definition means that teams' contributions to stadium construction lower their revenue-sharing burden to (or increase their revenue-sharing receipts from) other teams. Put differently, MLB as a whole is subsidizing the construction of stadiums.

Consider an example. The Yankees are proposing a new $800 million stadium that they would finance privately. If the Yankees were to amortize this sum over ten years, it would mean that they would be deducting an additional $80 million a year in stadium-construction expenditures. Since the Yankees face an estimated 39 percent marginal tax rate in baseball's revenue-sharing system, reducing net revenues by $80 million will save the team $31.2 million a year for ten years in revenue transfers. Using a 6 percent discount rate, this translates into a present value of roughly $230 million. That is, MLB is indirectly contributing $230 million to the construction of the new Yankee Stadium.

While the NFL's G3 program has been widely heralded (and with good reason), MLB's stadium policy may actually be more generous. The G3 program has provided a maximum of a $150 million loan to a team for building a new facility. The "loan" is paid back out of sharing 34 percent of club-seat revenues at the new stadium. Because the team would be obligated to share this 34 percent anyway, the loan is really a grant. The NFL, then, has been subsidizing stadium construction and thereby, helping to lower the public burden. As the Yankees example illustrates, however, MLB's program can actually provide more league financing than the NFL's.

Of course, it is true in both the MLB and NFL programs that the new stadiums help to generate new revenues that are subject to sharing. It is likely that the team will end up contributing more in absolute terms, despite the league's stadium subsidy. Nevertheless, to ascertain the size of the subsidy, the proper comparison is between the amount of the revenue-sharing obligation with the program and without the program. So if baseball still uses its monopoly power to leverage public subsidies for stadium deals, it seems to be practicing a more benevolent form of monopoly these days.

New York Facility Triad Is Good News

If bad news always happens in threes, then New York City is providing the exception to prove the rule. No sooner had Sheldon Silver, speaker of the New York State Assembly, vetoed the use of $300 million of state money to finance the Jets Stadium on Manhattan's West Side than the Yankees and the Mets announced plans for privately funded new stadiums. The Yanks and Mets now join the Ratner arena plan for Brooklyn to provide the prospect of three new sports facilities' opening in the five boroughs during 2008–2009.

Over the past fifteen years, the public share in total stadium development (facility plus infrastructure) costs has averaged about 70 percent. In each of these three New York facilities, the public share is below 25 percent.

The Mets are going to spend roughly $700 million for a new stadium next door to Shea. The city and state together are going to chip in approximately $180 million for infrastructure. In this case, the infrastructure is mostly directly beneficial to the Mets rather than to the general public. Nonetheless, the explicit public share of the total development cost of the new facility is 20.45 percent.

The Yankees are planning to spend $800 million for their stadium next door to the present one. The city and state together will pay out around $240 million, roughly 23 percent of the total. A large chunk of this "infrastructure" spending is for public purpose—the reconstruction and expansion of Macombs Dam Park, the parking facility, the boat slip, and a Metro North platform. Game-day parking revenues will all go to the state (unlike the Mets' arrangement, in which the money goes to the team) and will more than pay for the $70 million state investment. Moreover, the new development will facilitate the extension of the gentrification frontier naturally from Manhattan into the South Bronx.

The Nets will occupy a $500 million arena at Atlantic Yards in Brooklyn that is part of a twenty-one–acre, $3.5 billion residential and commercial development being undertaken by Bruce Ratner. In this case, the city and state will contribute $200 million in infrastructure money, or less than 6 percent of the total project costs.

In all three cases, a substantial portion of the funding will come from tax-exempt bonds issued by newly created local development corporations (LDCs). Debt service on these bonds will be covered by the teams via PILOTS to the LDCs. Some may object that if the teams cover the debt service instead of paying taxes, then in effect the public treasury is paying for the bonds and the facility through forfeited tax collections.

Sports Business Journal, June 27–July 5, 2005

This objection was valid in the case of the vetoed West Side stadium for the Jets. However, it applies only to a small degree for the Yankees, Mets, and Nets. The difference for the latter three is that the Bronx, Brooklyn, and Queens are all in tax-abatement zones (Manhattan is not). Under the Industrial and Commercial Incentive Program, commercial developers in these boroughs do not have to pay real-estate taxes on new projects for fifteen years. After that, the tax is phased in at 10 percent a year for ten years and only in years twenty-six to thirty are full taxes assessed.

I estimate the present value of the taxes that are being replaced by the PILOTS for the Yankees, Mets, and Nets at $44 million, $39 million, and $21 million, respectively. Thus, for instance, it could be argued that the Yankees are paying $756 million out of the $800 million for stadium construction, and the Mets are paying $661 million out of the roughly $700 million for their new ballpark. (All three teams benefit from an exemption on material sales during ballpark construction, but this is standard for large construction projects in New York.)

Of course, the Yankees and Mets will benefit from the MLB provision allowing them to deduct stadium capital and operating costs from their local revenue before revenue-sharing taxes are assessed.

The Nets' case is a bit different. The NBA has no program to subsidize team arena construction. Further, the Ratner project includes not only $500 million of private funds for the arena but an additional $3 billion in private funds for residential and commercial development.

When sports facilities are funded with public monies, the construction project itself generally does not add to the local economy. This is because the public spending on the stadiums is offset by the higher taxes, which lead to less disposable income and less spending by the local households.

In contrast, the three proposed New York facilities will be funded overwhelmingly with private funds that will constitute new monies to the local economy. There will be a net increase in local employment and income.

In the Yankees' and Mets' cases, the city also benefits because it no longer has to cover rising maintenance costs at aging facilities. These costs have been running at more than $10 million annually at Yankee Stadium in recent years and nearly that high at Shea. In the end, as in all large-scale construction projects, there will be some detractors. Yet back in 2001, Rudy Giuliani reached a tentative deal with the Yankees and Mets for the public to cover 50 percent of stadium-construction costs. Compared with the typical deal in the sports industry and previous proposals in New York, the new facility plans for the Yanks, Mets, and Nets are good news indeed.

Economic Impact of the Olympics Doesn't Match the Hype

The International Olympic Committee slapped the United States in the face twice two weeks ago: First, New York City lost out on its bid for the 2012 Olympics, and second, the IOC dropped baseball and softball as Olympic sports. It wouldn't take a paranoid personality to think that maybe somebody out there doesn't like us very much.

Baseball and softball are certainly not as popular as soccer, but they are more popular than the vast majority of Olympic sports. It was only twenty years ago that the Olympics did not allow professionals, and now they drop baseball because they insist on professionals. Ironically, this decision, if not reversed, will hurt Caribbean nations, South Korea, and Japan more than it will hurt the United States.

As for the 2012 bid, New York's Mayor Michael Bloomberg tried to put on a pretty face at the post-mortem news conference in Singapore. When asked how he felt personally about the decision, Bloomberg responded: "Two or three days from now there will be mea culpa stories. There will be some sports professor from Smith who will write a story, and by next week, it won't be a story anymore. It will drift out of the pages and it will come back, periodically."

Hmmm. I like Mayor Bloomberg and wouldn't want to make him a liar. So here's my story.

New York probably wins by losing. The evidence from past Olympic Games hardly suggests that there's a resounding economic gain from being the host city. Montreal's 1976 Olympics left the city with $2.7 billion of debt that it is still paying off. The financing of the Moscow Olympics in 1980 is opaque.

The Los Angeles games in 1984 left the organizing committee with a modest surplus of $335 million, but the Los Angeles Organizing Committee got 67 percent of the TV money and spent little on infrastructure or new facilities. The physical legacy of the 1984 games is close to nil.

The Barcelona Organizing Committee in 1992 broke even, but the public debt incurred rose to $6.1 billion.

Similarly, the Atlanta Organizing Committee in 1996 broke even, but the bottom line there is not encouraging. An econometric study using monthly data found that there was insignificant change in retail sales, hotel occupancy, and airport traffic during the games. The only variable that increased was hotel rates, and most of this money went to the headquarters of chain hotels located in other cities.

Interestingly, the director of planning and budgeting for the Atlanta games told Holger Preuss, author of the 2004 book *The Economics of Staging the Olympics*: "We can only give you the analyses which carry a positive image. Other analyses remain unpublished so as not to make the population insecure."

The Sydney Organizing Committee in 2000 also reports breaking even, but the Australian state auditor estimated that the games' true long-term cost was $2.2 billion. In part, this was because it is costing $30 million a year to operate the 90,000-seat Olympic Stadium.

When Athens won the right to host the 2004 games in 1997, its budget was $1.6 billion. The final public cost is estimated to be about $16 billion, ten times the original budget. Meanwhile, most of Athens's Olympics facilities today are reportedly underutilized. Maintenance costs on the facilities in 2005 will come in at about $124 million, and there is no interest in the two Olympic soccer stadiums.

The games are touted to bring in tens of thousands of tourists and, if things go according to the hype, to keep them coming into the indefinite future. Here, too, the evidence isn't rosy. Participants in and visitors to the Olympics often chase others away. In late 2004, Athens's tourism officials were talking about a 10 percent drop in tourist visitors to Greece in 2004.

The Utah Skier Survey found that nearly 50 percent of nonresidents would stay away from Utah in 2002 due to the expectation of more crowds and higher prices. A survey in Barcelona indicated that fully one-sixth of the city's residents planned to travel outside the city during the 1996 Olympics.

Today, much of the games' financing comes from the private sector. Companies buy sponsorships and naming rights or make donations. But companies usually have set public-relations and advertising budgets. If they spend money on the games, they won't spend on other activities. That is, the money they spend on the games is not free to the host economy.

Most important, there is the question of long-term land use. Olympic facilities can take up 15 or more acres each, often in a crowded urban setting. The proposed West Side Olympic Stadium in New York would have occupied prime land in the middle of Manhattan, overlooking the Hudson River. After the Olympics ended, the stadium would have been used for ten Jets game a year and maybe up to another thirty or forty additional days for convention-related business. Is this the best use of scarce and highly valuable urban real estate in a city with a significant housing shortage?

After the games, Olympic facilities also have to be either torn down or maintained. Operating and maintaining these facilities is expensive, especially since they are often used only for niche activities (think, for instance, of velodromes for bicycling). Today, facilities in Salt Lake City cost millions of dollars to operate, and many are in deficit.

None of this is to say that the Olympics always have a negative economic impact. Under the right circumstances, especially if they are held in cities without a modern infrastructure and with proper planning, they can have a salutary impact.

It is to say, however, that there is no automatic bonanza. Sometimes politicians and others lose sight of this, because the competition for the games itself takes on a life of its own. And we in the sports industry know better than most how thrilling and all-consuming the quest for victory can be.

IV

Antitrust and Labor Relations

Take Me Out to the Cleaners

The romantic view of Major League Baseball's relationship with cities—such as San Diego, where the All-Star Game will be played tonight—is that it is a benevolent partner. After all, a new old-fashioned stadium has revived Baltimore's fortunes. But the realistic view is that baseball squeezes revenues out of already impoverished urban areas.

Baseball franchises are not publicly held corporations. There is no functional separation between ownership and management and, hence, there is no pressure to produce book profits to please individual or institutional stockholders. Through accounting legerdemain, bloated front offices, and extensive perquisites, even baseball's most lucrative and successful franchises can show losses. Every year, eight to ten teams claim that they lose money.

But the industry is profitable. According to its most recent figures, baseball's return on sales was 10.6 percent in 1990, well above the 6.3 percent average in U.S. manufacturing. Part of baseball's success is due to the huge public subsidies it receives.

Why is baseball able to get away with this? Because demand by viable cities for major-league teams exceeds supply, restricted artificially by baseball's monopoly. In 1991, when two National League expansion franchises were auctioned for $95 million a piece, eighteen prospective ownership groups in ten cities paid a $100,000 application fee just to compete for the opportunity to own a team.

The result is that some worthy cities are denied teams, and the cities with teams are held hostage to threats of moving. Fiscally strapped cities are blackmailed into floating bonds or introducing taxes to finance new public stadiums. Typically, city guarantees on ticket sales and heavily subsidized rent are also part of the deal.

New York spent more than $100 million to refurbish Yankee Stadium during 1974 and 1975. Today, the franchise has annual revenues in excess of $100 million but pays less than $1 million a year in rent. Chicago built the White Sox a stadium two years ago and threw in a $2 million-a-year maintenance subsidy through 2001 and attendance guarantees thereafter.

Despite a record home attendance of 2.1 million in 1991, Seattle almost lost the Mariners this year. When San Jose, California, voters rejected an initiative to build the San Francisco Giants a new ballpark, Commissioner Fay Vincent gave the Giants' owner his blessing to consider another home for the team.

To keep its team in 1985, Pittsburgh put up $20 million to help finance the purchase of the Pirates by a group of private owners. In 1991, Montreal and Quebec put up $33 million to assist in the private acquisition of the Expos for

$98 million. In neither case did Major League Baseball allow the municipalities to retain an equity interest in the team. In 1990, Joan Kroc was prohibited from giving the Padres to San Diego. The old boys' club of baseball's owners says public ownership is inefficient.

But if inefficiency were truly their concern, baseball's barons would have banned themselves long ago. The real threat of public ownership is not inefficiency—several publicly owned minor-league franchises have been run profitably without political encumbrances for years—but accountability and financial exposure.

Baseball has abused the public trust. But how do we stop its mugging of our cities? For starters, cities should be given the right of first refusal to purchase a franchise before allowing a move. They could undertake municipal ownership or, like football's Green Bay Packers, arrange for fan ownership.

In 1952, Commissioner Happy Chandler said he "regarded baseball as our National Game that belongs to 150 million men, women and children, not to sixteen special people who happen to own big-league teams." A lovely thought!

Batter Up, Already

With two days to go until spring training, and with the Republican leadership in Congress apparently unwilling to lift a finger to settle baseball's paralyzing six-month labor dispute, fans must be in a state beyond despair. But the situation is not hopeless—at least, not yet.

To get real baseball in 1995, Congress needs to get involved now. *[**Note:** "Real baseball" here refers to major leaguers, as opposed to the replacement players that were used by the owners during spring training in 1995.]* It won't do to wait until June, when some have said they plan to revisit the issue, to see whether the players and owners come together. The current negotiations were opened by the owners in December 1992, and the sides are little closer today than they were then. The most significant movement has been toward ever greater rancor and distrust.

Speaker of the House Newt Gingrich and his Republican colleagues have offered several arguments for staying out of the baseball dispute. None hold water. Perhaps the silliest is that Congress has better things to do with its time.

President Bill Clinton proposed to submit the baseball dispute to a panel of arbitrators whose decision would be binding. Passing such a bill would establish a fair fact-finding process and get real baseball back on the field, and it would take Congress half an afternoon to pass it—far less time than Gingrich spent saying he didn't want to get involved.

Republicans say that Congress does not belong in the baseball industry, but that argument comes more than seventy years too late. Congress has repeatedly sanctioned baseball's anachronistic exemption from the antitrust laws, and rather than setting a clear and consistent policy, it threatens baseball with lifting the exemption every time a new senator wants an expansion franchise in his or her state.

Last June, the players' association said it wouldn't strike during the season if the owners promised not to impose a salary cap unilaterally after the season, but the owners said no deal. The players then told Congress that if the antitrust exemption was lifted (even only the part related to collective bargaining), they would not strike because they would be able to defend themselves in court. The bill died in committee, and the players went on strike. So Congress is not only involved. It is complicitous.

There is precedent, too, for imposing binding arbitration in labor disputes. Congress did so as recently as 1992, ending a dispute between the International Association of Machinists and Aerospace Workers and a rail-freight company. No, baseball is not crucial to the economy. But it is the only unregulated, legal monopoly we have in this country. If the Republicans really care about free markets, why do they have nothing to say about the baseball owners' attempts at price fixing through salary caps and intra-industry salary taxes that directly affront the idea of free labor markets?

Binding arbitration is a short-term solution. Lifting baseball's antitrust exemption—as proposed in limited form last week by Senators Daniel Patrick Moynihan and Orrin G. Hatch—would help in the long run, especially if it is a comprehensive measure that puts baseball on an equal footing with the other sports. (It would not, however, settle the labor dispute. The players' association would lift the strike, but the owners would almost certainly impose a lockout and go ahead with their plan for "temporary replacement" players.)

So to get real baseball back on the field in April, Congress must quickly revisit the issue of binding arbitration. And though the leadership's refusal to do so may have seemed final a week ago, perhaps the sight of overweight and undertalented athletes on exhibition fields in Florida and Arizona this week will give Gingrich and Company an ice-water bath of common sense.

As long as baseball faces neither competition nor regulation, the industry will remain in turmoil. If Newt Gingrich truly understood the teachings of Adam Smith, he would know this.

*[**Note:** Real baseball did return in late April 1995, thanks to a U.S. District Court decision that the owners were engaging in bad-faith bargaining.]*

Team Profitability and Labor Peace

The Florida Marlins lost more than $30 million last year. Right, and Dennis Rodman has no tattoos.

The NBA claims that more than half its teams are losing money. The National Basketball Players Association (NBPA) says that only five teams lost money last year, and four of those are getting new arenas. The NBA owners say that they need a hard cap to stop the bleeding. The players say it ain't so, and besides, if some teams on the bottom are really in the red year after year, then there are better ways to deal with it than creating still more restrictive labor markets. These issues, now extant in the NBA due to the lockout announced this week, plague labor relations in all of the major team sports.

In the NBA and the NFL, where an explicit salary cap restricts the payroll, the players have every reason to be concerned that team revenue is correctly identified. When the cap was introduced in the NBA in 1983, Larry Fleisher and the players' association were not very sophisticated about the ways owners could hide or rechannel revenue. The 1983 cap was defined as 53 percent of defined gross revenues (DGR), which in turn included only television, radio, and gate revenues. Following the 1988 collective-bargaining agreement that defined DGR as revenues "derived from, related to or arising out of the performance of players in NBA basketball games," a dispute arose about what sources of income should be included. Owners divided luxury-box revenue into two parts: the rental payment for the amenities of the comfort and convenience of the box and the ticket price for watching the game. The owners claimed the latter belonged to DGR and the former did not. This and similar issues led the players to bring an arbitration complaint against the owners, which they eventually won in 1992 for a settlement of some $60 million.

When the 1995 collective-bargaining agreement was signed, DGR was changed to basketball-related income (BRI), and the players accepted a lower share in return for a broader definition of revenues applicable to the cap. BRI now includes, for instance, 40 percent of luxury-box income, 40 percent of signage (but excludes naming rights, according to an arbitrator's curious decision in 1996), a pro rata share of permanent seat licenses (PSLs), and certain related-party transactions.

The collective-bargaining agreement takes eleven pages to define BRI, and it is still subject to regular disputation. Suppose you are an owner negotiating an arena lease and you are given a choice: pay $2 million in rent and receive 50 percent of a projected $4 million in signage income or pay no rent and receive no signage. It might seem that this is a choice between equals, but since the collective-bargaining agreement gives 40 percent of signage income to the players, the owner would do better with the second option of no rent–

no signage. Lease agreements offer manifold opportunities for such juggling, especially when the arena and team are owned by the same person or entity.

Related-party transactions are a central component to the finances for most teams. If the owner of the team also owns the arena, the arena management company, the concessionaire rights, a local TV or radio station, websites, local real estate, law or consulting firms, and so on that do business with the team, then the owner has tremendous latitude about where to make his or her profits appear. Abe Pollin, for example, owns the new MCI Center where both his NBA and NHL teams, the Washington Wizards and Capitals, play. He can retain arena revenue from naming rights, premium seats, signage, catering, theme activities, and so on, in his arena corporation, thereby reducing the revenues earned by his teams by tens of millions of dollars annually. Owners can also pay themselves exorbitant salaries and consulting fees, along with their extensive perks. Thus, Wayne Huizenga, owner of the Marlins, Dolphins, Panthers, Pro Player Stadium, Sportschannel Florida, and arena-management and concessionaire ventures can rechannel his teams' revenues to his other related businesses, making the world champion Marlins appear to lose money.

When there is a salary cap, such accounting legerdemain comes in handy to reduce directly player payrolls. When there is no cap, owners have still preferred to hide profits to reduce revenue-sharing payments or to argue for larger public-stadium subsidies, collective-bargaining concessions, or special treatment under the law.

As the sports industry globalizes, the opportunities to shuffle new income into different businesses will expand, and the potential for labor conflict will grow with it. If the NBA takes in millions of dollars from European or Asian advertisers on its website, is this, using the language from the 1995 collective-bargaining agreement, revenue that is "derived from, relating to or arising directly or indirectly out of the performance of Players in NBA basketball games or in NBA-related activities"?

The trend for media giants to buy up sports franchises so they can control their programming will further complicate matters. When Rupert Murdoch sends signals for Dodger games to hundreds of millions of Asian homes and is able to raise subscription or advertising fees on satellite TV service, how can baseball players lay any claim to this revenue they help to produce. How can other team owners include this income in the revenue-sharing base when there is no direct increase in Dodger revenues, especially when twenty-four teams are dependent on Fox-owned stations for their local TV revenue?

These are extraordinarily complex management and organizational issues. Put them together with the issues of competitive balance, single entity versus monopoly status, idiosyncratic personalities, among others, and you begin to sense the challenges that lie ahead for the business of team sports. Greater labor–management cooperation is an imperative first step in successfully confronting these challenges. Intelligent leadership and sensible public policy—both scarce commodities—would also help.

This Bud's for a Salary Cap

The coronation of Bud Selig as baseball's new commissioner brought yelps of acclamation from all corners. The owners even managed to turn their traditional trick of two votes: first the real vote, in which three owners dissented, and then the vote for public consumption, in which enthusiastic unanimity prevailed.

To be sure, Bud's promotion brings both good news and bad news. The good news is threefold. First, when referring to the office we will no longer have to take a deep breath and say "chairperson of the executive council." Now, it will just be "commissioner." Second, Selig is actually a sensible man with excellent social skills, and, most important, he leads by consensus—a felicitous trait in these litigious days of revenue disparities and fractious ownership. Third, Selig is joined by Paul Beeston as baseball's day-to-day chief operating officer. Beeston is smart and reasonable, and he gets along with Don Fehr of the MLB Players Association.

The bad news is also threefold. First, by naming an owner to the post, MLB is giving up all pretense of having an independent commissioner. The commissioner, of course, was never independent of the owners. He was always their employee. Yet some commissioners managed through their nominal independence to tip scales at crucial points by exercising "the best interests of baseball" clause. Fay Vincent did this in 1990 to end the owners' lockout. Given the stalemate that produced the 1994–95 strike, the inability of even President Clinton to put the game back on the field, and the ultimate bargain that seemed to favor neither side, one wonders whether Vincent, were he still in office, might have been able to bring that abomination to an earlier end. But the owners got rid of Vincent precisely so he wouldn't disrupt their assault on the players and, in a rare display of candor, said as much publicly.

Now MLB's ownership ranks are transformed. Earlier this year, the owners voted with one abstention to accept Rupert Murdoch as new owner of the Dodgers. Murdoch owns Fox, which has the long-term national TV contract with MLB as well as the local TV contract for twenty-three of the thirty teams. As one owner confided in me with a sigh about the vote to allow Murdoch into the baseball owners' club: "We didn't have any choice."

When the absence of a traditional "independent" commissioner is juxtaposed with Murdoch's financial clout, one wonders where the game might be headed. Certainly to Asia, but maybe also Murdoch will decide that two-and-a-half hours is enough of prime time and that a home-run derby should decide tied games after nine innings. Murdoch is not known for treating his employees with a soft touch, and what this augurs for labor peace in the future we will learn in two or three years.

Second, MLB tells us that since Selig is putting his shares of the Brewers in trusteeship, there will be no conflict of interest. Sure, and Rudy Giuliani isn't a Yankee fan. Selig's daughter Wendy is running the team in his absence, and Selig will reclaim his assets when he leaves the commissioner's job. How much the Brewers are worth five years from now will have a lot to do with how successful the team is between now and 2003. If I am the Tribune Corporation, I am not sure that I want Selig invalidating a trade the Cubs make with the Mets or upholding a player's suspension.

Third, baseball faces many challenges in the coming years, but none is more important than competitive balance. Since 1993, in large measure due to expansion by two teams in that year and again this year, dominance by big-city teams and teams with new stadiums has come to assert itself.

MLB's top-revenue teams earn about $150 million a year, and its bottom teams earn about $45 million. One positive outcome of the players' strike is that now baseball has a system of revenue sharing wherein the top-revenue teams transfer approximately $8 million–$10 million a year to the bottom teams. So now the range of the disparity becomes, say, $140 million to $55 million.

The top-revenue and bottom-revenue teams are expected to be able to compete with relative parity on the playing field. If the fans of the financially less fortunate team are to stay interested, they must believe that their team has a fair chance to win every game and to make it to post-season play.

Both the high- and low-revenue teams must compete in the same labor market for the same players. Signing a player for $10 million, even if he is expected to produce $11million in revenue, is risky. Low-revenue teams might find the risk too great.

Baseball is recovering from the ravages of the 1994–95 strike, and average attendance levels are almost back to where they were during the first two-thirds of the 1994 season. Yet the recovery is very uneven. Strong teams are now above their 1994 levels, but weak teams are at or below their levels immediately following the resumption of play in 1995.

In other words, MLB's revenue-sharing plan, while a step in the right direction, does not seem to go far enough. The reason the George Steinbrenners and Dick Jacobses of baseball accepted the new revenue-sharing plan is that the small-city teams said they would not confer local broadcast rights (the previous deal was expiring) to the home team without it. Now the rights have been conferred, and the small-city teams are left without leverage to take the revenue-sharing plan further. Even in the presence of the new 34 percent luxury tax on the top payrolls, competitive imbalance prevails.

Commissioner Selig has made it clear what he believes the solution is to this problem: a hard salary cap. This would enable small-city teams to compete with large-city teams for the best players. The players' association has also made it clear that it will not accept the cap. If Murdoch's past predicts his future, then he will urge the owners to beat the players into submission. In this context, what will it mean for Selig to rule by consensus? And what will it all mean for the future of baseball's ephemeral labor peace?

Let the Market Rule the Basketball Court

It's billionaire owners versus millionaire players, so who cares? A few years ago, people were reciting this mantra about baseball and hockey. Now it's about the NBA, a league that until last week had never missed a game due to a work stoppage.

With a lockout delaying the start of the season, owners and players are fighting over how to distribute the pie called "basketball-related income," a sum that excludes licensing revenue of more than $250 million a year as well as 60 percent of revenue from such sources as luxury suites and advertising in NBA arenas. As of last year, the players earned 57 percent of BRI, a figure the owners would like to cut.

Why are the sides explicitly fighting over the distribution of revenues? This isn't the way labor negotiations work in most industries. The answer is that unlike in every other industry (save the NFL), owners in the NBA are not always allowed to pay a player as much as they might think he is worth. Since 1983, the NBA has imposed on each of its teams a "salary cap," defined as a certain share of designated leaguewide revenues. Unless a player falls into a so-called exception category, the owner cannot pay the player a salary that would put the team over the cap.

This contrivance has produced predictable results: When one tampers with markets, black markets emerge. Black markets in the NBA take the form of owners' finding ways to beat the cap. Over the years, exceptions to the cap have been created, modified, eliminated, and created again, often with the result that players' salaries have grown more rapidly than revenues.

The owners, who locked out the players in May, are calling for a "hard" salary cap or "cost certainty"—a fixed share of revenues going to salaries, and this time not a penny more. Never mind that cost certainty is not a privilege afforded to other industries in a market economy. Never mind that owners are not willing to grant fans cost certainty by freezing ticket or concession prices.

A look at other sports shows why the NBA players have a point when they argue that the owners' demands are unfair. Cost certainty exists nowhere—not even in the NFL, which also functions with a salary cap. The NFL cap is set at 62 percent of a revenue base known as defined gross revenues, but loopholes have allowed players' salaries to grow to 67 percent of DGR (the NBA equivalent would be roughly 60 percent of BRI).

Baseball, which has no cap but instead imposes "luxury taxes" on team payrolls above a certain threshold, pays players some 58 percent of all baseball revenues. But baseball actually spends considerably more than this on players, since each major-league team runs a minor-league and scouting system on which it spends another 12 percent to 13 percent of its revenues. The NBA does not have player-development expenses: Division I universities do that job for the league. Moreover, baseball owners have shared licensing money with the players 50–50. In some years, the baseball players have received up to $90 million from that source. In contrast, the basketball players are given a fixed $25 million a year from licensing, and now owners want to do away with that.

The NBA owners say that a free market in salaries wouldn't work, because the league must maintain competitive balance among its teams to keep fans interested. According to the owners, some teams have a big advantage in hiring the top players because they play in larger cities or in newer arenas, or they have owners who own related businesses that also benefit from the star players. Thus, these teams will pay more, accumulate the best talent, and thereby dominate the league.

There is, of course, some sense to this argument. The question is what should be done about this possible tendency toward imbalance. The current system has not exactly been a great success, as shown by the Chicago Bulls' victories in six out of the last eight NBA championship series. Would the owners' proposed hard cap with absolute cost certainty do the trick? Not likely.

It turns out that the weak teams for which the owners profess concern already have low team payrolls and are below the cap. It is the strong teams that exploit loopholes and go above the cap. So the direct effect of installing a hard cap would be to lower the payrolls and increase the profits of the strong teams, not to aid the weak teams. The effect on competitive balance would be small.

Do the star players deserve their high salaries? Consider the Chicago Bulls' superstar Michael Jordan. He was paid $33 million last year by the Bulls' owner, Jerry Reinsdorf, presumably because Reinsdorf felt that Jordan would generate at least this much extra revenue for the Bulls—and by all signs, he did.

But Jordan also generates revenue for other owners by filling up their arenas when he plays there, by enriching the national television deals the league has signed with NBC and Time Warner, and by spurring growth in licensing revenue. In economics jargon, Jordan creates a large positive externality— estimated at well over $20 million—that the marketplace does not recognize. After all, Jordan does not sign a separate contract with the other owners or with the NBA.

The players' aim, however, is not to get Jordan or other superstars more income. Indeed, they have sought mechanisms to raise lower- and middle-level salaries disproportionately. The logical policy for the NBA is to abandon the salary cap and allow the market to work. If certain teams are exploiting their structural advantage to the detriment of competitive balance, then the league should follow the baseball model and levy a tax on individual salaries or team payrolls above a given threshold, as the players have also proposed.

The tax would provide a disincentive for the owners to overspend, but it would not prohibit them from competing for top talent. Any funds generated by such a tax could then be funneled to the weaker teams, provided that these teams maintained a payroll of at least, say, 85 percent of the league average. If the owners were truly concerned about the financial viability of the weaker teams and about competitive balance, this system would address these concerns and create the fewest distortions to underlying market forces.

The NBA Lockout: Who's Dropping the Ball?

On November 12, the *New York Times* ran a profile of the Washington Wizards' owner Abe Pollin. Pollin was quoted as saying that the NBA's present economic system does not work and that the owners deserve a fair rate of return on their investments. The same day, NBA Commissioner David Stern was quoted in *USA Today* stating that the fundamental issue was a fair share for the owners.

Interestingly, neither Pollin nor Stern alluded to a problem of competitive balance among the teams—the argument most often made on behalf of a salary-cap system. Rather, both seem to be concerned with team profitability.

Are NBA Teams Profitable?

Consider this: The NBA uses a revenue base known as basketball-related income (BRI) to set its salary cap. BRI includes most basketball revenue, but it excludes several important income sources. For instance, BRI does not include naming rights (often several million dollars per year per team), licensing income (about $300 million per year), parts of related-party income (when the team owner also owns the arena, concessions rights, or local TV station broadcasting the games and transfers income away from the team to these entities), and 60 percent of both arena-signage and luxury-box income. If we take BRI and subtract players' salaries and benefits each year from 1994–95 through 1997–98, we find that this sum grew from $371 million in 1994–95 to $765 million in 1997–98—a compound growth rate of 27.3 percent per year. That is, team income after deducting players' salaries more than doubled over three years. And the $765 million figure excludes the important income sources listed above.

The owners did not complain about being unprofitable back in 1994–95 or 1995–96. It is hard to believe that with this revenue growth after players' salaries they could have become unprofitable in the past two years.

The players received relatively detailed information from the owners about the 1996–97 season and concluded that perhaps four teams out of twenty-nine had a negative cash flow. The players asked for financial details about the 1997–98 season to verify the owners' claims but so far have received only cursory and largely meaningless summaries.

Besides the rapid growth in BRI after salaries, here's what the players know. The salaries of head coaches and general managers have more than tripled in the past four years. Fourteen head coaches receive more than $2.8 million a year, with some coaches reaching up to $8 million. Meanwhile, the highest-paid three head coaches in the NFL each earn less than $2.5 million a year, and each has won a Super Bowl. Asked to comment on the astronomical increases in coaches' salaries, David Stern commented to Sportsline USA: "If the owners spend all that money on coaches, that means they have it. Otherwise, they wouldn't do it." Stern himself reportedly earns almost $9 million a year.

The owners say that last year's player-salary share of BRI of 57 percent is too much, but the comparable share in football is about 60 percent, and in baseball it is more than 60 percent. Let us assume conservatively that the average NBA team in 1997–98 had the following financial results:

Team revenues: $60 million
Players' salaries: $34 million
Other costs: $23 million
Profit: $3 million

Now assume that revenues and salaries grow annually at 12 percent and other costs grow at 5 percent (more than double the current rate of inflation). Since revenues and salaries each grow at the same rate, the salary share will stay the same. Consider, however, what happens to profits under this scenario. By the year 2002–2003, the average team would have these results:

Team revenues: $105.8 million
Players' salaries: $59.9 million
Other costs: $29.3 million
Profit: $16.6 million

That is, profits would grow more than fivefold over the period—or the annual growth rate of profits would be 40.8 percent. Are these assumptions plausible? The owners' new television deals with NBC and Turner provide a guaranteed $662 million per year over the next four years. That's $22.8 million per team each year, compared with $9.5 million per year under the previous contract. Further, in the next two years, at least eight NBA teams will be playing in new arenas, each worth $10 million–$20 million or more per team annually. (The teams getting new arenas include all four teams with negative cash flows in 1996–97.)

Would $16.6 million of profit represent a fair return for a team owner? For the six years between 1990 and 1995, the average profit as a share of sales was 3.5 percent for all manufacturing corporations in the United States. A profit of $16.6 million would represent 15.7 percent of sales for an NBA team in 2002–2003. Even if we assumed that in 1997–98 the average team earned zero profit and other costs came to $26 million, at the assumed growth rates, average team profit in 2002–2003 would be $12.6 million, or 11.9 percent of sales.

But the definitive data on team profitability comes from another source: escalating franchise values. These values, determined in the marketplace, rise only when the economic return to ownership rises. Expansion fees for an NBA franchise were $32.5 million in 1988 and $125 million in 1994. In early November 1998, 80 percent of the New Jersey Nets sold for $150 million, implying that the entire franchise was worth $187.50 million. Thus, over the past ten years NBA teams have increased nearly sixfold in value. Simply put, this would not happen if there were not a substantial and growing economic return to ownership.

What about Competitive Balance?

If competitive balance is a concern of the owners, they are keeping it a big secret. Their first offer to the union called for the elimination of the Bird exception. This exception allows a team to re-sign one of its own free agents even if it put the team over the salary cap. It was because of the Bird exception, for instance, that the Bulls were able to sign Michael Jordan last year for $33 million when the team's salary cap was $26.9 million. It would have been impossible for any other team to sign Jordan to a one-year contract for this much money, because even if a team paid all of its other eleven players the minimum salary, it could not have offered Jordan more than about $23 million. The salary-cap system, then, actually prevented competitive bidding for Jordan and helped restrain his salary.

Significantly, the same exception gives all teams a big advantage in signing its own free agents. Combine this with the NBA's reverse-order–draft system (allowing teams with the worst win percentages to have earlier picks of the best players coming out of college and high school) and the system serves to enable small-market teams to retain superstars they select in the amateur draft. If Jordan originally had been drafted by the Milwaukee Bucks rather than Chicago, it is likely that he would be still playing for them. Of the eleven top-paid players in the NBA, seven are still with their original teams.

Further, if the owners are worried about competitive balance, why did they reject the players' suggestion that any revenue raised by a luxury tax on high salaries be redistributed to low-revenue clubs? And why don't the owners have a system to share local revenues as exists in the NFL and MLB?

What Is the Role of the Superstar Agents?

In early November, David Stern began blaming the owners' lockout on David Falk, the agent for Michael Jordan, Patrick Ewing, and other superstars. Stern claimed that Falk had magical powers over the NBPA's executive director, Billy Hunter, and the union, and the only thing that Falk cared about was high salaries for his marquee players. The union, whose president is Patrick Ewing, had transformed itself into a lobbying group for elite players. Stern's effort to divide and conquer eluded no one.

The facts are very different. First, Ewing and Jordan and several players on the union negotiating team are at the end of their careers. Existing long-term contracts will be grandfathered, and the league will find a way to pay Jordan. They have absolutely nothing to gain personally from this lockout. Indeed, with the highest salaries, they are losing more salary than anyone. Second, the union has proposed a stiff tax on high-end salaries, rapid increases in the minimum salary, and the introduction of an average salary exception (allowing teams to sign a player at the leaguewide average salary even if it goes over the cap), and it has fought against the owners' proposal to extend the rookie salary scale to five years. Each of these positions strongly benefit lower-end salaries. Third, anyone familiar with Billy Hunter and the operation of the union knows that the notion that he is controlled or even disproportionately influenced by David Falk is nonsense.

The owners' position is unreasonable. They want cost certainty, which exists for no other industry in this country, and large guaranteed profits for all teams no matter how they perform on the court. This is a recipe that not only is patently unfair to the players, but that will also weaken the game in the long run.

Waiting for players to miss paychecks, exhorting the rank and file to turn on the union leadership, and offering the union no substantive basis for owners' demands is wrongheaded and unproductive. There are many potential ways out of this lockout. They all begin with honest and open bargaining.

The NBA Lockout: A Postmortem

Some sportswriters and players' agents, and even the guru of sports-union leaders, Marvin Miller, have questioned the efficacy of union leadership during the recent NBA lockout. While the final collective-bargaining agreement makes some unfortunate concessions from the players' perspective, the deal also contains some important gains for the union. Moreover, both the structure of the deal and the union's accrued experience from the struggle augur well for the next confrontation six or seven years down the road. The critics are right when they argue that Billy Hunter and Patrick Ewing may have made some mistakes. They are wrong if they believe that Hunter and Ewing did not do a superlative job under the circumstances.

The two significant concessions made by the union were accepting a near-hard cap at 55 percent of defined revenues during years four through six of the agreement and accepting a limit on individual players' salaries. Miller critiqued the deal, asserting that the role of unions is to set minimum, not maximum, wages. Fair enough, but what Miller leaves out are the facts that (1) the NBA has had a salary cap, albeit porous, since 1983; (2) the union is coming off a nearly devastating bargaining process in 1995 that sharply divided the players and resulted in greater salary stratification; (3) the NBA players had no prior experience with work stoppages; (4) the economic conditions of the 1990s are far different from those that prevailed in baseball when Miller's players' union cut its teeth; and (5) the NBA owners conducted a very controlled, deliberate, and sophisticated lockout.

Under the new deal, the salary cap remains at 48.04 percent of defined revenues, and it remains subject to various exceptions. These exceptions will allow teams' payrolls to go up to 55 percent of defined revenues without any additional restraint. If aggregate payrolls go above this percentage, then the players will reimburse the owners dollar for dollar of any overage up to 61.1 percent of revenues. If payrolls go above this latter level, then the owners whose teams' payrolls exceed the 61.1 percent threshold will pay a 100 percent tax on every dollar of salary above this level. Thus, there are strong constraints built into the system to keep player-compensation expenses at 55 percent of defined revenues in net terms, but there is certainly some wiggle room. The point is that the current deal has evolved out of the existing salary-cap institution. It was not created out of thin air.

What is new, even to basketball, is the acceptance of an absolute limit on individual salaries. For this year, the limits are $9 million for players with less than seven years of service, $11 million for players with between seven and nine years, and $14 million for players with ten or more years. These limits will rise with NBA revenues, and no existing player will be forced to take a cut, thanks to a provision that allows any salary to grow by 5 percent over its previous level. Further, these limits apply to the first year of a contract, but contracts for Bird free agents can extend for seven years and grow at 12 percent of the base salary per year. If these limits had been in place during the last collective-bargaining agreement, only four players would have been affected directly. The problem here is not whether Patrick Ewing makes $20 million or $14 million (Ewing already forfeited $8 million of his salary this year). It is that historically the star players were the salary trailblazers for the entire league—the guarantors that salaries will follow increasing revenues.

While it is true that the owners stand to reap some handsome profits from these limitations, it is a stretch to think that this plan represents a direct threat to baseball or hockey, which have never operated with a cap. Indeed, it is likely that the NFL's constraints on the salaries of franchise players are more severe than the $14 million cap (in 1998–99) on veteran free agents in the NBA.

One problem that basketball has had for many years, and that was exacerbated by the 1995 collective-bargaining agreement, is that the cap system, without sufficient exceptions for midrange players, generated a sharp class system among the players. Rather than pulling up all salaries, by occupying increasing amounts of cap room, the superstars were forcing the salaries of most other players downward. This created not only a problem of equity but also a problem for union solidarity that did not go unnoticed by the owners.

The new collective-bargaining agreement scores appreciable gains for the players in this regard. For instance, a new "middle-class" exception was added at $1.75 million for this year, rising to the league average salary in year four. Teams will be able to sign one player per year under this exception (that is, even if the team has reached its 48 percent cap), each to six-year contracts. Thus, by year six of the deal, some teams will be able to have six of their twelve players paid the average league salary. The union also scored very significant gains in minimum salaries, which will now range from $287,500 to $1 million, depending on years of service, and substantial improvements in players' postretirement benefits.

Further, price regulation always creates strange outcomes. In the case of the NBA cap, we are already seeing the salaries of some excellent, but not superstar, players shoot up to the maximum. That is, instead of having, say, a Patrick Ewing at $18 million and a Latrell Sprewell at $10 million, we might have them both at $14 million. And other players whose salaries are effectively constrained by the maximum may find that the owners will give them a seven-year deal at the maximum, instead of what might have been a five-year deal at a few million more per year. This possibility will be especially beneficial to older veterans. In other words, the owners will find a way to pay the players.

It is apparent that in the short run, a majority of players will either gain from or be unaffected by this new collective-bargaining agreement. The 55 percent threshold is essentially the 57 percent the players attained in 1998 without Michael Jordan's salary. This is a key to understanding the union's dilemma and the eventual outcome.

When Marvin Miller fashioned the impressive solidarity and militance among baseball players in the early and mid-1970s, the minimum salary in baseball was $16,000 (in 1975), and the average salary was $44,676 (in 1975). An average baseball player who sat out a whole season in 1975, then, would lose less than one-fiftieth of what an average NBA player in 1998–99 would lose. Moreover, the potential gains in 1975 for the baseball players were astronomical if they could move from the reserve system to a system of free agency.

Billy Hunter did not have these advantages in 1998. Nor did he have the advantage of a union with any history of struggle and sacrifice. Instead, he inherited a union that was bitterly divided over a failed decertification vote in 1995 and acutely bifurcated salaries. To be sure, this is what Armen Keteyian and Harvey Araton had to say in their book *Money Players* about the state of union politics in 1994: "[Charlie] Grantham (then union director) knew his players were not about to strike or tolerate being locked out."

The absence of a history of collective-bargaining struggle is not just a matter of an abstract notion of solidarity. It involves the establishment of practices of cohesion and strategic communication.

Hunter faced strong criticism for being both too authoritarian and too democratic. On the owners' side, there was no issue of democracy. Commissioner David Stern called the shots and spoke for the twenty-nine owners with one voice. Hunter needed to lead, but he couldn't get too far out in front of his constituency of more than 400 players.

Early on, Hunter called a meeting for all union members in Las Vegas. The issues and positions were exhaustively debated in small and large groups. The meetings were open only to players and union staff, but it was clear within days that Stern knew what was being discussed and decided on in Las Vegas. Indeed, individuals from the commissioner's office have suggested that they had informants all along and knew about every move the union would make.

Hunter was also accused of being a puppet to the players' agent David Falk and, sometimes, the agent Arn Tellum. Large parts of the media uncritically regurgitated these claims. Yet anyone involved in the process, who spent time in the union office, or who knew the deep integrity of Billy Hunter knew that these charges were utter nonsense. To be sure, the willingness of the union initially to discuss and then to accept limits on high-end salaries run diametrically counter to the interests of the big-time agents.

Hunter developed a wonderful rapport with the players and his staff. He fashioned a strong unity out of division, and he held the players together for several months of the lockout—itself a Herculean feat. While not everything the union wanted, the final settlement terms are a very long way from where the owners' demands started, or even where they were when the owners supposedly made their last offer in late December. What is remarkable about both the process and the outcome is that under the circumstances, Billy Hunter and the union were able to accomplish as much as they did.

Next time around, the union will have this experience under its belt, and players' salaries will be more compressed. Both augur well for union solidarity and strength. Most important, the vast majority of NBA players are pleased with the present deal.

*[**Note:** The next collective-bargaining agreement was signed in 2005 and contained what are generally acknowledged to be improved terms for the union.]*

"Jordan Effect" Won't Rescue the NBA

Michael Jordan announced his return to the NBA last week—not as a player but as part-owner and general manager of the Washington Wizards (formerly the Bullets). He also vows to participate in team practices so he can look closely into the players' eyes and see what they are made of. And if Gar Heard, the Wizards' coach, doesn't like it? "I'm his boss and so I can do it," Jordan pronounced at a press conference.

Understandably, the second coming of basketball's greatest player generated a lot of excitement. The news was the lead story in both the *Washington Post* and *USA Today*. President Bill Clinton even showed up at the MCI Center to embrace Jordan and the Wizards' majority owner, Abe Pollin.

But how will Jordan fare in his new role? We've already seen that his hoops prowess doesn't translate on the baseball diamond. Will it help him evaluate talent, hire good scouts, manage the NBA draft, and be an effective communicator? If he's even one-tenth as good a manager as he was a basketball player, Jordan will easily surpass the performance of Wes Unseld, the Wizards' erstwhile head of basketball operations.

I've worked with Jordan in the players' union and learned to respect his intelligence and business acumen, but even so I remain skeptical about how he will do. Most of the precedents aren't encouraging. Remember Magic Johnson, another retired superstar, trying to coach the Los Angeles Lakers for a few miserable games? The only great player who has become a great executive is Jerry West, the Lakers' general manager.

Maybe Jordan will prove as successful, but in Washington he faces a challenge more formidable than breaking down the New York Knicks' defense (which he used to do with some regularity). The last time the Wizards won a playoff series was during Ronald Reagan's first term. This year the team has 13 wins and 29 defeats.

Despite this miserable performance, the team has the sixth-highest payroll in the NBA at $53 million. Nearly $41 million—$7 million above the official salary cap of $34 million this year—goes to four players: Juwan Howard, Mitch Richmond, Rod Strickland, and Ike Austin. Each is on a long-term contract, and none is playing up to expectations. If Jordan wanted to get contract concessions out of Howard or Strickland, he would have to deal with their agent, David Falk, who also happens to be Jordan's long-time agent. It's unclear how the Wizards will resolve this potential conflict of interest.

The peculiarities of the NBA salary-cap system make it practically impossible for Jordan to hire high-priced talent for at least the next two years. And unless the Wizards get one of the first three lottery picks after this season, they will lose their first-round draft pick to the Golden State Warriors as a result of a 1995 trade.

Will Jordan's arrival improve the Wizards' finances and the NBA's fortunes? Both could use a boost. The Wizards, perennial doormats, play to half-empty arenas. The NBA is still trying to recover from 1998's double-whammy of the owners' lockout and Jordan's retirement. TV ratings and attendance are down 5–10 percent, and licensing revenue is off by even more. Jordan's return may provide a temporary boost to the Wizards and the league.

But fans get excited by who's on the court, not who's in the boardroom. Broadcasters won't be showing slow-motion replays of Jordan making incisive points during salary-arbitration meetings. The Jordan effect on attendance and TV ratings is likely to be small.

The real winners in this deal appear to be Jordan and Pollin. Jordan gets a reported 20 percent of Ted Leonsis's sports holdings (which include 40 percent of the Wizards and the WNBA Mystics, a minority stake in the MCI Center, and full ownership of the NHL Capitals), along with a handsome salary. Plus, all this publicity should boost Jordan's flagging line of Nike sneakers. Pollin, who apparently surrendered no assets in the deal, gets to associate with one of the world's most famous people.

If by some miracle the Wizards quickly turn into winners, it would be a clear sign that fortune smiles on retired NBA players. Bill Bradley, take heart.

NBA Players Are Doing Fine, Thank You

If all goes according to plan, after the January 28 Super Bowl, U.S. sports fans will focus renewed attention on the NBA. It will come none too soon for most NBA arenas, where empty seats have been more visible than usual this season. NBA television ratings on Turner are averaging only a 1.2 Neilson rating, down 14 percent from last year.

Yet there are also signs of success. The NBA is approaching the midpoint in its present collective-bargaining agreement whose negotiation delayed by three months the start of the 1998–99 season. When the accord was reached in early January 1999, many commentators claimed that the union's chief, Billy Hunter, had sold the players short. The critics pointed to new caps on individual players' salaries and the hardened team cap via the introduction of the escrow and luxury-payroll taxes.

If results matter, then it is time for the detractors to do some reassessing. Consider the evidence.

When the owners locked the players out in 1998, they said such a decisive measure was necessary because the salary share in BRI had risen to the unacceptably high level of 57 percent during the 1997–98 season. Two years earlier, it had been at 53 percent.

Based on extended rosters (roughly 420 players), the NBPA estimates that average salaries, which were a lofty $2.37 million in 1997–98, rose to $2.64 million in 1998–99, $3.27 million in 1999–2000, and $3.93 million this season. That is, over the past three years, average salaries have grown by 65.8 percent, or by 18.4 percent per year—and that despite the subtraction of Michael Jordan and his $34 million salary with the Bulls in 1997–98.

NBA revenues have also continued to grow, but at a slower pace. Consequently, the share of salary in BRI has risen—from 57 percent in 1997–98, to 59 percent in 1998–99, to 62 percent in 1999–2000, and to an estimated 64 percent in 2000–2001. Not bad results for a labor contract that some called a sellout.

Next year, however, is the first year of the new escrow tax. Here's how it works. The players place 10 percent of their total salaries and benefits in an escrow fund. For every dollar that the players' total remuneration exceeds 55 percent of BRI, a dollar is taken out of the escrow fund and given to ownership until the escrow fund is exhausted. Thus, if the players' share of BRI is between 55 percent and 61.1 percent, the owners collectively will be reimbursed to bring their net payments to players down to 55 percent. If, however, the players' share exceeds 61.1 percent prior to the escrow reimbursement, there is no further reduction of players' income.

The owners also have a second line of defense: the luxury tax. If an individual team's payroll exceeds 61.1 percent of team BRI, the owner pays a 100 percent tax on the overage. These two mechanisms, many thought, would contain players' net salaries and benefits within 55 percent of BRI.

Early returns suggest otherwise. Based on long-term contracts currently in place and other provisions in the collective-bargaining agreement, the NBPA estimates that the average salary will increase to $4.5 million next year. Given projected leaguewide revenues, the players' pre-escrow share in 2001–2002 will come to 67 percent of BRI. Players will then have to surrender the entire sum in escrow, and their post-escrow share will be 60.9 percent—3.9 percentage points above the players' 57 percent prior to the lockout.

And there is other, significant good news for the players. Largely as a result of the poor contract agreed to by the former NBA chief Simon Gourdine in 1995, which eliminated a middle-range exception to the salary cap, players' salaries became increasingly bifurcated. The growing salary gap created a problem for union solidarity.

The 1998 collective-bargaining agreement, by reintroducing middle-range exceptions, has gone a long way toward narrowing the divide in players' salaries and re-creating a middle class. The median salary increased from $1.4 million in 1997–98 to $2 million in 1999–2000. This represents 19.4 percent annual growth. With the median salary-growth rate exceeding that of the average salary, and with the sharp increases in minimum salary, the middle class of players is back. The number of players with salaries below $1 million was reduced from 151 in 1997–98 to just 95 in 1999–2000. This bodes well for ongoing union strength.

So the players are happy, and the owners have stopped complaining. Now it only remains to make the fans happy again.

Contraction and Baseball's Antitrust Exemption?

Should MLB scorn common sense and its fans by proceeding with contraction plans, it will find a variety of challenges to its special antitrust-exempt status. These challenges will come from attorneys-general of states seeking to retain existing clubs or to attract relocating clubs and from the MLB Players Association, among other possible sources.

Several weeks ago, I was having lunch with a group that included a few owners of Major League Baseball teams. One of the owners inquired whether MLB's antitrust exemption still mattered. It is a reasonable question—after all, each of the major team-sports leagues is a monopoly, but the NFL, NBA, and NHL all survive without a blanket exemption.

The question is complicated, but the answer is clear in the end. Bear with me. First, since 1961, all of the team sports leagues have enjoyed a legislated exemption that allows their teams to package national rights for over-the-air television. The legislative history of this broadcasting exemption, as well as subsequent judicial interpretation, make it apparent that this law applies only to free television. Thus, national packages with satellite distributors (such as DirecTV) or possibly even with cable stations (such as ESPN) are subject to antitrust challenge. The NFL's Sunday Ticket was recently challenged, resulting in a pretrial settlement that, among other things, obligates the NFL and DirecTV to offer individual weekend deals along with the full-season package. The NBA and NHL full-season packages are currently being challenged in court. Significantly, no litigation has yet been brought against MLB's Extra Innings package with DirecTV because it is presumed that baseball is protected by its blanket exemption.

Second, in 1998 the U.S. Congress partially lifted MLB's exemption as it applies to collective bargaining. The players' association had long argued that baseball's exemption was partly to blame for the game's turbulent labor relations. In particular, the exemption made it impossible for the players to defend themselves in court if the owners unilaterally imposed restrictions on the operation of the player market (such as a salary cap). Prior to the 1994–95 strike, Don Fehr stated that he would not recommend a strike to the players if either (1) the owners pledged not to impose unilateral restrictions during the off-season; or (2) Congress passed a partial lifting of the exemption so the players could defend themselves against such restrictions with antitrust litigation. The owners made no such pledge, and Congress did not act. Players viewed the midseason strike as the only effective way to defend themselves against new, limiting labor-market rules.

Sports Business Journal, July 9–15, 2001

As part of the 1996 collective-bargaining agreement, the owners and players agreed that it was in the game's interest to have baseball's exemption lifted with respect to collective bargaining. With this bilateral support, Congress finally acted in 1998. Now the players can defend themselves, as the football players did in the McNeil free-agency case, via litigation and without a work stoppage.

Under the recent Supreme Court Brown decision, the union must first decertify itself before it can bring an antitrust suit, which makes the option less attractive. Nonetheless, the 1998 legislation makes a players' strike considerably less likely this time around.

Third, and most important, MLB's exemption underwrites the present minor-league system. Under union shop rules, depending on the collective-bargaining agreement, workers can be obliged to join a union after accepting employment. In these workplaces, the union can bargain over the conditions of entry into the union. Thus, in the NFL, NBA, and NHL, the union bargains over the reverse-order amateur draft, and the leagues gain a nonstatutory labor exemption that permits them to limit severely the labor-market rights of drafted players. (The nonstatutory labor exemption allows unions in arms-length collective bargaining to give up certain labor-market rights in exchange for other gains.)

In MLB, however, with very few exceptions, drafted amateurs go to the minor leagues, which are not unionized. The players' association therefore has no right to bargain away amateurs' labor-market rights via draft rules. (The association, however, does bargain over certain drafting rules because draft picks are involved in some free-agent signings.) Without a nonstatutory labor exemption, baseball needs its blanket antitrust exemption to implement its restrictive draft.

Once drafted, players enter into the minor leagues, where they are paid set salaries. They may also be forced to remain in the minor-league system of a given team for up to six-and-a-half years. These restrictions, akin to indentured servitude, would constitute flagrant violations of free–labor-market principles were it not for baseball's exemption. Minor-league players would gain higher remuneration and more flexibility, both of which would threaten the existence of minor-league baseball as we know it.

In the final analysis, it is baseball's present and future fans who will be most aggrieved by contraction. There are millions of fans who would love to be able to root for a home team and see live action. Imagine General Motors buying up its competitors, then declaring that it has decided to stop selling cars in Washington, D.C., Portland, Oregon, and Las Vegas.

Recently, the *Wall Street Journal* ran a story that cited several indicators that Little League baseball is on the decline. Perhaps President Bush's youth baseball initiative will help, but the better way to interest youngsters in our national pastime is to put a major-league team in their area. MLB ought to be debating expansion, not contraction.

Baseball's Addition through Subtraction Just Doesn't Add Up

The lords of baseball gave us one full day to relish the most electrifying World Series in recent memory. Then, out of nowhere, came the "C" word.

Baseball is a monopoly, and like all monopolies it is fond of limiting output to raise the price of its product. In this case, baseball is reducing the number of franchises and, it hopes, raising franchise values.

Meanwhile, the consumers in Minnesota, Montreal, and greater Washington, D.C., get shafted. It is as if GM had bought up Ford, Chrysler, and Toyota and announced it would cease to sell cars in Oregon.

Some say baseball should be able to do what it wants. After all, if Mc-Donald's has a franchise that is underperforming, it shuts it down. Sure, but McDonald's participates in a competitive industry. If it decides there will be no McDonald's in the nation's capital, then it cedes the market to Burger King and Wendy's, and consumers are still serviced. Further, if McDonald's was experiencing nationwide revenue-growth rates of 14.5 percent annually, as MLB has since 1995, then even if it closed down a franchise in one location, it would open up new franchises in other locations. And McDonald's does not require cities that want its golden arches to subsidize with public funds the construction of its restaurants. Nor does it benefit from free, extensive, daily coverage in the local media of its business.

Baseball has an antitrust exemption, but its scope is ambiguous. The most recent federal ruling, from the U.S. District Court in Philadelphia in 1993, interpreted the exemption to apply only to labor. Thus, many believe that baseball is vulnerable in the federal courts, as well as in the state courts and U.S. Congress.

Baseball owners have sprung this new plan on us because they cannot agree among themselves about any other plan—not even the plan that their hand-picked mavens on the Blue Ribbon Panel suggested. The Blue Ribbon Boys, by the way, did not recommend contraction.

The owners hope that contraction will improve the finances and competitive balance among the remaining twenty-eight teams. Not likely.

Jeff Luria and Carl Pohlad can ask for more in compensation than their franchises are worth in Montreal and Minneapolis. Why? Because the prospect of a new stadium in the country's eighth-largest media market beckons. A new team in greater Washington, D.C., might be worth $400 million–$500 million. Sure, Luria or Pohlad would have to sue MLB to get to that market, but in the proper venue such litigation could loom rather threatening. So if MLB buys each owner out for a compromise $200 million–$250 million and then buys out the five minor-league franchises associated with each team (another $25 million–$30 million), the relevant stadium leases (including spring-training sites), and commercial contracts—and maybe a few players' contracts—the bill is likely to approach $300 million per team.

On the plus side of the ledger, MLB would save annually $40 million–$45 million per team in revenue sharing and national media and licensing income. If MLB invested the $300 million in a mutual fund yielding 14 percent (instead of buying out one franchise), it would generate $42 million a year—close to a financial wash.

But MLB also has to deal with the fact that with two fewer markets, national media ratings (and, hence, future contracts) will fall, as will national licensing and sponsorship revenues. And it will have to deal with the financial and public-relations costs of litigation, not to mention the fact that MLB might have its antitrust exemption narrowed.

So what is in it for MLB? First, it seems likely that MLB will decide to put an expansion team in Washington, D.C., in the near future. (Peter Angelos is on tenuous legal ground and, in any case, is less important than the U.S. Congress and can be paid off, if necessary.) Rather than have Luria reap the bonanza from this market by relocating the Expos, MLB can sell the franchise for half a billion dollars and divide the booty. Of course, this means that some other team will be contracted, and it is likely to be Miami, unless Jeb and George Bush can pull a stadium rabbit out of the hat. If they can't, Luria, who will probably own the Marlins at the time, can earn the distinction of being the only owner to be contracted twice.

Second, MLB apparently believes that competitive balance will be ameliorated by lopping off two bottom dwellers. Think about the lowly Detroit Tigers, for instance, who are playing in a two-year-old facility (built with the aid of more than $160 million in public funds). With a 66 wins and 96 losses record in 2001, the team was able to draw only 1.9 million fans to the ballpark. If the Minnesota Twins stayed in baseball and Pohlad kept his payroll below $25 million, the Tigers would have a good chance to improve their record by beating the lowly Twins. Without the Twins, the Tigers will face, on average, tougher competition and, other things equal, will have a still worse record. Their attendance and revenue will dwindle further. There's a comforting thought that should make Jesse Ventura reconsider his opposition to building the Twins a new ballpark.

Of course, MLB Commissioner Bud Selig's disclaimers to the contrary, perhaps the real agenda here is to break the union. Why else would Selig have refused to put union representatives on the Blue Ribbon Panel studying the game's economics? Why else would Selig have not initiated formal collective-bargaining sessions at least six months in advance of the end of the expiring collective-bargaining agreement? Why else would Selig not have attempted to negotiate the contraction plan and its terms (for example, the dispersal draft) with the union before announcing it to the public?

And one word for the dozens of sportswriters who support contraction on the grounds that baseball talent has become too diluted. If the number of major-league ballplayers is reduced from 750 to 700, the share of the U.S. population playing top-level baseball will drop from .000002678 to .0000025. This movement along the normal curve of talent is no more likely to produce differential performance that is perceptible to the naked eye than Jim Bouton is apt to win the Cy Young Award next year.

Alas, there is also some good news. Among the Conyers–Wellstone bill to narrow baseball's antitrust exemption; the Minneapolis Metropolitan Sports Commission's legal challenge; the union's grievance and potential actions before the National Labor Relations Board (NLRB) and the U.S. District Court; the antitrust claims and calls for injunction by state attorneys-general and many others; and operational difficulties, there appear to be too many obstacles in the way of contraction for the 2002 season. Senate Majority Leader Tom Daschle, in requesting that MLB delay contraction for a year and reconsider its options, has given Selig the opportunity to take a graceful way out. In these heady days of political compromise and unity, there is hope that the commissioner will heed the Senator's plea and initiate a more constructive process of collective bargaining.

Baseball's Game of Smoke and Mirrors

Ever since the last days of Peter Ueberroth's commissionership, it has been hard to suspect the barons of baseball of conspiring to do anything. Conspiracy implies foresight, organization, and cohesion—qualities that have eluded the owners as a group.

The owners' present leader, team owner–commissioner Bud Selig, is sufficiently confused that, after being accused of a conflict of interest in trying to eliminate the Twins, he assured the national media that Minneapolis was closer to St. Louis (621 miles) than it was to Milwaukee (337 miles). Then the good commissioner proclaimed that Carl Pohlad had offered to pay 80 percent of the costs to construct a new stadium in Minneapolis when the true share was below 60 percent (and less still if infrastructure is included). And when the commissioner's handpicked mavens studied the economics of baseball for a year and made a set of reform recommendations that excluded contraction, the owners opted only to contract. Or did they?

Did the owners really believe on November 6 that they would be able to eliminate the Expos and Twins before the opening of training camps for the 2002 season in mid-February? They knew that the Twins had a specific performance clause in their signed contract to play the 2002 season at the Metrodome. They knew that the players have three levels of defense (internal arbitration appeal, unfair labor practices before the NLRB and various actions before U.S. District Courts) to impede contraction. They knew that various affected states and parties would also sue in state and district courts. They knew that there are very complicated operational matters regarding the dispersal of players and scheduling to be worked out.

Even if MLB does not succeed in eliminating two teams, the contraction gambit clearly does generate significant uncertainty during the 2001–2002 off-season. This uncertainty, together with the country's recessionary economic conditions, has become the basis for the clubs' mantra that they will wait before signing free agents (Jason Giambi, Barry Bonds, John Smoltz, and perhaps a few others aside). That is, the clubs do not need a dispersal draft to flood the free-agent market; they only need the pretext of a prospective player dispersion to restrain their competitive behavior in the labor market. It should surprise no one that a "high-ranking baseball official" told Buster Olney of the *New York Times*, "It's amazing. You could probably count the number of teams on one hand who are going to be aggressive financially in this market." Since the owners apparently can't agree among themselves on a strategy for collective bargaining and revenue sharing, the contraction ploy is a convenient holding action (conspiracy?) to reduce players' salaries.

One might be tempted to ask: Whom do these guys think they're kidding? MLB's revenues have grown from $1.4 billion in 1995 to $3.5 billion in 2001, or nearly 17 percent per year (or 14.5 percent per year if one adjusts for the shortened season in 1995). And MLB is proposing not to grow or stabilize its industry's output and employment but to shrink them.

Revenues may be growing, but, the owners moan, twenty-five of thirty teams lost money in 2001, and together the teams lost more than $500 million. To demonstrate its case for the necessity of contraction, MLB has told the media that it will release the clubs' summary income statements to the House of Representatives for its antitrust hearings on December 6.

There is little doubt that MLB could release statements that would support its contention of large losses. The problem, however, is threefold.

First, income statements can be juggled in a variety of ways to make profits disappear. Owners can put themselves or family members on the payroll, lend money to the partnership that owns the team, amortize the purported value of player contracts, and engage in transfer pricing schemes, among others. *[**Note:** See Part I of this volume for detailed illustrations of this point.]*

Second, owners reap the return on their investments in baseball teams in numerous ways that are not revealed on the bottom line. They include direct benefits to related businesses, special access to politicians and corporate executives, tax advantages, potential capital gains, perquisites, personal notoriety, ego promotion, and fun.

Third, even if it were objectively true that a majority of franchises were losing money, it would make less sense to contract than to attempt to restructure the game's economics.

So, when Selig glibly tells the fans in Minneapolis to "look in the mirror," he is really inviting them to submit to baseball's game of smoke and mirrors. Perhaps MLB thinks that all of its problems will go away because it spends a million dollars in political lobbying or in setting up its own PAC. Buying votes in Washington is one thing. Earning the support of fans is quite another.

Baseball and D.C. for All the Wrong Reasons

Congratulations Washington, D.C., you have been anointed. Last week, MLB Commissioner Selig indicated that Washington, D.C., after a thirty-year hiatus, once again might be a worthy host for Major League Baseball.

One might wonder by what logic the nation's capital and eighth-largest media market merits a team after MLB's planned contraction to twenty-eight teams but did not before, when there were thirty franchises. Of course, contraction is not a reality; it is only an ownership gambit, and one that has no place in a sane economic world. MLB, as the only producer of top-level, professional baseball in the country, is a monopoly. Like most monopolies, it finds that it can maximize profits by reducing output below competitive levels and raising its price above such levels.

However, most monopolies raise output when demand grows—just not the baseball monopoly. MLB's revenues grew at a compound rate of 14.5 percent annually from 1995 to 2001. Yet two days after one of the most scintillating World Series in memory, and less than two months after the devastation of September 11, Selig slapped American baseball fans in the face. MLB not only would not increase its output; it would not even maintain it at the same level. Instead, MLB would reduce its output by 6.7 percent for the 2002 season by "contracting" two teams. Selig even stated that additional cuts may be forthcoming in subsequent years. A reasonable inference would be that fans should be grateful that he was being so cautious and responsible by doing only two at a time.

Of course, as fate would have it, and as we all know, baseball will not contract by two teams for the 2002 season. The U.S. Congress called hearings to look into MLB's presumed antitrust exemption. The players' association, threatened with the loss of eighty union jobs, brought a grievance against the owners. The Minneapolis stadium authority sued for an injunction against eliminating the Twins and won in state district and appeals courts. Florida's attorney-general began an investigation, and dozens more suits were waiting to be filed.

Selig told the House Judiciary Committee in November that one of the reasons contraction was necessary was that the industry was bleeding red ink. Prior to testifying, the commissioner assured the media that MLB had no financial secrets and all would be shared with Judiciary Committee. Indeed, during the hearing Selig told the committee that no relevant financial information was being withheld, prompting Congresswoman Maxine Waters to remind the commissioner twice that he was under oath.

Washington Post, January 27, 2002

But MLB shared only summary data. Newspapers printed it on less than one page in the next day's editions. Yet to make any sense out of the industry's financial condition, minimally it would be necessary to have individual team financial reports, each about fifteen pages in length. The bottom line is that when one adjusts for amortization, interest payments, centralized Internet investments, the accumulation of a war chest for the possibility of a work stoppage, related party transactions, ownership perquisites and income, expensing of signing bonuses, and other items, the data released by MLB tell us little that is useful about the industry's economic health.

Absent meaningful financial information about the teams, it is perfectly reasonable to apply the market test of economic well-being: revealed asset value. The Red Sox (along with 80 percent of NESN and Fenway Park) just sold for more than $700 million, and two rejected bids reportedly nearly reached to $800 million. And this despite the fact that, according to the figures MLB gave to Congress, the Red Sox experienced $22 million in cumulative operating losses between 1995 and 2001.

The other reason baseball says that it wants to eliminate two teams is to improve competitive balance. The logic is clear enough. Think of a ladder. Cut off the bottom two rungs and the distance between the top and bottom is shorter. Presto: more balance. (Or, cut off the top two rungs and you not only get a shorter distance, but you preclude the Yankees and Mariners bidding up the price of free agents each winter.)

But the strategy of fewer but better comrades didn't work for Stalin, and it is not the way to build a better baseball industry, either. Baseball remains more popular in the over-fifty than in the under-fifteen crowd. Little League participation is diminishing. The best way to turn on America's youth, tomorrow's fans, is by bringing the major-league game and its stars to the largest cities.

Why should ten year olds in greater Washington, D.C., be deprived of seeing Barry Bonds, Alex Rodriguez, or Randy Johnson in live action? Imagine McDonald's buying up Burger King and Wendy's and telling Washington, D.C.: Either build our restaurants for us and exempt us from property taxes or we shall sell no hamburgers in your city.

Most businesses, even monopolies, like to expand to new markets. Wouldn't MLB's national TV ratings go up if there were more baseball fans in Washington, D.C./northern Virginia; Portland, Oregon; Las Vegas; and elsewhere? Wouldn't national licensing of MLB products be given a fillip?

Has anyone taken notice that the McGwire, Sosa, and Bonds assaults on the home-run record have all come after the 1998 expansion to thirty teams? There is a good statistical reason for this. The so-called talent dilution from adding fifty major leaguers was just enough to give these sluggers an edge to put them over the top. Challenges to longstanding records are fun, and they excite fans' interest. Go back to twenty-eight teams and baseball loses this dimension.

The proper way to deal with imbalance is through a combination of enhanced revenue sharing across the teams, a luxury tax on the highest payrolls, the internationalization of the amateur player draft, and a more open policy regarding team relocations. Oddly enough, this is precisely what Selig's hand-picked Blue Ribbon Panel on the Economics of Baseball recommended. The panel did not recommend contraction.

Of course, if it is to improve competitive balance, revenue sharing must be designed sensibly, unlike the system MLB installed in 1996. In that system, the lower a team's revenues, the more sharing it gets from central funds. The problem is that team owners who perceive that their team has little or no chance to compete for a divisional title, much less the World Series championship, have a direct incentive to lowball team payrolls. They maximize their profits by paying low salaries, accumulating less talent and receiving larger revenue transfers from MLB. That is, the current system encourages roughly the bottom half of teams to perform more poorly. An appropriate revenue-sharing scheme either has to be based on projected, not actual, revenues (linked to the local media-market population, income per capita, and stadium situation) or it has to stipulate reaching a minimum payroll threshold before teams can be beneficiaries of revenue sharing.

So contraction is not about solving baseball's economic problems, and it is not about competitive balance. Indeed, one wonders if the owners really want to contract anyway. If they did, and if Selig's claim that the owners have been on board on the contraction issue for the past year, why didn't they announce their intentions prior to November 6, and why didn't they begin bargaining with the players over contraction and its effects last spring?

The contraction gambit had other motives. One of them seems to be to find a way to transfer the Expos from Montreal (where they are worth about $100 million or less) to Washington, D.C. (where they may be worth $400 million or more), without allowing the team's owner, Jeff Luria, to appropriate the financial gain from the move. The gain instead would accrue to all of baseball's owners if MLB could first eliminate the Expos or effectively take them over. Now that Luria is about to buy the Marlins, MLB has found a way to take over the Expos without contraction.

What about the poor Peter Angelos, who will no longer have a monopoly in the Washington, D.C., and Baltimore area if a team returns to the nation's capital? Baseball's rules grant teams only territorial (areas with a seventy-five–mile radius) monopolies within the same league. With modest compensation and a supramajority vote of owners, they can place a team in D.C.

The end game for Washington, D.C., will be the same. MLB will not commit to the area until it has taken advantage of its monopoly position. The threat of contraction means that it can eliminate the Expos without granting Washington a team (never mind the possibility of putting a team in Portland,

Sacramento, Las Vegas, Charlotte, or elsewhere—a possibility that becomes more viable as MLB increases its revenue sharing).

Gabe Paul of the northern Virginia group thinks it will cost $12 million a year in public stadium subsidies to get a team. How state and local budgets will produce this sum in the current economic environment is not MLB's concern. But for now Washington, D.C., you can gloat. You've been anointed.

All Right All You Lawyers, Play Ball!

This season, the owners have pledged that they will not lock out players or unilaterally try to impose an agreement. The players, rather than striking as in 1994, are likely to take a decidedly different tack, too: decertify their union and sue the owners on antitrust grounds. They can do that because in 1998, Congress lifted MLB's antitrust exemption as it applies to collective bargaining.

How does the owners' behavior violate antimonopoly rules? First, to increase revenue sharing, and purportedly to promote competitive balance, the owners want to impose a nominal 50 percent tax on the net local revenue of each club (the net rate is 48.33 percent). The effective tax is actually much lower than that because teams get to hide substantial revenue from stadium and local-TV deals and also to liberally deduct expenses related to stadium operations. The Yankees' owner, George Steinbrenner, for instance, is likely to pull in more than $200 million from his YES Network but reportedly will claim only $54 million as local-TV revenue.

For every dollar of extra revenue that a star player brings in, then, the team has to share 50 percent with other clubs. That makes a star 50 percent less valuable to the team. And guess what: Other things being equal, his salary offer will likely fall by about 50 percent. Although lower salaries may be a desirable outcome, that is nonetheless a restraint on free labor markets.

Second, Commissioner Bud Selig, after not enforcing the rule about one team providing another with financing when his Brewers got a loan from the Minnesota Twins' owner, Carl Pohlad, has decided that he is going to enforce a different financing rule that has been honored in the breach in recent history. It states that a team's debt cannot exceed 40 percent of asset value. On the surface, the rule smacks of financial prudence, but the devil is in the details—two of them in particular.

Selig has declared that a team's asset value shall be set at two times annual revenue, adjusted for baseball's internal sharing. For instance, the Boston Red Sox in 2001 had adjusted revenue of $160.5 million, according to figures that Selig provided to Congress. By the Selig valuation rule, the Red Sox would be worth $321 million and allowed a debt of $128.4 million.

Yet the market tells us that the Red Sox—recently sold for $700 million—are worth much more. Even subtracting the value of the real estate and the 80 percent of NESN that came with the team, the Red Sox would be worth as much as $500 million. In this range, the appropriate revenue multiple is around three, not two. And allowable debt would be in the neighborhood of $190 million, not $128.4 million.

The other detail is that teams must count long-term contracts as debt. (There's a strong irony here: When they file taxes, teams count them as amortizable assets.) For instance, in late 2000, the Red Sox signed the outfielder Manny Ramirez to an eight-year, $160 million deal. As of June, when the Selig rule kicks in, the Red Sox will have a long-term obligation to Ramirez of about $120 million, which will be included in its allowable debt—plus about $66 million more in obligations to seven other players. It also had $40 million of pre-existing debt that was assumed by the new owners, the John Henry group. So even before Henry and Company's own financing of its purchase is counted, under the Selig rule the Red Sox are over their debt (read, salary) limit.

That means the team must apply for a short-term exemption. And then, for the remainder of 2002 and the next off-season, it will have no flexibility in its payroll. In practice, therefore, MLB is imposing a salary cap that was not collectively bargained, constituting a restraint of trade not subject to the nonstatutory labor exemption.

Then there is the matter of Major League Baseball's threat to ax two teams. Expect lawsuits from state attorneys-general, prospective owners, and the players. In short, prognosticating about the baseball season is simple: mountains of litigation, and the Yanks in seven.

Baseball: A Deal Can Get Done

In July 2000, Commissioner Selig's hand-picked Blue Ribbon Panel, after fifteen months of study, issued its report on baseball's economic problems and what to do about them. The panel's principal recommendations were threefold: increase revenue sharing, reintroduce a luxury tax on high payrolls, and modify the draft system by internationalizing the amateur draft and establishing a competitive balance draft off the major-league rosters.

With minor tweaking, Selig has put these recommendations on the bargaining table. Press reports suggest that he has put four other significant economic issues on the table, as well: a rule stipulating that no more than 40 percent of a team's capitalization can be in debt, with long-term player contracts counting as debt; the establishment of a fund of upward of $85 million to be deployed at the commissioner's discretion; granting the right to owners to walk away from salary-arbitration awards they find unreasonable; and, of course, contraction of two teams.

It is possible that the last four matters were put on the table as bargaining chips to derive more leverage for the owners. If not, I suspect that they will be resisted tooth and nail by the players' association and, ultimately, will impede a settlement.

If so, the main issues to be resolved are the luxury tax and the magnitude (and form) of revenue sharing. There is good news here. Though the players thus far have resisted the luxury tax, they accepted it (albeit under different conditions) in 1996, and it did not seem to have a major deterring impact on salary growth. My guess is that when the brinkmanship of bargaining plays itself out, a compromise on a new version of the luxury tax can be worked out.

The remaining issue, then, is revenue sharing. The press informs us that the owners want to increase the tax on net local revenue (local revenue minus stadium expenses, which have mysteriously grown since MLB's existing revenue-sharing system was introduced) from the present 20 percent up to 50 percent.

The players have offered to increase the tax rate up to 22.5 percent. They are reluctant to increase the rate too rapidly or too far because higher tax rates undermine an owner's incentive to win and to pay salaries commensurate with a player's value. That is, revenue sharing has two effects: it equalizes team revenues and it depresses player salaries.

For instance, if George Steinbrenner thinks that Jason Giambi will increase his team's revenues by $20 million a year, he may be happy to pay him $18 million. If, however, half of Giambi's revenue generation will be taxed away, then his net value to the Yankees is only $10 million (actually $10.33 million; see discussion later), and Steinbrenner would reduce his salary offer accordingly.

Sports Business Journal, July 29–August 4, 2002

The proposed tax rates of 50 percent and 22.5 percent seem ominously miles apart. In fact, they are not. Here's why.

The players are suggesting 22.5 percent on the current split-pool system, while the owners' 50 percent is on a straight-pool basis. Under the split pool, every team's net local revenue is taxed at the same rate. Of the resulting collection of funds, 75 percent is distributed equally across all the teams, and 25 percent is distributed only to teams with below-average revenues. Under the straight pool, 100 percent of the collected funds is distributed equally across all the teams. Because the split-pool system disproportionately redistributes to lower-revenue clubs, it does considerably more to equalize revenues than the straight-pool system.

Thus, last year, under the split pool system at a 20 percent tax rate, MLB's revenue-sharing system redistributed $163 million from clubs in the top half to revenue to those in the bottom half of revenue. If the straight-pool system had been used, only $100 million would have been redistributed. At the same tax rate, the split pool redistributed 63 percent more revenues. And if we consider the amount going to the bottom seven clubs (rather than the bottom fifteen), the split pool increases their take by 76.5 percent.

Using the 2001 data Selig provided to the U.S. Congress, I performed several simulations on the impact of different revenue-sharing schemes. It turns out that under the players' proposed 22.5 percent split pool, the total revenue redistributed to the bottom fifteen teams is only $66 million less than under the straight pool at 50 percent, and redistribution to the bottom seven teams is only $33 million less.

Further, if the players conceded to a 30 percent split pool, the total revenue redistributed to the bottom fifteen teams would be $244.8 million, compared with $250.1 million under the straight pool at 50 percent. The revenue redistributed to the bottom seven teams would be $171.5 million under the split pool at 30 percent and $161.9 million under the straight pool at 50 percent. More specifically, under the split pool at 30 percent, the Expos, Twins, and Marlins would receive $41.5 million, $27.6 million, and $27.4 million, respectively, while under the straight pool at 50 percent, these teams' shares would fall to $36 million, $25.5 million, and $25.3 million.

Alternatively, if the players accepted a 25 percent split pool and the owners accepted a 40 percent straight pool, the former would redistribute $204 million to the bottom half of teams (and $143 million to the bottom seven). The 40 percent straight pool would actually redistribute less: $200 million to the bottom half (and $130 million to the bottom seven).

Since the owners' 50 percent proposal was only an opening bargaining gambit, as was the players' 22.5 percent, it is apparent that modest compromise could bring them to a meeting of the minds. There are other components to the plan, such as the minimum payroll a team would have to meet to qualify for participation in the system (owners are proposing a $45 million threshold for the forty-man roster) and the handling of related-party revenues, but these, too, should not present insurmountable obstacles.

In short, acerbic and extreme rhetoric to the contrary, there is a middle ground that would work for baseball. Fans still have a reason to hope.

Labor Relations Heating Up in the NBA

Three weeks ago, the NBPA filed an appeal of the September 25 ruling of the system arbitrator Charles Renfrew. Renfrew denied the NBPA's claim that the NBA had circumvented the 1999 collective-bargaining agreement.

The NBPA discovered at the beginning of 2002 that the owners were intending to use a distribution system that, in essence, would increase the lux-ury-tax rate substantially above the already high 100 percent stipulated in the collective-bargaining agreement. (By way of comparison, the luxury-tax rate in the new baseball collective-bargaining agreement starts at 17 percent and can go as high as 40 percent in the third year for some teams.)

Let's take a step back to put the dispute in context. NBA owners feel that their basic salary cap is too porous. Several exceptions—most notably, the Larry Bird exception—enable teams to go way above the nominal cap of 48 percent of basketball-related income (BRI). The Portland Trailblazers, for instance, currently have a team salary of $105 million, more than 2.5 times the salary-cap level.

So in the 1999 collective-bargaining agreement, the owners negotiated some controls. Two of the more important controls are the escrow and the luxury tax. The escrow, which kicked in for the 2001–2002 season, allows the owners to hold up to 10 percent of the players' salaries in escrow if total player salaries and benefits go above 55 percent of BRI. For the 2001–2002 season, the own-ers retained $131 million of taxed escrow money. The escrow money to be retained by the owners this year will be approximately $160 million.

The luxury tax kicks in if total salaries and benefits go above 61.1 percent of BRI. The current season, 2002–2003, is the first year that the luxury tax may take effect. For every dollar an individual team's payroll exceeds the 61.1 per-cent threshold (projected at $52.4 million this year), the team must pay one dollar in tax. Thus, the Trailblazers are $52.6 million over the threshold and they will have to pay this much in luxury taxes. It is anticipated that there will be eighteen (of twenty-nine) teams over the threshold this year that will pay a total of $207 million in luxury taxes.

Together, there will be approximately $367 million in escrow and luxury-tax monies to be distributed among the owners. This is where the dispute comes in.

The owners have decided not to distribute this largesse equally to each of the twenty-nine teams. Rather, those teams that go over the luxury-tax thresh-old will get less than a full share. The details of the plan are still incomplete, but it seems to work something like this: If a team's payroll is within a $3 million window of the luxury-tax threshold (between $52.4 million and $55.4 million), it will get 62 percent of a full share (the full share being one-twenty-ninth of the $367 million, or $12.7 million per team). If it is above the window, it will not receive any direct distribution. (It will get an indirect distribution through the so-called surplus fund.)

True to NBA caponomics, this system is unbearably complex. So let's make it simple and consider a hypothetical example. Suppose a team with $52.4 million of salary already committed to eleven players is contemplating re-signing one of its own free agents for $10 million a year. The cost to the team of doing so is roughly the following: $10 million in salary, plus $10 million in luxury taxes, plus not receiving its share of $12.7 million in distribution payments out of the escrow and luxury-tax fund. That is, it will cost the team $32.7 million to sign this player to a $10 million contract. The implied luxury-tax rate is not 100 percent, as stipulated in the collective-bargaining agreement, but 227 percent!

This rate, almost 2.3 times higher than that specified in the collective-bargaining agreement, provides a strong disincentive to owners to hire free agents (lowering competition for players and putting downward pressure on salaries). This disincentive is stronger for teams around the luxury-tax threshold.

Understandably, the NBPA objects to the owners' distribution plan because it creates a significantly higher de facto luxury tax and lower salaries. As my friend Clark Griffith has already instructed *Sports Business Journal* readers (September 30–October 6), the owners claim that the collective-bargaining agreement (in Article 7, Section 12[h][1]) gives them "sole discretion" to distribute the escrow and luxury-tax monies as they see fit. The players say that this discretion does not encompass the right to circumvent the clear agreement between the parties that the luxury tax shall be 100 percent—a rate that was established after long, hard, and contentious bargaining.

The underlying legal issues are complicated and cannot be resolved here, but the arbitrator's decision in favor of the owners' position seems to be flawed in two crucial ways. First, the arbitrator writes: "However, there is a difference between paying a tax and not receiving a benefit or payment. … The failure to receive a payment does not constitute an economic tax or economic penalty." This is plain and simple economic nonsense. Economically, there is no distinction between the two: Each provides the same disincentive to increase payroll.

Second, the arbitrator argues that by implementing their distribution plan, the owners are preserving an "essential benefit" of the collective-bargaining agreement, which is the promotion of competitive balance. But the way the plan is structured, the strongest disincentive falls not on the top-payroll teams whose payrolls are already well above the threshold (for example, the Kings' payroll is about $66 million, the Mavericks' is about $72 million, the 76ers' is about

$77 million, and the Knicks'—may God bless them—is about $93 million) and will not qualify to receive distribution payments anyway, but on those teams whose payrolls lie close to the threshold. That is, it prevents the middle teams from rising to the level of the top teams. This is not a reasonable strategy to address concerns about competitive balance.

So here comes the NBPA appeal. And to think that just a few months ago sports fans thought it was baseball that had labor-relations problems.

*[**Note:** In the 2005 labor agreement, a neutral distribution system for escrow and luxury-tax funds was put in place. The effective top rate can no longer exceed 100 percent.]*

The New Baseball Labor Agreement Is Already at Work

The smells of spring are buried under two to three feet of snow on much of the East Coast, but the crack of the bat and pop of the glove are being heard in Florida and Arizona. The new baseball season is about to begin, and it is a reasonable time to ask whether baseball in 2003 will be different from baseball in 2002.

It is clear that MLB's new collective-bargaining agreement is already having an impact on the game. The question is whether it is the desired impact.

The owners had two professed goals for the new collective-bargaining agreement: improved competitive balance and salary control. With assists from a dismal national economy, a limp stock market, tougher insurance-policy rules, and a tighter budget for the MLB-owned Expos, the collective-bargaining agreement seems to be doing just fine in restraining player payroll. Guaranteed salaries fell by an average $626,141, or 16.5 percent, for the sixty-five free agents who had signed major-league contracts as of January 8, 2003. Thirty-four of the sixty-five free agents took pay cuts relative to their previous year's salary. At the same time last year, only fourteen of fifty-five free agents had taken pay cuts, and average salaries for free agents had increased 23.6 percent.

The new collective-bargaining agreement has several provisions that are contributing to this outcome: significantly higher tax rates on local revenues, the luxury tax on high payrolls, the new rule that deferred salary must be fully funded within eighteen months of the year in which it is earned, and, importantly, the new regulation stipulating that a club's debt cannot exceed ten times its EBITDA in 2006. Since most clubs report negative EBITDA, this means that teams will have to overhaul their financial operations, their accounting practices, or both over the next three years.

The early signs on the second goal of enhanced competitive balance are a bit shakier. Although the Yankees' revenue-sharing contribution will increase by nearly $20 million this year and its luxury tax payments will surpass $11 million, the Yankees' projected forty-man payroll for 2003 is $182 million—$7 million above last year.

On the other end, the MLB-owned Expos will see its revenue-sharing receipts rise by some $4 million, to more than $31 million. Despite this increase, the Expos' payroll is flat-budgeted at $40 million. Tampa Bay is projected to increase its receipts by some $5 million, yet when asked whether the increase in transfers under the new system would all go into payroll, the team's owner, Vince Naimoli, stated that, rather than use the funds to increase payroll, he "might instead use some to pay down the team's revolving line of credit."

And the Kansas City Royals, who will see their revenue-sharing transfers rise from about $16 million to $19 million, are cutting payroll by $10 million in 2003. The highest-paid pitcher on the Royals' staff is Jason Grimsley at $2 million, with no other pitcher earning a seven-figure salary. Meanwhile, Grimsley is rumored to be on the trading block. Not one starter on the current staff won as many as five games in 2002.

So what has gone wrong with the collective-bargaining agreement's design? The revenue-sharing system's marginal tax rates rise above 40 percent and are actually higher for low-revenue than for high-revenue teams. If David Glass of the Royals spends an extra $10 million on payroll and in consequence the team improves and revenues grow by $12 million, then Glass loses roughly $5 million in revenue sharing and his net result is negative $3 million. There's no incentive here for Glass for improve his team, particularly since the collective-bargaining agreement does not have a minimum payroll mandated to qualify for revenue-sharing transfers.

It could not have helped matters that the collective-bargaining agreement was crafted under inordinate time pressure—pressure that baseball brought upon itself. Next time, let's hope that productive bargaining can begin before the expiration of the existing collective-bargaining agreement rather than after the players set a strike deadline.

NHL: Time to Stop Blowing Smoke and Start Real Bargaining

The NHL's collective-bargaining agreement runs out after this year. Contrary to the tough rhetoric out of the commissioner's office, the league can ill afford a work stoppage, let alone a protracted one. With the very real prospect of a smaller national TV contract, lower sponsorship agreements, and growing competition from the broader entertainment industry, a lockout could have devastating effects. The good news is that, despite the present escalating war of words between Gary Bettman and Bill Daly on the owners' side and Bob Goodenow and Ted Saskin from the players' association, a lockout is eminently avoidable.

Let's begin by deconstructing the recent, multilayered smoke blowing over the league's financial status. Layer one is the debate about how much faster salaries have grown than revenues during the course of the present collective-bargaining agreement, dating back to the 1994–95 season, when thirty-two of eighty-two games were lost due to the lockout. As with all time-series data, the growth rate you get depends on the years you pick to start and end your period.

The union picked 1994–95 as the starting point, arguing that it was the first year of the agreement. True enough, but it was also an atypical year. Salaries were disproportionately higher because (1) the size of prorated signing bonuses was not diminished by the work stoppage; and (2) injured players generally continued to be paid. So if you start with 1994–95, when the salary share was artificially inflated, you get very little difference in the growth of salaries and revenues through 2002–2003.

The proper statistical procedure is to "smooth out" the start and finish by taking the average of two or three years at each end. If we average the player-cost share in revenues for 1993–94 and 1995–96 (leaving out the distorted year) and compare it with the average player cost share during 2001–2002 and 2002–2003, the player cost increases from 62 percent to 73.8 percent of reported revenues. Thus, by reasonable standards, salaries have been growing considerably more rapidly than revenues—though perhaps not as much as originally portrayed by the owners.

One further caveat is important here. Player cost can be defined in various ways (depending on, for instance, the discount rate used for deferred salaries, the treatment of amateur signing bonuses or the drafting rights fees paid to international organizations). The 73.8 percent share uses a very inclusive definition of salaries.

Sports Business Journal, November 10–16 and November 17–23, 2003

The next layer of dispute concerns revenues. The union asserts that, because teams sometimes own the arenas, media companies, or other businesses connected to the team, they can arrange to have the team underpaid for its rights or services. Such contracts are called related party transactions. The union, in fact, was given access to the books of four teams of their choice. The union selected these four teams because they expected them to be more heavily engaged in related-party transactions. The union says it found $50 million in hidden revenue in just these four teams—or $12.5 million per team.

For argument's sake, let us assume that the other twenty-six teams (less suspected by the union) together hid an additional $100 million in revenues. If we added the $50 million and $100 million to the revenue figures from the commissioner's office, the share of player costs in total revenues would fall to 68.4 percent—still well above the 62 percent share at the beginning of the period and well above the roughly 60 percent player-cost shares in the NBA, the NFL, and MLB.

Similarly, the league figures suggest losses last year of $300 million. If we add back $150 million in hidden revenues, the league still lost $150 million—suggesting the likelihood of an overall financial problem (even allowing for some manipulation of reported franchise costs).

In any event, the union seems to recognize that there is a structural financial problem. Reportedly, the union has proposed to the league (1) an across-the-board 5 percent cut in all salaries; (2) increased revenue sharing; and, (3) luxury taxes on high team payrolls.

So the debate is not about whether something needs to be done to restrain salaries. Rather, it is about how best to achieve the restraint.

Commissioner Bettman has repeated the mantra of cost certainty over and over. He says that other businesses have it. Perhaps he is referring to businesses in the former Soviet Union. Under capitalism, there is risk and neither cost nor revenue certainty.

In the NHL's "Collective Bargaining Agreement Backgrounder" report, the league states that cost certainty is "a sensible and enforceable relationship between revenues and expenses." It goes on to state that "there are numerous ways to achieve cost certainty." Taken at its word, the league is saying that it does not need a hard salary cap.

That's a start. After all, the two U.S. sports leagues that have a cap system, the NFL and NBA, each have loopholes so teams have some room to maneuver in setting their yearly payroll.

It is also clear that even with a hard cap, the NHL would not solve its economic problems. Last year, the average team's payroll was $45.8 million. If the team cap were somehow set as low as $35 million, based on last year's payrolls, there were still fourteen small-market teams with payrolls below this level. Thus, the cap would not help them become profitable if they are not already; it would only make some of the high-payroll teams more profitable.

Whatever the system of salary restraint that the league puts in place, the NHL also needs to introduce a significant degree of revenue sharing. Currently, other than the revenue from its relatively small national television deals and licensing (approximately $6 million per team) and modest subsidies to Canadian teams, no revenue in the NHL is shared.

While the commissioner's office appears to accept that revenue sharing is needed, its backgrounder report states that "increased revenue sharing in the absence of 'cost certainty' would serve only to reallocate the league's current level of financial loss—it would do nothing to reduce losses."

This statement is partly true, partly false. The league wants salary restraint together with revenue sharing. Fair enough. But revenue sharing by itself, as it is practiced in MLB and the NFL, does help to restrain salaries and to reduce losses or grow profits.

Why? Suppose each team pays a tax of 33 percent into a pool that then gets redistributed to the low-revenue clubs. Now suppose that the New York Rangers are thinking of signing Ilya Kovalchuk (imagine he is eleven years older and is a free agent) and the team estimates that he would raise its revenues by $12 million. Without a revenue-sharing tax, the team would be willing to pay Kovalchuk up to $12 million. With the tax, the net contribution of Kovalchuk is only $8 million, and the team's offer would be correspondingly reduced. Thus, revenue sharing based on team revenue decidedly does reduce salaries.

Further, to the extent that revenue sharing will balance the competition on the rink, fans will be more interested in the games, and league revenue should grow. The NHL should rethink its position on revenue sharing. (There are superior ways to design revenue-sharing systems that will provide a greater boost to competitive balance than those practiced in MLB and the NFL, but that is a subject for another piece.)

The union also reportedly offered luxury taxes on high payrolls. The luxury tax in MLB's new agreement provided for teams with payrolls in 2003 above $117 million to pay a 17.5 percent tax. This is a very low tax rate compared with the nominal rate of 100 percent for teams above the NBA payroll threshold—and even more so when compared with the effective luxury-tax rate in the NBA, which can surpass 300 percent. Yet the low rate set in MLB was sufficiently effective that only one team—you can guess which one—surpassed the $117 million threshold in 2003. It is not clear why this happened, but it is likely that one of the reasons is that teams used the threshold as a hortatory budget limit.

The new MLB agreement, which combines luxury taxes with revenue sharing and some new team debt limits, seems to have been rather effective in reversing the upward salary momentum in the labor market. Last winter, free agents' salaries fell some 16 percent. They appear headed down again this off-season.

MLB's system of parametric controls rather than a strict payroll limit has a number of advantages. First, it preserves a significant degree of market determination of a player's value. There is, after all, no fairer method to value one's labor in a market economy. It also gives owners more entrepreneurial leeway. They can always sign a player if they want to. They just have to pay more to do so. The system is based on incentives, not quotas.

Second, it avoids the Byzantine system of cap exceptions and capology that creates a variety of distortions and headaches for the NBA and, to a lesser extent, the NFL.

Third, it avoids having to define revenue. Since salary caps set payroll limits as a share of revenue, in cap systems the union has a right to certify that revenues are being properly reported. This entails not only looking at teams' financial statements but also looking at financial statements of related businesses with overlapping ownership—and sometimes detailed financial ledgers. It can be, to be blunt, a can of worms.

Fourth, union politics and ideology make a salary cap extremely difficult to get to, even if these and other problems can be overcome.

The obvious choice, especially since the commissioner's office says it is willing to consider systems of salary restraint other than a cap, is to bargain over the design and degree of revenue-sharing, luxury-tax, and debt-restriction policies. Perhaps new preferences for weak teams can be added to the draft system, as well.

The sooner the two sides can do this, the better off the NHL will be. Not only will it give the league more time to reach an agreement and more time to design the proper incentives into the system, but it will ensure present and prospective corporate sponsors that the hockey industry is on the right path. Equally important, it will let the fans know that the game will go on uninterrupted.

The NHL faces enough serious challenges in the entertainment marketplace without adding more problems of its own making. Spending the next ten months bluffing and posturing will not accomplish anything positive for either the owners or the players. It is time to start real bargaining in a spirit of cooperation.

A-Rod Capture Makes Dollars and Sense

John Henry, owner of the Red Sox, reacted to the Yankees' acquisition of Alex Rodriguez by stating that he was now convinced that baseball needed a salary cap. Henry said that the Yankees' resources so far outstripped those of all other teams that a cap was the only way to level the playing field.

The irony, however, is that the Yankees' financial clout had next to nothing to do with landing A-Rod. Over the past month, the Yanks have rid themselves of nearly $10 million in salary obligations to two of the organization's former third basemen: Aaron Boone and Drew Henson.

Boone tore his anterior cruciate ligament in a basketball game. Boone's contract does not allow him to play contact sports without the team's permission. This indiscretion voided the guarantee in his contract.

Henson, erstwhile prodigy from the University of Michigan, never learned how to hit a curveball in the Yanks' minor-league system. And he wasn't having that easy a time with fastballs or fielding grounders, either. Henson is heading to the NFL.

Throw in the $5.4 million the Yanks would have paid Alfonso Soriano in 2004 and the team roughly has the $15 million it will need to pay A-Rod. There's also a $1 million deferred payment, but the balance is being picked up by Tom Hicks, owner of the Texas Rangers. In fact, Hicks is picking up $67 million of the remaining $179 million on the last seven years of A-Rod's contract—the point being that any team could have afforded to trade for A-Rod under these circumstances.

The special circumstance on the Yankees that attracted A-Rod was not a higher salary, but the team's playing strength. One would presume that his Ruthian presence on the New York media and endorsement stage and the opportunity to play in his native city also carried some appeal.

So the Yanks paid next to nothing in net terms to get A-Rod. What can they expect to receive in return for their negligible investment? The biggest kick will come from additional gate revenues. In 2003, the Yanks led the majors in attendance, with 3.47 million fans who paid an average ticket price of $24.86 (excluding luxury suites). In 2004, the Yanks' average ticket price will rise approximately 10 percent, to $27.35.

The Yanks filled about 77 percent of the capacity at Yankee Stadium last year. Judging by the pace of ticket sales earlier this week after the A-Rod announcement, that number could rise to 82 percent, despite the hike in ticket prices. This would lift attendance to 3.69 million and yield $100.9 million in gate revenue (without luxury suites) versus $86 million in 2003—a gain of almost $15 million.

If attendance at the stadium increases by 220,000, each fan on average spends $12 on concessions and memorabilia, and the Yanks net 40 percent of this, then there's another $1.1 million. Beyond this, ratings for Yanks games on the YES network should undoubtedly rise, and this will lead to higher rates for advertising spots—potentially adding a few million more dollars.

Depending on the outcome of the pending arbitration between YES and Cablevision and whether the YES Network resides on expanded basic or premium cable, the acquisition of A-Rod could also lift subscription revenue. Other than merchandising sales at the stadium and the Yanks' outlets in town, any increase in licensing income is shared equally among all thirty MLB clubs. (This is also true for merchandising sales in Japan and elsewhere in the world, so the signing of Hideki Matsui was a boon to all clubs last year.)

Of course, if A-Rod helps the Yanks get to and win in the post-season, then he also adds post-season revenues. Who knows whether the Yanks would have gotten there without him or, even with him, whether their pitching staff could carry the team that far. And if they do get to the post-season or World Series, there are other new players on the team who might be as responsible as A-Rod.

It is impossible to know with any precision, but these numbers suggest that A-Rod may boost Yanks' local revenues by some $20 million, or perhaps more. That's the good news for George Steinbrenner. The bad news is that under MLB's new revenue-sharing system, Steinbrenner will have to give approximately $8 million of that back to MLB.

Overall, the Yanks probably will pay revenue-sharing and payroll luxury taxes to MLB of $70 million–$75 million in 2004. John Henry in Boston will likely make payments in excess of $40 million. No wonder he'd prefer a salary cap to the present system.

What to Do about the Hockey Mess

In the past few months I have been asked by players' agents, law professors, sports talk-show hosts, and others whether I would consider becoming involved in resolving the NHL's labor dispute. Guess what? The owners aren't interested in mediation, much less arbitration.

The owners, under Gary Bettman's leadership, made a bad compromise in 1995 and now seem to be determined to resist any compromise. Bettman has made clear what the owners want: something he calls "cost certainty," as if such a thing exists in a capitalist economy. Even the salary-cap systems in the NFL and NBA do not have cost certainty.

The owners don't want any independent people looking at their books or messing with their plans. They are willing to proclaim losses of $270 million in 2002–2003 or $230 million in 2003–2004 (stating that the modest improvement was due to the rising Canadian dollar) and to pay hired guns a reported $1 million to confirm the proclamations, but they are unwilling to have the NHLPA participate in these financial audits.

To be sure, the NHLPA was allowed to look at the books of four franchises and found some $50 million of hidden revenues. When the team owner also owns (or has a master lease on) the arena, or owns a local television station or cable-distribution service or concessions company, then it is a relatively simple matter to transfer revenue generated by the team to these other entities.

In its annual financial survey, *Forbes* estimated the NHL's losses during 2002–2003 at $123 million. Though *Forbes*'s team-by-team estimates are imprecise and often uneven, the magazine does a good job of identifying many hidden revenue streams. In my view, it is likely that the NHL's real losses are closer to those estimated by *Forbes* than those claimed by the league. But no matter—one way or the other, the NHL is in financial trouble, and something must be done.

One plausible interpretation of the owners' plan is that they are seeking to break the union. The owners, after all, have not budged from their cost-certainty plan. The prospective scenario has the owners declaring an impasse in collective bargaining and then unilaterally imposing their own contract terms. Players would be invited to bolt the union and return to the rink.

For this to be successful, at least two things have to happen. First, the owners have to get the NLRB to sanction their declared impasse. To do this, the NLRB has to be convinced that the owners had been bargaining in good faith. Though the NLRB today has a more conservative slant than it did in the 1990s, it still seems a stretch to judge that the owners' unflinching demand for a hard cap of about $31 million per team (when the average team payroll has been about $45 million) constitutes good-faith bargaining.

Second, assuming that the owners get their impasse, they still would have to induce a significant number of players to return to the ice. I have no way to assess the likelihood of this.

The next question is whether this confrontational approach is really necessary and sufficient to resolve the league's economic woes. I think it is neither necessary nor sufficient.

It is not sufficient because, even with a $31 million hard cap, there would still be at least five to ten teams that would lose money. The NHL, without a sizeable national television contract and vast income inequalities across its teams, desperately needs a system of local revenue sharing.

It is not necessary because a system of luxury taxes, revenue sharing, and team debt controls would be adequate to bring salaries down to reasonable levels. Such a system would at least preserve a semblance of market determination of salaries, which is important for both vertical and horizontal equity among the players.

Bettman says that he does not want such a system because it contains no cost guarantees. Yet the system has worked very effectively to reduce salaries in baseball, despite the initial resistance of MLB owners to accept anything but a cap. Since the 2002 baseball labor agreement, new signings of free-agent contracts have seen declines of 16 percent before the 2003 season and 26 percent before the 2004 season.

To be sure, the hockey union is offering something never offered in baseball. As an initial bargaining position, it offered to have a 5 percent across-the-board salary reduction along with restrictive changes to the entry-level system. Even without further negotiating, these changes stand to save the owners well over $100 million.

Moreover, any system of taxes and other parametric controls can contain automatic adjustments according to yearly results. For instance, it might be decided that luxury taxes will be 40 percent for payrolls between $40 million and $50 million and 50 percent for payrolls above $50 million.

However, if under this system the players' share in revenue exceeds, say, 60 percent, the rates might be adjusted upward to 60 percent and 70 percent. And so on.

Still no guarantee, I'm afraid. But I wonder whether Bettman meant it when he told ESPN.com back in June: "Is it a hard cap? It doesn't have to be. ... All we've said is link salaries to revenues." If he did mean it, then a system of parametric controls will do just fine to establish such a linkage.

And as a bonus, he will minimize the substantial short- and long-run costs associated with the owners' present strategy.

*[**Note:** The 2005 labor agreement does contain a salary cap with a band of some $8 million per team on either side. It also contains a very modest degree of revenue sharing, which is likely to be insufficient for many small-market franchises.]*

Hockey Owners Give Their Sport a Slap Shot

Looking for a new economic system, the NHL owners have been locking out the players since September.

Just in case you forgot, metropolitan New York hosts three National Hockey League teams. Does anyone in the five boroughs and its environs believe that New York City's cultural life has been diminished by the absence of hockey? Has anyone noticed a drop in the area's economic activity without Rangers, Devils, or Islanders games being played?

And as you ponder these not-so-complex questions, think about the NHL's expansion teams in Charlotte, Nashville, Atlanta, Tampa Bay, Broward County (Florida), Dallas, Anaheim, Phoenix, Los Angeles, and San Jose, where it is not even cold enough to skate outdoors in the winter time. Are the denizens of these climes feeling hockey-deprived?

Not likely. The NHL, forgive the metaphor, is skating on thin ice. Its share of the North American sports audience has been in decline for decades, and it has been passed over by the explosion of national television revenues since the 1980s. Whereas each NFL team receives more than $90 million annually from its league in national media revenues, and each MLB and NBA team receives about $30 million, under its last contract, each NHL team scarcely averaged $5 million. When the NHL owners are ready to play again, the league will face a diminished national television contract—some predict as low as $3 million per team.

No one—save, perhaps, Commissioner Gary Bettman—expects America to rush back to the arenas when the NHL finally decides to open for business. Baseball recovered from its 1994–95 work stoppage, but it took the heroics of Cal Ripken's consecutive-game streak plus the performance-enhanced home run chases of Mark McGwire and Barry Bonds to bring it back. And hockey has none of baseball's cultural cachet.

So by pulling hockey off the shelves, Bettman and his owners are playing with fire. They are engaging in an anti-marketing campaign, hoping against hope that forced abstinence will intensify the lust of hockey fans.

Of course, Bettman has done all he can to convince hockey aficionados that the owners' lockout is justified. He reportedly spent a million dollars to hire Arthur Levitt, former chief of the Securities and Exchange Commission, to confirm that the league was losing large sums of money. Levitt's report was issued with few financial details but much fanfare.

If Bettman wanted to persuade the players of the league's financial difficulties, it might have made sense to invite them or their representatives to participate in the Levitt study. But Bettman excluded the players, leaving one to infer that he was more interested in molding public opinion than in promoting a collective-bargaining agreement. *[Note: The 2005 labor agreement acknowledges an additional $100 million–$150 million in league revenues not previously recognized.]*

Bettman says the NHL needs cost certainty and will accept nothing less. He overlooks that cost certainty does not exist in capitalism—not even in the NFL and NBA, where salary-cap systems (with exceptions) have been negotiated with the unions.

With hopes of salvaging part of the 2004–2005 hockey season, the hockey players' union made an unprecedented giveback proposal two weeks ago. Among other things, the union offered an across-the-board 24 percent reduction in players' salaries, together with a luxury tax on high team payrolls, revenue sharing among the teams (which puts downward pressure on salaries), and constraints on salaries for rookies and salary arbitration.

Despite the evidence that revenue sharing and luxury taxes work to restrain salaries in baseball and basketball, Bettman refused to accept the union's offer even as a basis for negotiation. If it hadn't been obvious earlier, now it became clear that Bettman's plan is to break the union.

In one possible scenario, Bettman and the owners will declare a bargaining impasse and hope that the Republican staff at the NLRB and the increasingly conservative U.S. judiciary will let them get away with it. The owners will then impose their own labor-market system, sign up some replacement players, and invite the old players to return.

Matters could then get complicated and ugly. Any attempt to use replacement players in Canada will be impeded by the country's more progressive labor laws. Players may divide, and union solidarity may fracture. It's a battle that Bettman is betting he can win.

Yet he may find that he has won the battle but lost the war. When one plays with fire on thin ice, it is likely that something will sink.

Monopoly's Money

Never mind the drivers—NASCAR's rulers seem to be spinning out of control. A few weeks ago, NASCAR's chairman and chief executive, Brian France, proposed a plan to limit the number of cars that team owners may control to three. This could reduce the stable of cars owned by Roush Racing, which has five, and Hendrick Motorsports, which has four.

France says he is concerned about equity and competitive balance. As the argument goes, when one owner controls several cars, the drivers can share information about track conditions and car technology, giving them an advantage over other drivers. And as it becomes more and more expensive to build cars and sponsor teams, owners with less capital will suffer, as will the fortunes of their drivers.

It is nice to see that France, who may soon be leaving the family business, has discovered an interest in competition and fairness. His family, after all, owns NASCAR; the Motor Racing Network, the radio network that broadcasts all NASCAR races; and Americrown, the catering company that sells food at most NASCAR tracks. It also owns a share of Action Performance, the dominant motor-car–memorabilia company, and a controlling interest in the publicly traded International Speedway Corporation.

The corporation owns twelve of the twenty-two racetracks that are host to the Nextel Cup, NASCAR's premier series. It also has economic ties to the owner of five more tracks where Nextel Cup races are run.

The only new tracks NASCAR has sanctioned for cup races since 1998 are owned by the International Speedway Corporation. One of the most modern and well-equipped tracks in the country, Kentucky Speedway, has been trying to get a cup race for the past five years. NASCAR has put off Kentucky each year. Meanwhile, NASCAR holds races at inferior and more dangerous tracks owned by the speedway corporation.

What about large teams with multi-car entries? From 1990 to 1995, only 7 percent of all entries were from multi-car teams. This proportion grew to 38 percent from 2000 to 2004.

Yet as multi-car teams have become more prominent, the outcome of races has become more balanced. During the past five years, no driver has repeated as the top earner or the points champion. From 1990 to 1994, there was an average of twelve different winners each season. From 2000 to 2004, there was an average of seventeen different winners a season.

Multi-car owners also seem to make it easier for new drivers to enter the top circuits. As the expenses associated with building and maintaining a race car skyrocket, individual drivers or car owners increasingly find the cost prohibitive. The economies of scale associated with multi-car teams facilitate new entries.

So what is France really worried about? About 25 percent of Nextel race revenue is paid to the drivers and their teams. This compares with the more than 50 percent of revenue paid to players in the NFL, the NBA, the NHL, and MLB. NASCAR is earning a bundle by being the monopoly sanctioning agency, then controlling the production process.

If the drivers are united by multi-car teams, NASCAR will lose some of its leverage over the producers. The Roush and Hendricks teams, for instance, could come together and boycott certain Nextel Cup events if the drivers and teams were not offered a larger share of the spoils. Worse still, they could threaten to form a new racing circuit.

They may also begin to demand that races be transferred to the more modern and longer tracks that are not owned by the speedway corporation. And if race sites were selected based on merit rather than on ownership, the profits of the NASCAR–International Speedway Corporation cartel would shrink. If France were truly concerned about new drivers' getting a fair shake, there would be a straightforward solution. The cup series today has thirty-six official races. France says he is reluctant to expand the number because drivers need time off.

Fair enough. NASCAR could mandate that each driver be limited to thirty-six official races a year but still sanction, say, forty-five Nextel Cup races. That would be a 25 percent expansion in the number of races and potential entries, and new drivers would have a greater opportunity to win.

NASCAR output would expand to new tracks and new regions of the country. Higher output and service to new areas would improve consumers' satisfaction. It would be a victory for fans, for drivers, for independent track owners, and for the economies of new regions. The only loser would be the France family.

V

College Sports and Gender Equity

College Sports: Surplus or Deficit?

The NCAA publishes financial surveys of its 930-odd member schools every two years. The 600-plus schools in Divisions II and III run substantial deficits in their athletic departments. The 200-odd schools in Divisions IAA and IAAA also run large athletic deficits. But approximately three-quarters of the 110 "big-time" schools in Division IA report an athletic surplus, and the NCAA is not loathe to trumpet this apparent success. The front-page headline of the November 18, 1996, issue of the *NCAA News* read: "Study: Typical IA Program Is $1.2 Million in the Black."

If the association wanted to leave a different impression, the headline instead could have read accurately: "Study: Excluding Institutional Subsidies, Typical Program Is $237,000 in the Red." That is, when you take away explicit subsidies from the university and the state, the average surplus is turned into an average deficit, and 52 percent of the schools are in the red. But the full story is considerably gloomier.

A few years ago, the Major League Baseball executive Paul Beeston described the chimerical nature of income reports for baseball franchises: "Anyone who quotes profits of a baseball club is missing the point. Under generally accepted accounting principles, I can turn a $4 million profit into a $2 million loss, and I can get every national accounting firm to agree with me." The same point applies to college athletics, with one exception. There are no generally accepted accounting principles.

One of the favorite ploys of professional sports teams' accountants is to use related-party transactions to diminish the apparent profits of the team. If the same individual or entity owns the franchise and related business entities (for example, the stadium or arena, the local television station, the facility- or concession-management firm, a beer company), the owner can alter the prices that one entity charges another to shift costs and revenues between them. Thus, Time Warner can pay its subsidiary the Atlanta Braves a below-market price for the right to broadcast Braves games on another subsidiary, WTBS, thereby lowering the Braves' revenues and WTBS's costs. The Braves' profits will shrink, and those of WTBS will grow. For Time Warner, it is money in one pocket or the other.

College athletic departments have built-in related-party transactions for almost all of their costs. For instance, grants-in-aid (scholarships) for athletes can appear as an expense to the athletic department or the college financial-aid office. Salaries for coaches can be assigned to the athletics budget or the faculty salary pool, or sometimes considered an off-budget item covered by the booster club. Debt service on facility construction can be paid by athletics, by the college's facilities' budget, or by the state. Maintenance, utilities, sanitation, and security for the sports facilities can go to athletics or the general budget. Expenses for the college band (uniforms, travel, conductor's salary, maintenance of and rent for practice rooms) can be attributed to athletics or the music department or considered off-budget and defrayed by booster funds. Likewise for rent and utilities for athletic offices; tutoring and special course sections for athletes; extra medical and health insurance expenses for athletes; facilities insurance; film and video costs; special meal preparation and scheduling for athletes; laundry for uniforms; phone, mail, and traveling expenses of athletic-department personnel; and much more.

Consider the following examples. In September 1991, the Arkansas State Legislature, after experiencing years of dubious and variable accounting practices in the athletic departments of its various state campuses, passed a law mandating uniform procedures. One such procedure was to require all sports programs to take on a facility-maintenance expense equal to 10.65 percent of its budget (the average maintenance share at state colleges for all facilities). This change alone tripled the athletic department's facility expenses at one school and engendered a sevenfold rise at another. The law also limited the annual state athletic subsidy per school to $450,000.

Unlike at many other Division I universities where facilities use is not charged to athletics, at the University of Massachusetts in Amherst some of the facilities expense is absorbed by the athletic department in the form of modest rental payments for the use of the Mullens Center arena. Yet when the direct operating costs of the facility are put against the rental and other revenues, the facility incurred an annual operating loss that ran between $356,000 and $537,000 during 1994–96. Moreover, the university annually sets aside $408,000 in its facility-maintenance budget for the Mullens Center, so that the total net cost of the facility to the university has averaged more than $800,000 a year. This is an athletic expense that is covered outside the athletic budget. Yet the true subsidy from the Mullens Center is even greater because the facility cost $50 million to build, for which yearly debt service and opportunity cost of capital is in the neighborhood of $4 million–$5 million.

The athletics program at Vanderbilt University has been suffering a long-standing malaise. Attendance at football games is waning; booster-club membership dropped from 5,600 in 1991 to 3,700 in 1996; and the program ran an estimated $4 million deficit during 1995–96. Part of the solution was found in card shuffling: The university decided to pick up the cost of 150 athletics scholarships on its budget (worth about $3 million for the 1996–97 year) and to take over the operation of two money-losing enterprises (the parking garage and the eating and social club at the stadium) from the athletics program.

Yet another indication of irregular accounting practices is provided by the huge disparities among Big Ten Conference schools for the 1994–95 year.

Maintenance expenses on athletic facilities went from a low of $18,092 for Illinois to a high of $1.05 million for Purdue. Physical-plant costs were zero for Iowa, Michigan State, and Minnesota, but $883,123 for Northwestern and $878,320 for Penn State. Debt service varied from zero for Indiana and Purdue to $1.98 million for Ohio State and $2.95 million for Penn State. Medical expenses went from zero at Ohio State to $370,831 at Purdue.

Similar examples of accounting irregularities abound. The absence of common accounting practices makes a rigorous assessment of the bottom line in big-time college sports virtually impossible. It is clear that certain big-time schools with first-class facilities and teams perennially ranked among the nation's best regularly generate net income from the athletic programs, but there are probably no more than a dozen such schools. The other schools must provide subsidies for their intercollegiate sports—just as they do for their economics departments.

Make Freshmen Ineligible: Only Good Can Come of It

A few weeks ago in *Sports Business Journal*, Bryan Burwell ridiculed the NCAA for considering the reintroduction of freshman ineligibility for intercollegiate basketball. He argued that if freshman basketball players are made ineligible, it will lead to an earlier flight to the NBA, as well as to restraint-of-trade and race-related lawsuits. Burwell said the way to insure academic integrity is to make the athletes take real classes.

The struggle over freshman eligibility in college sports goes back at least to 1869. In that year, with the help of ten freshmen, three of whom were failing algebra, Rutgers beat Princeton in the first intercollegiate football game. Twenty years later, Harvard's President Charles Eliot commissioned a study on the relationship between academic success and football participation among Harvard freshmen. The finding: Freshman football players had nearly four times as many Ds and Fs as As and Bs. Eliot reasoned that first-year students should be ineligible for athletics while they sought their social bearings and established themselves intellectually. In 1895, the Big Ten declared that transfer students must be enrolled for six months prior to playing in a game and that athletes delinquent in their coursework would be ineligible. During the next decade, Harvard, Amherst, Wesleyan, Williams, and the Big Ten all introduced rules restricting athletic participation for freshmen.

Many other schools and conferences followed suit in the ensuing years, but the NCAA never established an association-wide policy until the 1960s. In 1968, the NCAA declared freshmen to be eligible in all sports but basketball and football. In 1972, football and basketball eligibility were added.

Burwell argues that since black players are most heavily concentrated in the sport of basketball, making freshmen ineligible only in basketball and not the other sports would be racist. If this is so, then Burwell must call the decision in 1972 an act of reverse racism. Besides, if racist overtones is what concerns the NCAA, then it would be far better to extend the restriction on freshmen's participation to all sports than not to extend it to basketball.

The discussion about restricting first-year students from playing basketball, though, has nothing to do with racism. It has to do with maintaining the theoretical primacy of one's studies over one's sports participation in college. College basketball in Division I has become professionalized in every regard except the paying of its players. Players dedicate 40–80 hours a week to playing basketball, training with weights, watching films, traveling with the team, and dealing with the media. And unlike football, basketball spans both semesters. It is hard enough to imagine an upperclassman having the maturity, discipline, study habits, and confidence to handle the time and emotional demands of playing on the basketball team and still keep his head above water as a student. For a freshman, except in the rarest of instances, it is a near-impossibility.

The NCAA, despite the profoundly contradictory project of big-time college sports, still tries to reconcile the demands of amateurism and professionalism on its "student athletes." The courts have made it clear that they see regulations to protect the NCAA's amateur and educational ideals as legitimate. Restricting the participation of freshmen won't run afoul of antitrust laws. The NCAA gets in trouble when its regulations are designed to reduce the costs of operating an athletic program. In the case of freshman ineligibility, costs will actually rise if scholarships are given to students who are ineligible to play.

Burwell also frets that some high-school athletes, rather than sit out their first year in the university, will skip college altogether. This is unlikely to be a problem, because the number of high schoolers nationwide who would be drafted by NBA teams can be counted on one hand. Others, who do not belong in college in the first place, will form a player pool to support a new, basketball minor league. If any of the three new leagues trying to establish themselves this year succeed, then the problem solves itself. If they fail, then there will be pressure for the NBA to begin to fund its own player-development leagues, as does Major League Baseball.

College is not for everyone. It appears little different for Allen Iverson to leave Georgetown after his sophomore year than for Bill Gates to drop out of Harvard to found Microsoft, Steve Jobs to drop out of San Jose State to form Apple, or Jan and Dean to drop out of the University of Southern California to sing surfer songs.

Burwell is right on one point. Student athletes should be made to take real classes. The recent cheating scandal at the University of Minnesota, however, once again makes it clear that such a reform in isolation will accomplish little. The NCAA will have to do a lot more to right the ship of college athletics, and making freshmen ineligible to play basketball is a useful start.

Real Reform, Not Tinkering, Is Needed in College Sports

Another season of big-time college football has kicked off. Once again, the first games were played a week or two before classes began. Who ever said that universities don't have their priorities straight?

Carrying its $303 million budget, the NCAA has moved its offices into plush new quarters in Indianapolis. The sports-marketing agency ISL has offered $380 million annually for rights to a sixteen-team post-season college football tournament (2.7 times the amount paid out for bowl games in 1999), and the networks are reportedly offering several billion dollars for a long-term contract to broadcast March Madness.

Yet television ratings for men's football and basketball are declining. Tutors are writing term papers for student athletes at the University of Minnesota and the University of Tennessee. The basketball coach at Rutgers is making his players strip buck naked during practice. Athletes at Northwestern are betting with bookies. Some students at Michigan State are rioting in East Lansing because their team lost, while others at Colorado State are rioting because their team won.

Self-serving proclamations to the contrary, the overwhelming majority of college athletic programs are running in deficit. Without explicit institutional subsidies, the average Division IA athletic program lost $823,000 in 1997. To be sure, the University of Michigan, with its 108,000-capacity stadium sold out for all its games, $5 million in yearly licensing income, and a perennially dominant power in both basketball and football, reportedly lost $2 million on its athletic program last year.

Meanwhile, the NCAA settled its restricted-earnings case in March at a cost of $54.5 million (one fifth of its annual budget), had its test-score criterion for freshman eligibility invalidated in District Court, and is waiting to hear from another tribunal whether it is subject to Title IX. The restricted-earnings case has called into question whether many of the association's regulations are violations of the nation's antitrust statutes. Is it legal, for instance, for the NCAA to proscribe paying salaries to student athletes, to limit their ability to earn more than $2,000 during the school year in outside jobs, and to prohibit a student from earning summer income with his or her athletic talents? If the NCAA is subject to Title IX, are the association's scholarship limits per sport legal, and is its differential spending to promote post-season tournaments for men and women a violation of gender-equity rules?

Some practitioners have grave concerns about the NCAA's future. San Diego State's athletic director, Rick Bay, says: "I don't want to be a doomsayer. But I think we're headed, if not toward the elimination of the NCAA, toward an NCAA that's far different."

The NCAA itself knows that it must change the way it does business. Among other things, the association hired a law firm to review its bylaws to anticipate where it might run afoul of antitrust rules, and it set up a commission to recommend how to change college basketball to make it more congruent with the association's proclaimed academic mission.

The NCAA expected its basketball commission to propose serious changes. Back in July, Cedric Dempsey, the NCAA's executive director, stated: "A lot of kids are coming to school now just to get exposure for a year or two, with no interest in moving through the academic program. That's a real concern for me, and that's where I think freshman ineligibility would be helpful."

Many wonder how it is feasible for a first-year student to set his or her intellectual and social bearings, develop good study habits, and devote thirty to sixty hours a week to a sport—especially when upward of 80 percent or 90 percent of men's basketball and football players are "special admits" without proper qualifications to be in college in the first place. But the basketball commission not only let freshman eligibility stand; it recommended that students who do not meet the grade-point and SAT standards be allowed to receive a full-ride athletic scholarship for the first time.

The commission did make an interesting recommendation regarding scholarship limits and incentives to graduate. Currently, only 41 percent of Division I basketball players graduate college after six years, and each men's team is allowed thirteen full-ride scholarships. The proposal is to link the number of scholarships with the team's graduation rate over the previous four years.

This is a worthy idea if implemented with proper incentives. The commission, however, suggests that, for teams with graduation rates above 75 percent, the number of allowed scholarships be raised to fourteen; for teams with rates between 33 percent and 75 percent, the number should stay at thirteen; and for teams with rates below 33 percent, the number be reduced to twelve. The problem here is twofold. First, the message that it is OK to have a graduation rate of 33 percent is wrongheaded. Second, the incentives are too diluted to have a significant impact on behavior. The payoff to the coach from winning is much greater than the cost of losing a scholarship. Moreover, measuring academic success solely by the graduation rate in an environment where athletes do not take serious classes and have tutors do much of their work is misleading, at best.

Vanderbilt University's Chancellor Joe Wyatt has a much simpler and more effective plan. Every time an athlete drops out of school in bad academic standing, the school loses a scholarship slot for the balance of the player's eligibility. The Southeastern Conference has already endorsed Wyatt's plan but will not implement it without the NCAA's approval.

But college sports suffer from more than superficial wounds. Any effective reform must begin with a repudiation of tinkering. The underlying incentive system must be attacked, and real resources need to be dedicated to its enforce-ment. (Fifteen investigators with no power of subpoena to oversee 950-plus universities and 1,300-plus pages of regulations does not work.)

Here are some ideas for starters: Loosen restrictions on athletes' testing their value in professional markets and earning summer income; eliminate freshman eligibility; establish clear criteria for students in good standing; sub-stantially cut the number of scholarships in Division IA football; take control over the summer camps in basketball; shorten the length of seasons and hours per week; give coaches long-term contracts but no sneaker money; and set up minor leagues in basketball and football with financial support from the NBA and NFL.

The NCAA Has Lost Its Way

On page one of the 1997–98 *NCAA Manual*, the basic purpose of the National Collegiate Athletic Association is written: "to maintain intercollegiate athletics as an integral part of the educational program and the athlete as an integral part of the student body and, by doing so, retain a clear line of demarcation between intercollegiate athletics and professional sports." Some may wonder whom they think they are kidding.

In December 1996, Notre Dame was playing its final regular-season football game against the University of Southern California. The Notre Dame place-kicker missed an extra point at the end of the fourth quarter, and the game went into overtime, where Notre Dame lost, 27–21. The loss quashed Notre Dame's bid to go to an Alliance Bowl game, which would have been worth $8 million to the school. The Fighting Irish turned down an invitation to the $800,000 Independence Bowl. The place kicker blew an $8 million extra point.

Notre Dame has a $45 million contract with NBC to televise its regular-season football games. The major conferences have a $700 million contract with ABC to televise the Bowl Championship Series (BCS) beginning in 1998–99. The NCAA has a $1.725 billion contract with CBS to broadcast its annual men's basketball tournament.

Like the professional leagues, the NCAA promotes its own line of licensed clothing, as do its leading colleges. Like the NBA and the NFL, the NCAA has its own traveling tent show—NCAA Hoop City. It has its own marketing division. Its corporate sponsorships have increased roughly sevenfold in the 1990s, with guaranteed income of $75 million between 1997 and 2002. It has its own real-estate subsidiary and even its own Learjet. In 1997, the NCAA cut a deal with the city of Indianapolis to build it a new headquarters and provide an estimated $50 million in subsidies, leaving three hundred employees and forty-five years behind in Kansas City.

The NCAA's total budget, which surpassed $270 million in 1997–98, has grown at an annual rate of 15 percent since 1982. Its executive director, Cedric Dempsey, has done even better than this. His salary and benefits package grew 30.2 percent in fiscal 1997, to $647,000, as part of a new five-year deal. Dempsey replaced Dick Schultz in 1993 when Schultz ran into ethical problems. As punishment, the association gave Schultz a golden parachute worth at least $700,000.

Dempsey also gets treated well when he attends the Final Four of the annual basketball tournament. The *Kansas City Star* reports that "the manual for cities holding Final Fours requires a series of gifts to be delivered every night to the hotel rooms of NCAA officials. These mementos cost Indianapolis an estimated $25,000 [in March 1997]. ... At a minimum, gifts for each official included a Samsonite suit bag, a Final Four ticket embedded in Lucite, a Limoges porcelain basketball and Steuben glass." To maximize revenue at the Final Four, the NCAA has spurned normal basketball-size venues and instead has chosen cavernous arenas such as the New Orleans Superdome, the San Antonio Alamodome, the St. Louis Trans World Dome, the Indianapolis RCA Dome, and the Georgia Dome, all with seating capacities in excess of 40,000.

With big bucks dangling before their eyes, many NCAA schools find the temptations of success too alluring to worry about the rules. Schools cheat. They cheat by arranging to help their prospective athletes pass standardized tests. They cheat by providing illegal payments to their recruits. They cheat by setting up special rinky-dink curricula so their athletes can stay qualified. And when one school cheats, others feel compelled to do the same. Then the NCAA passes new rules to curtail the cheating. Sometimes these rules are enforced; sometimes they are not. But rarely is the penalty harsh enough to be a serious deterrent. The solution, it turns out, is more rules. The *NCAA Manual* grew in size from 161 pages in 1970–71 to 579 pages in 1996–97 (and the pages increased in size from six-by-eight inches prior to 1989 to eight-and-a-half-by-eleven inches after). In 1998–99, the manual became so long that the NCAA broke it into three volumes, with 1,268 pages (some are repeats).

So what is "the clear line of demarcation between intercollegiate athletics and professional sports"? It certainly is not the presence or absence of commercialism and corporate interests. Rather, two differences stand out. First, unlike their handsomely remunerated coaches and athletic directors, college athletes don't get paid. Second, the NCAA and its member schools, construed to be amateur organizations promoting an educational mission, do not pay taxes on their millions from TV deals, sponsorships, licensing, or Final Four tickets.

The tension between professional and amateur in college sports creates myriad contradictions. And as the NCAA can well attest, contradictions in 1990s America mean litigation.

Consider the legal toll on the NCAA during 1997–98. It settled a long-standing dispute with the basketball coach Jerry Tarkanian over due process for a hefty $2.5 million in the coach's favor. It was told by the Third Circuit Court of Appeals in Philadelphia that since NCAA schools receive federal funds, the NCAA itself is subject to Title IX (federal gender-equity rules). Among other things, this ruling called into question the legality of NCAA regulations about scholarships for athletes. And potentially most significant, the NCAA was hit with a $67 million court judgment over one of its rules that restricts the earnings of certain coaches. This ruling, if it stands, might be used to challenge a panoply of NCAA restrictions on the operation of markets, including prohibitions on paying athletes, restrictions on how much they may earn outside their sport, and limitations on the number of games played or the number of players on a team. In the end, it may challenge the modus operandi of the association. As I write in late summer of 1998, the NCAA faces a new $267 million antitrust suit by Easton Sports over proposed specifications to reduce the pop in aluminum bats.

In the end, college sports leads a schizophrenic existence, encompassing both amateur and professional elements. The courts, the IRS, and sometimes the universities themselves cannot seem to decide whether to treat intercollegiate athletics as part of the educational process or as a business. The NCAA claims that it manages college sports in a way that promotes both the goals of higher education and the financial condition of the university. Critics say it does neither.

The NCAA wants it both ways. When confronted by the challenges of Title IX and gender equity, the NCAA and its member schools want to be treated as a business. Athletic directors argue that it is justifiable to put more resources into men's than women's sports, because men's sports generate more revenue. But when the IRS knocks on its door, the NCAA and its member schools want their special tax exemptions as part of the nonprofit educational establishment, and they claim special amateur status to avoid paying their athletes.

Unsportsmanlike Conduct

Claude Rains's Inspector Louie Renault in Casablanca was "shocked, shocked" to learn that gambling was going on at Rick's Café. Now it is time for administrators at the NCAA, the University of Tennessee, and scores of sports writers to be shocked that academic fraud was going on among the players on the Volunteers national champion football team during 1998–99.

According to ESPN, it appears that four or more tutors were writing papers and doing other schoolwork for at least five football players last year. A few months ago, we learned that one tutor at the University of Minnesota completed more than one hundred class assignments for as many as twenty basketball players over a five-year period. Sooner or later, someone will catch on that there is nothing at all unusual about the universities of Tennessee and Minnesota, except, perhaps, that they got caught.

Scratch the surface and you see a system of incentives that guarantee academic cheating will be virtually ubiquitous. Having a winning Division IA team basketball or football often brings coaches contracts of $1 million or more, while athletic directors can look forward to half that much. Most coaches admit that upward of 80–90 percent of the students they recruit are "special admits" (formerly known as "tramp athletes") who are likely to have joint SAT scores 200–400 points below the rest of their class along with barely passing grade-point averages (GPAs) in high school. Moreover, a large share of them has no interest in academics. College for them is the route to the pros.

Then consider that these "student athletes" are spending 30–60 hours a week on their sport and that they have to make some academic progress (usually pass two or three specially selected classes) to stay eligible to play. Is cheating avoidable?

What are the countervailing pressures? The NCAA has a budget of more than $300 million but dedicates less than $2 million to enforcement of its 1,300 pages of rules and regulations. David Berst, the NCAA's enforcement chief from 1988 to 1998, estimated that every day there are at least ten major schools that engage in a serious violation of association rules. Yet the enforcement staff has only fifteen investigators, with a high rate of turnover. When all is said and done, the NCAA enforcement office conducts twenty to twenty-five investigations a year—not much if there are 3,650-plus serious violations.

So on one side, a coach is offered fame and fortune for cheating and winning, and on the other, he is led to believe that his chances of being caught are slight. The few who are caught can expect a light slap on the wrist. If the school is sufficiently embarrassed by the coach's transgressions, such as those of Jim Harrick of the University of California, Los Angeles, who indulged in giving gifts to recruits and players and filing false expense accounts, then the school may fire him. Harrick got a several-hundred-thousand-dollar golden handshake from UCLA and ended up coaching basketball the next academic year at the University of Rhode Island. Clem Haskins, the basketball coach at the University of Minnesota who reportedly encouraged tutors to provide all necessary help to his players (nonetheless, his team had an average 1.68 GPA in 1998), was let go by Minnesota and given a severance check for $1.5 million.

If the University of Tennessee is found guilty and castigated (say, by reducing the number of football-recruiting visits and grants-in-aid by five per year for two years), then legend has it that all will be right in the world of college athletics once again. In fact, nothing will have changed. As long as the charade of student athletes is tolerated and self-serving athletic administrators run the show, dishonesty and hypocrisy will rule the day. Token punishments and tinkering reforms have not worked for the past fifty years, and they will not work for the next fifty.

In the meantime, maintaining this charade costs money. Out of the 974 colleges that are active members of the NCAA, only a dozen or so athletic departments turn a surplus in any given year. Even the football and basketball powerhouse Michigan, with its sold-out 108,000-capacity stadium, lost $2 million last year.

Here's an alternative. Allow Division IA schools to have ten players on their football teams and three on their basketball teams who do not matriculate as students. Pay them as minor-league athletes and give them a free education voucher for possible future use. Major League Baseball teams spend an average of nearly $10 million apiece on their player-development systems. The NBA and NFL are getting a free ride from the colleges today. At the very least, they should pick up the cost of paying these nonmatriculated athletes. The schools would save money on their academic support and scholarship programs, and they could maintain realistic admissions standards and do away with their phony courses. The players could avoid the degradation of pretending to be something they are not and begin to concentrate on developing their professional athletic skills. Other changes are needed, but this would be a good start.

CBS's Big NCAA Deal Is No Cure for What's Ailing College Sports

The sports world is in the midst of a media-rights explosion. Falling ratings to the contrary, the new NFL, NBA, NHL, and MLB/ESPN television contacts have all more than doubled their previous levels.

Last month, CBS offered the NCAA $6 billion commencing in 2003 for eleven years of broadcast, Internet, sponsorship, and licensing rights to the annual men's basketball tournament in March, plus several smaller events. The annual average revenue from this deal is $545 million—two and a half times the existing 1995–2002 contract of $216 million.

These riches were bestowed on the NCAA despite (1) the fact that the tournament ratings hit an all-time low in 1999, thus falling by 28 percent since 1990; and (2) the likelihood of the emergence of professional basketball minor leagues that will sap some of the talent from Division I basketball. CBS will be paying $3 million more per ratings point for its NCAA deal than it is paying for its NFL package.

The media-rights explosion seems to be driven by several factors. First, new technology has vastly expanded the number of television stations, and hence has engendered stronger competition for potential viewers. This competition puts a premium on the premier programming that major sports represent. Second, the emergence of a fourth national network, along with several cable networks, has increased the competition to land sports programming. Third, restrictions on network ownership of local stations have been relaxed, producing a larger prospective return to a network from popular programming. Fourth, the U.S. economy is in its longest uninterrupted expansion in post–World War II history, which, together with the spectacular stock-market boom, has created a singularly strong advertising market. Fifth, the blossoming of the Internet and its apparent destiny to replace television are leading media companies to tie up as much attractive software as possible, so that these companies can attract an audience to their websites and insure their prominence in anticipated Internet competition.

It was largely this fifth factor that inspired CBS to open its wallet so widely for the NCAA. CBS recently lost out on the bidding for NASCAR and racing's Triple Crown and has no rights for the NBA, the NHL, MLB, or the collegiate Bowl Championship Series. CBS's strategy to secure software for the transition to the Internet is understandable.

The eventual question, however, is: How will the Internet generate the advertising revenues to justify these rights fees? With or without the Internet, roughly the same number of companies will be hawking products, and the same number of consumers will ultimately purchase the products being hawked. The only change is that there are now more advertising venues to share the advertising fees.

Thus, each of the five reasons for the explosion in media-rights fees will likely have run their course over the next several years. Expect an era of greater rights-fees sobriety.

But the NCAA has already landed its bonanza and has money in the bank through 2013. What does this apparent bonanza mean for the troubled finances of intercollegiate athletics?

Most observers have made sanguine proclamations. Some have even asserted that the financial constraints blocking the fuller implementation of Title IX will fade away in the wake of the new CBS deal. Don't count on it.

In fact, the CBS contract will have precious little impact on the economics of college sports. Consider the following. First, the new money does not kick in until 2003, when it will be $360 million, compared with $300 million to be paid out in 2002 under the current contract (between 2003 and 2013, the annual fees will then grow by about 8 percent per year). Second, the NCAA will take 6–10 percent off the top for administrative overhead and another 7.5 percent that will have to be shared with Divisions II and III. Third, the CBS payments are gross of sponsorship revenues that the NCAA currently receives separately under a deal with Host Communications. Fourth, the balance that is left will have to be divided among the 318 colleges in Division I, meaning that the net increment per school in 2003 will average less than $200,000. Rising coaches' salaries alone between now and 2003 will more than eat up this gain, not to mention increasing costs for facilities, transportation, and medical insurance, among others.

Out of 318 Division I schools, there might be a dozen or so where the athletic program generates black ink in any given year. The prudent bet is that college sports will be in the same financial mess or worse in 2003.

Win One for the Gipper

Last month, the NCAA hit Notre Dame with the first major infraction penalty in the school's history. Long viewed as the collegiate sports model to emulate because of their ability to maintain a strong commitment to academics at the same time that they excelled athletically, the mighty Fighting Irish seem to have fallen from grace. If Notre Dame has succumbed to the pressures of commercialization, many wonder, is there any Division IA school left that has resisted corruption?

Notre Dame's recent transgressions were threefold. First and foremost, a booster showered extravagant gifts (airline tickets, accommodations, events in Las Vegas, meals, money, and more) on certain members of the football team during 1995–98. Second, another member of the team exchanged complimentary tickets for cancellation of a debt. Third, still another student athlete paid a tutor to prepare an academic paper for a course in which he was enrolled. The NCAA Infractions Committee penalized the team by reducing the number of football scholarships from eighty-five to eight-four for the next two years.

Notre Dame's reputation for purity goes back at least to 1924, when the college refused to accept rights fees for the radio broadcast of its games. Instead, the school followed the clever policy of inviting all radio stations around the country to carry its games for free. The result was a national following and the spreading of the Notre Dame legend. In 1925, after appearing in the Rose Bowl, the college declared that it would no longer allow its football team to play in post-season bowl games because they made the season too long and interfered with academics. (A novel thought!)

The administration also announced that, while the normal student needed a 70 percent average to graduate, athletes would need a 77 percent average. Moreover, the school would open its academic records to the public to confirm that athletes were taking real courses. To the present day, Notre Dame has maintained a graduation rate for its football players that is well above the Division IA average.

Yet beneath Notre Dame's veneer of propriety there has resided an athletic program riddled with compromises and contradictions. Consider, for instance, the legendary Fighting Irish kicker and runner George Gipp ("the Gipper"). Gipp did not show up at Notre Dame until the team's third game of the 1917 season. Gipp lived off-campus in the best hotel in South Bend, where he worked for a time as a high-stakes card player and pool shark. Two years of his academic transcript are blank.

In the 1940s, the football team sold advertising space to cigarette companies and for several years played an annual game against Army at Yankee Stadium that brought in $200,000 a pop (roughly $2 million in today's dollars). In the early 1950s, still against bowl games, Notre Dame lobbied for the creation of a super-conference for the nation's top football schools.

In 1986, the school hired Lou Holtz to coach. Holtz promptly instituted grueling 5 A.M. practices, which the players came to call "puke sessions." After the practices, the players were so exhausted they went straight to bed and missed their morning classes. Holtz recruited John Foley, national high-school "Defenseman of the Year," who was accepted into the school even though he had received a joint SAT score of 680.

In 1995, the joint SAT scores of all entering students averaged 1,260, while for football players it averaged 890. And the most recently released figures show that graduation rates are 28 percentage points lower for football players than for the average student. A recent legal suit by a retired assistant coach revealed incidents of physical fighting among the coaches and of coaches' striking players. Thus, Notre Dame does run a program with relatively more integrity than most, but despite the absence of officially designated major violations until now, the program long ago yielded to commercial pressures.

Why was Notre Dame not sanctioned before December 1999? The NCAA devotes less than 1 percent of its budget to enforcing its 1,281-page manual of rules and regulations. It has only fifteen investigators, and they are given no power of subpoena. David Berst, who moved on in 1988 after heading enforcement for ten years, estimated at least ten significant infractions were committed every day by a major university—that is, more than 3,650 serious violations per year—and the NCAA budgets the resources to investigate twenty to twenty-five cases. With these odds, it is hardly remarkable that Notre Dame has been unscathed until now.

In predictable fashion, having been caught, Notre Dame received just a mild rebuke for its "major" infraction. Other than the fleeting embarrassment and obligatory self-righteous pronouncements of shock, the football team's only concrete loss is one scholarship out of eighty-five over a two-year period. One in eighty-five—and the team has a few dozen additional players who are walk-ons.

Division IA coaches and athletic directors face the following incentives. Assemble a football team that wins and earn fame and fortune. If you cheat in the process, do not worry: Your odds of getting caught are slim. If you should be caught, you can count on no more than a gentle slap on your wrist.

Without real enforcement and real punishment from the NCAA, Notre Dame can no more escape the corruption of academic values than can any other school. As the big-time schools spend tens of millions of dollars on new arenas and stadiums, their single-minded pursuit of winning grows more intense. Onward to victory!

Backlash against Title IX:
An End Run around Female Athletes

After an initial burst of progress following its passage in 1972, Title IX did little to promote gender equity in intercollegiate athletics during the 1980s. The Civil Rights Restoration Act of 1987 and subsequent court cases, however, reinvigorated the advance during the 1990s. The share of women among all intercollegiate athletes increased from 33.4 percent in 1990–91 to 39.9 percent in 1997–98.

While this growth marks substantial improvement, it is clear that women still have a long road to travel before gender equity is attained. In Division I during 1997–98, women accounted for 41 percent of all athletic-scholarship money, 40 percent of all athletes, 33 percent of all sports-operating expenditures, 30 percent of recruitment spending, and 27 percent of base salaries for head coaches. Beyond this, female athletes still play in inferior facilities, stay in lower-category hotels on the road, eat in cheaper restaurants, benefit from smaller promotional budgets, have fewer assistant coaches, and so on. Cedric Dempsey, the NCAA's executive director, assessed the status of gender equity in college sports in October 1999 as follows: "Improvements are being made, but being made much too slowly. ... We must continue to add programs for women and dedicate more resources to women's programs on our campuses at a faster rate."

Yet the progress toward gender equity is too rapid for some. The Center for Individual Rights, the Independent Women's Forum, and members of the collegiate wrestling community are pressing the presidential candidates, the courts, and other constituencies to reinterpret Title IX or change the law. They argue that it is wrong for the number of participants in some men's sports to be capped or for other men's sports to be eliminated in the furtherance of meeting quantitative Title IX standards.

While it is easy to sympathize with those who would prefer to see more opportunities for male athletes, it is unrealistic to think that growing women's sports alone will be sufficient to achieve gender equity in the near or intermediate future. The problem, of course, is money. Of the 973 colleges in the NCAA, only a dozen or so have athletic programs that run a true surplus in any given year. The accounting imbroglios of college sports finances are too pervasive to permit an elucidation of this claim here. Suffice it to say that the University of Michigan, which perennially ranks in the top twenty in both football and basketball, has a football stadium with a capacity of 111,000 that has sold out every game since the mid-1980s, and earns more than $5 million annually in licensing revenues, ran a reported $2.5 million deficit in athletics last year. Thus, unless universities and state governments are willing to subsidize further intercollegiate athletic programs at the expense of other educational activities, there must some redistribution of resources within athletics.

The Title IX critics claim that men are being shafted. While it is true that some men's teams have had the number of players capped, and a few sports at some schools have been cut, the larger picture does not suggest significant net losses for male athletes. Hardest hit has been men's wrestling, where the number of colleges sponsoring teams has fallen from 264 in 1993–94 to 246 in 1997–98, a modest 6.8 percent decline. Some schools have limited the number of walk-ons in football and other men's sports, but the average Division I football team still has 103 players.

Overall, between 1978 and 1996 the total number of men's sports teams in all three NCAA divisions increased by seventy-four. After falling 12 percent between 1985 and 1996, the number of male athletes grew 6 percent during the past three years. In 1997–98, 203,686 male and 135,110 female athletes were playing college sports.

The Title IX detractors argue that it is both understandable and acceptable for men's sports to receive differential resources because it is men's basketball and football that produce the net revenues to fund the other sports. First, this argument ignores the fact that men's wrestling, swimming, squash, tennis, track and field, etc., all are net revenue losers, and if a market criterion is applied, any one of them may be subject to reduction or elimination. Second, both Title IX and the courts' interpretation of it make clear that market forces do not alter the goal of gender equity. Indeed, college sports programs happily enjoy numerous tax benefits as well as the privilege of not paying their athletes a salary on the grounds that they are sponsoring amateur activities. Prevailing college ethos requires that academic resources be equally available to men and women. It is duplicitous for universities to accept the fruits of amateurism for men's sports and then invoke business principles when it comes to funding for women's sports. Third, although the absolute measures of women's participation and scholarship support are higher at Division IA schools, the relative measures are lower than they are at Division IAAA (programs without football) and Division II schools.

More important, there are more attractive options available than reducing or eliminating men's sports. Currently, men's programs are extravagantly funded. Men's coaches on the leading basketball and football teams receive compensation packages routinely between $700,000 and $1.4 million (although their base salaries, to which women's coaches' salaries are compared, will normally be in the $125,000–$200,000 range). The coaches are getting paid with the money saved by not paying the players they (or their assistants) recruit. It is well beyond the salary that a competitive market would offer them. What free market would pay strikingly similar total salaries to the coaches on the top three dozen football and basketball teams when the average revenue generated by a Division IA football team is 2.7 times that of a Division IA basketball team? And what market would pay a Division IA football coach roughly the same total salary as an NFL team coach, when an average NFL generates ten times the revenue of an average Division IA football team?

So one obvious place to find resources to promote gender equity without diminishing men's sports is the coaches' salaries. Would it be too radical to require that a head coach's compensation package not exceed that of the university president? Such a reform would save dozens of schools in the neighborhood of $1 million—enough to finance two Division I swimming and diving teams or one ice-hockey team.

Another place to find resources is in the excess number of coaches in certain sports. The average Division IA football team carries 10.3 assistant coaches, at an average salary of more than $60,000, plus benefits and perquisites. Cutting the number here by three would save enough to support a college tennis team.

The scholarship limit for men's football is eighty-five. There are eleven players on the field at a time. Even with three separate platoons with different players for offense, defense, and special teams and a punter and place kicker, a team needs only thirty-five players. NFL teams have forty-five–man rosters with a taxi squad of seven players. Why do Division IA teams need eighty-five scholarship players? College coaches will maintain that they need more players than the NFL because of injuries. When an NFL player is hurt, the team adds a player. College football does not have the same flexibility, the coaches say. But what about the fact that most Division IA teams carry twenty to fifty walk-ons (nonscholarship players), bringing the total rosters to well over one hundred? There is no compelling reason why the number of scholarships could not be reduced to sixty, saving each school $350,000 or more—approximately the budget of a Division I wrestling team.

Finally, a long shot—but one worth pursuing—is that MLB teams spend nearly $10 million each on their minor-league and player-development systems. NFL and NBA teams don't have minor leagues; universities do it for them. The NCAA also cooperates with the leagues in player draft and eligibility regulations. Is there any reason why the NFL and NBA should not be contributing to the player-development programs at U.S. colleges?

It is heartening that Cedric Dempsey issues public declarations that the progress of Title IX is too slow. When the NCAA feels strongly about a matter, it has devoted resources to ensure its development. During 1972–74, for instance, the NCAA spent $300,000 lobbying against the full implementation of Title IX. In 1976, it invested additional funds in challenging Title IX in the courts. One hopes that this time around, the NCAA will convert its words into actions on behalf of Title IX.

Kimberly Schuld, manager for special projects at the Independent Women's Forum, asserts that the implementation of Title IX has created a quota system and that colleges are starting "women's programs like bowling, squash and tiddlywinks to say they have more women's programs and are in compliance." Schuld's sarcasm to the contrary, women have showed that they are interested in participating in intercollegiate sports when the opportunities are there. Currently, more than 2.25 million girls are playing interscholastic sports in high school—more than enough to supply enthusiastic players for larger numbers of women's college teams. Attendance at women's sporting contests is growing every year, as are television ratings. Until women's college sports are supported at levels similar to those of the men for close to a generation in time, it will be impossible to assess their long-run potential. In the meantime, those concerned with the modest shrinking of men's sports should think more carefully about wasted resources and less about taking resources away from female athletes.

Has March Madness Gone Mad?

The NCAA March basketball tournament is the culmination of the college basketball season. The association recently sold the television, radio, and Internet rights for this sixty-four–team tournament to CBS for $6 billion over
eleven years, commencing in 2003. This year, the NCAA will earn approximately $225 million from the tournament's television rights and another $19
million from arena revenues, generating just over 80 percent of the NCAA's
annual budget.

Maybe these riches embarrass the association. Rather than basking in
year-end celebration, the NCAA has chosen to enforce one of the thousands
of regulations in its 1,281-page manual. Seven players have been suspended
recently at leading basketball programs for violating an amateurism rule.
Erick Barkley at St. John's, Andre Williams at Oklahoma State, DerMarr
Johnson at Cincinnati, and Kevin Lyde at Temple were suspended when it
was discovered that boosters connected to Amateur Athletic Union summer
basketball teams paid part of their tuition at private high schools, where
they had been sent principally to enhance their basketball skills and visibility. As a variation on the theme, Kareem Rush at Missouri, his brother JaRon
Rush at UCLA, and Jamal Crawford at Michigan were suspended when it was
learned that they had received material benefits besides tuition while in high
school.

Some wonder how the NCAA, an association of U.S. colleges, arrogates the
right to dictate how people may behave when they are not in college. If one
accepted the NCAA's amateur code as legitimate, then there would at least be
some consistency in the treatment of the Rush brothers and Jamal Crawford
with the treatment of players while they are in college. No payment or material benefit in return for athletic skills is permissible.

The treatment of Barkley, Williams, Johnson, and Lyde, however, is entirely
inconsistent with the treatment of players while in college. In the cases of
Barkley et al., the players were suspended for having received a tuition benefit while in high school. By sanctioning them, the NCAA is in effect taking the
position that it is consistent with the principles of amateurism to receive a
tuition benefit while in college, but it is not consistent to do so while in high
school.

Thus, the NCAA has added one more curious wrinkle in its ever shifting
definition of amateurism. When the NCAA was first formed in 1906, amateurism was defined to be an activity engaged in for pleasure; hence, any form
of compensation (even a tuition benefit) was considered to contravene the

precepts of amateurism. This definition persisted until 1948, when the NCAA allowed that an athlete might receive a tuition benefit (but not room and board) if he was fully qualified academically and in need financially. Then the concept morphed again in 1955, this time permitting scholarships (including room and board) for athletic skills alone and with no financial-need criterion.

In 1972, automatic four-year athletic scholarships were abolished. Thenceforth, all athletic scholarships would be one year at a time. Thus, if a player was not performing up to a coach's standards, he could be cut off from his scholarship no matter how well he was performing academically. The 1972 twist made it clear that athletic performance was a quid pro quo for the scholarship, lending greater credence to those who argued that college athletes were in an employment relationship with their schools.

The definition of amateurism has been tweaked several times since 1972, but the present innovation heaps greater indignity on the exploited athletes and greater hypocrisy on the NCAA. The NCAA has sought legitimacy over the years as an enforcer of the amateur code by going after the little guy or slapping the big guy on the wrist.

Until the rudimentary principles of college sports are straightened out, however, the contradictions of the system will persist. In the meantime, the NCAA will reflect the insight of the Cheshire Cat in Alice in Wonderland: "If you don't know where you are going, any road will take you there." And fans will continue to go crazy in March.

Pay for Play in College Sports: Think Twice

There's a new and growing movement among students, coaches, and analysts in favor of paying college athletes. Everyone knows that the only thing amateur about intercollegiate sports is that the athletes don't get paid. The coaches on the top men's basketball and football teams make a million dollars a year and more. The colleges in the BCS games take home $13 million–$15 million per appearance. The new CBS contract to broadcast the NCAA basketball tournament is worth $6 billion over eleven years. Surely, there's enough here to pay the workers.

Economic studies estimate that the star players on the leading teams in men's basketball and football might generate a million dollars or more in revenue each year for the schools. In return, they get tuition, room, board, books, some clothes, first-class hotels and meals on the road, and potentially up to several hundred dollars per person in emergency funds. Yet a large proportion of them never get a college degree, which raises the question of what their free tuition is ultimately worth to them. (Recent numbers show that only 40 percent of basketball and 50 percent of football players in Division I get their degrees within six years.)

Are the star football and basketball players being exploited? You bet.

What happens to the surplus they create? It does not go to the bottom line of the athletics department. Rather, the player-generated revenue goes to the coaches who recruit the star players and to the 400–550 other student athletes on sports scholarships at the school.

So what happens if we pay the athletes real money? First, probably only five to seven basketball players and ten to fifteen football players generate revenue in excess of the $30,000 annually or so that their scholarship is worth. Thus, if the players were paid a market wage, half the basketball team and three-quarters of the football team might not even get a full scholarship. The ones who get paid the real money would receive anywhere from a few thousand to several hundred thousand dollars above their scholarships.

Second, the coaches, who currently get paid much of the value produced by the players they (or their assistants) recruit, will be paid salaries more commensurate with what they are worth. It is mind-boggling, for instance, that a Division IA football coach may earn upward of $1 million (Florida's Steve Spurrier earns $2 million), as much as many coaches in the NFL, even though the average NFL team generates more than ten times as much revenue as the average Division IA team. If we paid the players, some top basketball and football coaches might even get paid less than the college president. Perish the thought!

Third, the male and female student athletes on the tennis, golf, water polo, hockey, soccer, lacrosse, track and field, gymnastics, or crew teams will no longer receive scholarships to attend college. The present system of cross-subsidies, wherein mostly poor African American basketball or football players generate the revenues to pay for scholarships to middle-class, white squash players, will end. More dramatically, the funds for supporting women's sports will be diminished, and schools will have a harder time meeting gender-equity goals. One likely result will be a significant reduction in the number of "non-revenue" sports for both sexes.

The prospects of cutting back on non-revenue sports and halting or reversing progress toward gender equity are not comforting. Colleges would probably also be impelled to increase the subsidies to their athletic programs.

There is also the question of how paying the top athletes would affect college culture. Will other student activities also be subjected to the laws of supply and demand? What about the first violinist in the orchestra or the lead actress in the school musical? Will they be paid their share of ticket sales? What about professors? Will they be paid more for enrolling more students in their classes?

In the end, only a few student athletes would get substantial remuneration above their fellowships. Yet many of these college athletes are being trained, and gaining exposure, for future careers as professional athletes, where they will receive very handsome salaries. Is it practical to disrupt the entire fabric of college life to pay these few athletes?

Perhaps other reforms should come first. Allow student athletes to use their athletic skills to be gainfully employed during the summer months. Allow them to enter professional drafts and return to college with their eligibility intact if they do not like the team that drafted them or the salary they are offered. Allow them to borrow money from the NCAA itself to take out insurance policies if they are injured playing college ball and their professional careers are aborted. Allow them to receive athletic scholarships to attend private high schools. These and other reforms are at least as consistent with the basic amateur concept of not paying the athlete for playing a sport as is the current practice of allowing student athletes to receive scholarships in college.

It is time to acknowledge that Division I college sports are a rare hybrid of professionalism and amateurism. As such, they have grown to be enormously popular in our society. If the athletes are paid, will the team have the same relationship to the university, and will fan appreciation be sustained? Before we undertake radical surgery, we should think carefully about the consequences for college culture and sports consumers.

College Athletic Success and Donations: Evidence Is Not Encouraging

Out of the 300-plus schools that play in the NCAA's Division I, in any given year there are probably no more than a dozen whose athletic departments turn a surplus when all their operating costs are taken into account. Acknowledging this, many supporters of big-time college sports argue that successful athletic programs pay for themselves indirectly by inducing alumnae and others to increase their giving to the university's general fund

The logic is reasonable enough. A school goes to the Rose Bowl or to the Final Four. Alumni and boosters feel proud and open up their pocketbooks.

Indeed, this is one of the conclusions of a study published a few months ago in the journal *Contemporary Economic Policy*. The results of the study were also summarized in the August 7, 2000, issue of *BusinessWeek* magazine. The article, "Educational Contributions, Academic Quality and Athletic Success," by Thomas Rhoads and Shelby Gerking, found a weak statistical relationship between winning a football bowl game and alumnae giving in individual years and between strong athletic traditions and alumnae giving over time. One could raise a number of questions about their results, but the most telling problem is that the authors use a dataset that does not distinguish between giving to athletics and giving to the general fund. Since it is generally accepted that athletic success may lead to increased giving to athletics, it follows that a measurement of giving that includes both athletic- and general-fund donations might be positively correlated with certain measurements of athletic success. This result, however, does not mean that athletic success increases donations to the general fund.

To be sure, apart from two very limited and statistically sloppy studies, all the published literature suggests that there is no reliably positive impact of athletic success on giving to the general endowment of a university. This literature consists of at least twelve separate studies. In some cases, a significantly negative effect is found.

There are several possible reasons why there is no statistical relationship between athletic success and general endowment gifts. The main contributors who seem to respond to athletic prominence are boosters, not the normal alumnus or academic philanthropist. Boosters tend not to be graduates of the school but, rather, local businesspeople who also happen to be avid sports fans. The boosters at the University of Iowa, for instance, include more than 8,000 individuals who were not students at the school.

Boosters give to athletics, not to the general fund. Richard Conklin, a top administrator at Notre Dame, has commented: "We at Notre Dame have had extensive experience trying to turn athletic interests of 'subway alumni' [read, boosters] to academic development purposes, and we have had no success. There is no evidence that the typical, non-alumnus fan of Notre Dame has much interest in the educational mission." John D. Biaggio, former president of Michigan State University and member of the Knight Commission on College Athletic Reform, reaffirms this: "No data support the oft-heard claim that wins on the field or on the court bring in more private dollars or more state and federal funding. Losses do not result in decreased financial support, either. To be sure, wins can and do often bring in more support for athletic programs. But the myth of institutional dependency on athletic revenues—therefore, on athletic victories—needs to be aggressively refuted."

Yet if normal alumni are approached about giving specifically to athletics, some seem to respond positively. Unfortunately, this comes at the expense of giving to the general fund. Consider the following concern expressed in the minority report of the University of Massachusetts task force about upgrading to Division IA: "Major fundraising around support of a major upgrade for football and a capital campaign is likely to lure dollars away from general University giving and toward athletics. Related to this concern is athletic department information from [the University of Connecticut], where athletic department giving rose from $0.9 million in 1988–89 to $4.29 million in 1992–93. At the same time, a decrease from $7.5 million down to $4.5 million took place for total university giving."

Even if it were true that upticks in donations occasionally followed stellar athletic years (particularly teams that rise from oblivion to prominence over the course of one or two years), it is probable that downticks in donations would offset these gains when the teams dropped from prominence. It is also likely that a team penalized by the NCAA for rule infractions would face a degree of ignominy, resulting in diminutions of academic giving.

Finally, it is no secret that most, if not all, Division I (and many Divisions II and III) schools follow an admissions policy of accepting "special admits." That is, gifted athletes who do not meet the school's academic criteria for admission are nonetheless admitted. Some schools are more shameless than others in this regard. The consequences of this practice are twofold: first, the educational and intellectual environment is vitiated; and second, SAT scores drop, which hurts the college's ranking and diminishes its reputation. Each of these outcomes might reduce academic giving.

The NCAA's New Financial Status Report: Good News or Bad?

Last week, the NCAA came out with the latest edition of its biannual report on the financial performance of its Division IA schools. As always, if the report is read uncritically, it seems that most big-time sports universities are having no economic difficulties in running their athletic programs. Consider the following apparently sanguine news.

Of the 104 Division IA schools responding, average revenue of the athletics program grew from $17.7 million in 1997 to $21.9 million in 1999, an impressive 24 percent growth over the two years. The reported profit of the average program increased almost fivefold, from $400,000 in 1997 to $1.9 million in 1999. And 71 percent of the programs reported revenues exceeding expenses.

What's wrong with this picture? First, it turns out that virtually all of the revenue growth is at a small group of select schools. For instance, the revenue of the top school rose from $47.6 million in 1997 to $73 million in 1999, a 53 percent increase. The revenue of the top program was 3.33 times as large as the average revenue of the 104 reporting schools with Division IA.

Second, these figures include institutional subsidies. When these subsidies are excluded, the average profit of $1.9 million becomes an average profit of zero, and the share of the reporting Division IA schools earning a profit declines from 71 percent to 46 percent. The numbers also exclude student-activity fees allocated to athletics and support from the state government. Student-activity fees to athletics averaged $1.262 million, and reported direct government support averaged $314,000. Thus, deducting all reported subsidies leaves the average Division IA athletics budget more than $1.5 million in the red.

Third, there are 114 Division IA schools, yet only 104 responded to the NCAA survey. In previous years, the nonresponding schools had well below average financial performance. Thus, if past patterns hold, the averages for the full division would be inferior to those described in the NCAA report.

Fourth, there are no common accounting practices in college athletics. No schools count all athletics-related expenses in their athletics budget, and most schools omit important expenditures. For example, it is commonplace for capital and maintenance expenditures for sports facilities to appear under the buildings and grounds—rather than the athletics—budget and for legal expenses connected to athletics to be absorbed under the administration's legal budget. The same goes for the school's marching band and the music department, special team meals and the institution's food-services budget, team uniforms and the laundry budget, and so on.

Jim Duderstadt, former president of the University of Michigan, told the Knight Commission last week that in the early 1990s the presidents of the Big Ten universities got tired of reading the faulty budget reports from their athletics departments. Collectively, they decided to ask their chief financial officers to do a proper study of athletic-department revenue and expenses for several different years. Their conclusion: Not one school in the Big Ten had an athletic program that was generating a true surplus, and at some schools the actual deficit ran more than $7 million annually.

Economic difficulties notwithstanding, the big-time college programs behave as if they are in an arms race to hire the most expensive coaches and build the fanciest facilities. A handful of successful and glamorous programs seem to be sufficient to entice hundreds of universities to chase the Holy Grail of athletic prominence. A September 2000 special report on college athletics in the *Philadelphia Inquirer* estimated that more than $4 billion has been spent over the past ten years on college sports facilities. Meanwhile, compensation packages for men's basketball and football coaches now routinely exceed $1 million a year, several times more than the university presidents are earning.

Without stockholders to hold the athletic directors accountable, even athletically successful schools find ways to spend all of their revenue and more. Until serious reform is undertaken, the financial picture of big-time college sports will only grow more bleak.

College Is Not for Everyone

In a rather intemperate and poorly informed piece (*Sports Business Journal*, January 8–14, 2001), Len Elmore accused the Knight Commission of promoting a wrongheaded and possibly racist policy regarding young, minority basketball players. Elmore objected to the suggestion by a few members of the commission that the NBA should reconsider its intention to have a minimum age of twenty for players in the new National Basketball Developmental League (NBDL), scheduled to begin next fall.

In fact, the Knight Commission is in the process of holding hearings on the problems in college sports. It has yet to issue any recommendations.

That said, it is true that certain commission members believe that college is not for everyone. For instance, Mary Sue Coleman, president of the University of Iowa, told the NBA's Russ Granik that she would "rather see kids who have no interest in college go directly" to the pros. *[**Note:** Mary Sue Coleman is now president of the University of Michigan.]*

Elmore accused Coleman of being blinded by the Ivory Tower and failing to understand the background and needs of the kids she would have skip college. Elmore expressed concern that the majority of kids who go directly to the NBDL, instead of college, would never make it to the NBA and would end up with "a future not much better than flipping burgers."

Elmore's concerns for the futures of these kids are appropriate, but it is he who exists in an Ivory Tower. In recent years, the six-year graduation rate of Division I male college basketball players has hovered around 40 percent— and lower still for minorities. These abysmal rates are recorded despite the fact that the big-time athletic programs these days spend a million dollars or more each year on special tutoring programs for their intercollegiate athletes.

Too often, the tutors in these programs do more than assist the athlete in learning. Sometimes they go to classes for the athlete, take notes, read books, and even write papers. And too often, the athletes are put in jock-friendly classes and majors that demand little, if any, academic rigor.

Elmore says that these kids need college—its education and its inspiration. But what kind of education and inspiration do these kids get from participating in a hypocritical charade that exists to keep them eligible? What kind of inspiration do they get from an ethos and practice that separates them from normal students? What kind of value for education do they learn from an incentive structure where the basketball coach gets paid five to ten times more than the highest-paid professor on campus?

Actually, the majority of these kids are asked to live a lie. They are inadequately prepared for college—not just because they achieve low scores on standardized tests, but because they have not learned proper study habits and basic skills.

They are interested in basketball. The present system makes them go to college. And Elmore thinks it might be some kind of racist conspiracy to give these kids the option of playing professional basketball when they reach eighteen or nineteen.

Meanwhile, colleges debase themselves and their curricula to admit these athletes and then retain their eligibility. This debasement undermines the intended intellectual spirit and mission of the school, and it vitiates the educational experience for large numbers of undergraduates. (See the excellent treatment of this phenomenon in James Shulman and William Bowen's 2001 book, *The Game of Life: College Sports and Educational Values*). This, in short, is a system that helps no one.

To be sure, the system's ills run much deeper than the misplacement of these student athletes, and its reform will require profound measures. That is what the Knight Commission is trying to study.

There is a much more sensible plan to deal with providing educational opportunity to underprivileged, minority children. Colleges should use the money that is currently bringing underqualified and uninterested teenagers to their schools to play sports to fund academic scholarships for poor kids who have shown a clear interest and capacity to succeed in college studies.

Let the pure athletes go to the NBDL. The NBDL, in turn, should offer a compensation package that includes a scholarship for college in the future, if and when the athlete is ready to be a student.

Should College Athletes Be Paid?

Star college athletes on top Division I basketball and football teams produce revenues of $1 million a year or higher. What do they get in return?

Ignoring illicit payments and benefits, the star athlete gets a free-ride scholarship that includes tuition, room and board, book money, and emergency funds. This value can run upward of $35,000 annually. The star athlete often stays in special housing, eats well, travels first class, benefits from extensive tutoring in his classes, and may receive Pell Grant money of more than $3,000 a year.

To qualify for these benefits, the star athlete is generally expected to devote forty to sixty hours a week, year-round, to his sport. He is under intense pressure to perform competitively in his sport and stay eligible. Graduation rates in Division I hover around 50 percent for football players and 40 percent for basketball players.

Is this star athlete paid a value that is commensurate to the value he is producing for his school? No way. He is exploited big time. But professionalization isn't the solution.

If we pay the star football player, do we also pay the first violinist in the school orchestra? Will other academic relationships be similarly mercantilized? And if we pay the star athlete, how much do we pay him? Do we use market standards? If we use market standards, then a few players would be paid hundreds of thousands of dollars; a few would be paid between $50,000 and $100,000; a few would earn their full-ride scholarship; and hundreds of student athletes per school would lose their scholarships.

And, of course, along with professionalization comes workers' insurance payments, the loss of a panoply of tax privileges currently benefiting college sports, and the threat to undermine the branding of college sports as amateur events.

Further, in any given year, no more than one or two dozen colleges of the 970-plus schools in the NCAA turn a true surplus in their athletic programs. Put simply, colleges cannot afford to pay their top athletes without further draining their academic budgets.

There are more sensible reforms that should be attempted first. Allow student athletes to be real students by reducing the number of games and hours of training and practice. Allow the star student athletes to earn money using their athletic skills in the summertime. Allow them to test the waters in professional drafts and to retain their eligibility to play college sports until they receive their first professional paycheck. Allow them to borrow money to buy career-ending–injury insurance. These and other changes make sense. They should be given the old college try before we throw in the towel on the hybrid model of intercollegiate athletics.

American Teacher, September 2001

Making the (Up)Grade: Tougher Than It Looks

Since 1990, approximately a dozen schools have attempted to upgrade from Division IAA to Division IA in college football. The lure is the expectation of greater media exposure and the hope of an elusive financial payoff.

Typically, however, costs rise much faster than revenues for the metamorphosed schools. To be in Division IA, universities must sponsor at least fourteen varsity sports, play at least 60 percent of their games against other Division IA teams, have a football stadium with a minimum capacity of 30,000, and experience an average attendance of more than 17,000 at least once in the previous four years. These requirements are scheduled to become even more stringent in 2004–2005.

Division IA schools also allow eighty-five football scholarships rather than the sixty-three in Division IAA. If men's scholarships grow by twenty-two, then Title IX mandates that women's grow by twenty-two, as well. Indeed, Title IX mandates that all the upgrades for the men's programs (increased expenditures on recruitment, team travel, coaching, training facilities, academic support, and so on) eventually find a counterpart in the women's programs. In his 1996 book *Keeping Score: The Economics of Big-Time Sports*, Richard Sheehan surveyed the colleges that have made the jump from Division IAA to IA and concluded that "no school has made significant profits."

When the University of Akron played in Division IAA in 1986, the football team sold 5,000 season tickets. The school upgraded to Division IA in 1987. Going from being a leading team in Division IAA to a bottom dweller in Division IA, by 1994 the team had sold only 2,500 season tickets. Jacksonville State University upgraded in 1996, and its athletic director, Jerry Cole, reported on the transition to Division IA: "However expensive you think it may be, however much trouble you think it may be, double that."

Now a major scandal appears to be brewing at Arkansas State University. Dreaming of replicating the dubious success of the Razorbacks at the University of Arkansas, in 1992 Arkansas State upgraded to Division IA. Since going "big time," the football team's record has been a dreadful 28–82–1. In that time, the team has gone through five head coaches and five athletic directors. (No, George Steinbrenner is not on the Board of Trustees.) Last year, its enlarged, 30,000-capacity stadium notwithstanding, the team sold only 4,500 season tickets.

With football leading the way, the athletic-department deficit has grown by leaps and bounds. Student athletic fees have risen by 67 percent since 1992.

Sports Business Journal, May 27–June 2, 2002

Today, these fees, together with institutional subsidies to athletics, cover more than 60 percent of the athletic budget.

When the Arkansas State administration announced its budget this year, it included a 2 percent decrease in academic funding but a whopping 15 percent increase in the athletics budget. It also planned to transfer $2.6 million from academic funds to cover the remaining athletics deficit and to temporarily increase student fees another 75 percent.

It turns out that, with this budgetary plan, the university administration had taken one step too many. The state's attorney-general ruled that the plan violated state funding rules.

As the administration juggles its funding sources, it does not seem deterred in its quest for the holy grail of athletic success. It has hired a new athletic director who is due to receive a $100,000 bonus if Arkansas State maintains its Division IA status in 2004, which will require higher attendance at the games. Since this bonus payment is not contingent on a reduction in the football deficit, the new athletic director can simply increase expenditures on marketing the team and lower ticket prices to stimulate attendance. This appears to set the school up for a larger financial hit in the years to come.

And beware: As schools invest more and more in athletics, they become more desperate for success. When standard methods fail, they are wont to transgress NCAA rules. Academic-integrity scandals ensue, raising the school's legal and reputational costs.

As the NCAA debates modifying its rules of amateurism and other needed reforms, it might consider calling a moratorium on school upgrades to Division IA. Division IA needs to get its own house in order before it further enlarges its family. In the meantime, Arkansas State, the University of Connecticut, the University of Massachusetts, and other aspirants to the big time should think about using their scarce resources to upgrade academically.

Another Bowl Game Is Not What the NCAA Needs

The NCAA has approved another college football bowl game, the ConAgra Bowl, to be held on Christmas Day in Hawaii for the 2002–2003 season. This makes twenty-eight certified post-season bowl games.

Thus, fifty-six schools will go to bowl games next year. With only 115 Division IA schools playing football, this means that 48.7 percent of the teams will make the post-season. More precisely, with two or three schools typically sanctioned against playing in bowl games each year for NCAA violations, more than half of the eligible schools play in bowl games.

Some might say that this is a good sign. The NCAA is behaving in an egalitarian manner, befitting its stated commitment to amateurism and academics. Of course, if this is the goal, one wonders, why not have fifty-seven bowl games?

Others say that the proliferation of bowl games is good for no one. It detracts from the top contests, hurting the best teams and diminishing the value of college football's richest asset. Aside from the four BCS games, going to a bowl game is a money-losing proposition for a school. Travel, lodging, entertainment, and food costs, plus the obligation to guarantee thousands of ticket sales, almost always outpace the meager revenues going to the school. Since the athletics programs of these schools are virtually always several million in the red anyway, the extra deficit from the bowl appearances just requires increasing subsidies from the university budget.

Well, some do benefit. The athletic and academic administrators at the participating schools get a free, perk-laden trip to a warm clime for themselves, and often their families, in midwinter. The sponsoring bowl committee, assorted businesspeople from the local community, enjoy increased spending at the hotels and restaurants in their city. And athletic directors delude themselves into believing that they will have an easier time recruiting when they tell their prospects that their school played in a bowl game.

Why not just admit the fact that fans really care only about the national championship? Even for the BCS, ratings are strong only for the top one or two games, depending on the ambiguity in the computer rankings.

MLB takes eight of thirty teams, or 27 percent, for its post-season. The NFL takes twelve of thirty-two teams, or 38%. Based on those ratios, college football can support fifteen to twenty bowl games with thirty or forty teams.

But there is a crucial difference. In MLB and the NFL, an elimination tournament is played, working down to the winner. Currently, the NCAA bowls are isolated events.

Although various alternatives have been suggested, the most obvious is to have the NCAA run a national championship tournament, as it does in basketball and in Division IAA, Division II, and Division III football. The Division III championship, for instance, began in 1973 as a single-elimination tournament for four teams. It became an eight-team single-elimination tournament in 1975, and the current format has sixteen teams.

An eight-team format would involve three games to determine a national champion. The Bowl Alliance argues that three games in the post-season prolong the season two extra weeks, and this would take up too much time for the student athletes. Not a bad thought, but in the past decade three Alliance conferences have added conference championship games, and two pre-season games have been created. If those two weeks were used instead to support a championship tournament, sponsored by the NCAA, the selection of participants could be open and the distribution of revenues could be more equal, similar perhaps to the NCAA basketball tournament. If the regular-season schedule could be tightened to save one additional week, the final tournament could include four rounds with sixteen teams.

Furthermore, if the NCAA were to add games, it would be far less disruptive for student athletes to play during the first two or three weeks of January, when school is not in session, than is the scheduling of the March basketball tournament.

Many fans would prefer a playoff system for football, as in basketball, because it is more interesting to have real competition decide championships than to have it done by computer. Moreover, many writers have cited possible anomalies with the bowl-championship formula that will result in the crowning of an ambiguous or disputed champion.

In a playoff format, the greater the number of rounds included, the greater would be the financial bonanza to the NCAA. DeLoss Dodds, athletic director at the University of Texas, believes that a playoff system would be so popular that it would add at least an extra $1 million in revenue for every team playing Division IA football. Schools clamoring for resources to meet the demands of Title IX might welcome such a financial windfall.

But the politics of change are not encouraging. The bowl committees would lose control if a playoff format were adopted; hence, they resist such a change. The Alliance members would lose privileged access to their self-proclaimed championship games, and they would be forced to share their post-season revenues with dozens, if not hundreds, of other NCAA schools. They, too, would resist the change. Conference commissioners, athletic directors, coaches, and sometimes college presidents and trustees from the Alliance would lose the enticing perquisites provided by the bowl committees.

Conference commissioners may also prefer to defer to the NFL wishes to have no intrusion of competition during its playoffs and Super Bowl. Unfortunately, these groups are already sufficiently powerful to make such a reform unlikely. Without serious governance reform, college sports will continue to operate against the best interests of the student athletes and the fans.

Numbers, Facts Don't Back Title IX Critics

In January 2002, the National Wrestling Coaches Association (NWCA) sued the U.S. Department of Education for the way in which its Office of Civil Rights has implemented Title IX regulations and enforcement. The NWCA, along with other anti–Title IX groups, has vigorously lobbied the Bush administration and Speaker of the House Dennis Hastert (a former wrestling coach) to weaken existing procedures that support gender equity in college athletics. This commission appears to be the product of these pressures.

Like other critics, the NWCA charges that Title IX regulations function as an illegal quota system. To meet the Title IX "quotas" for female athletes, schools have eliminated wrestling, gymnastics, and other men's sports, to the detriment of gender fairness. While it is true that the number of men's wrestling and gymnastics teams has been sharply reduced since Title IX's passage in 1972, it makes little sense to blame Title IX for these cuts. Further, even though some men's teams have been diminished in number, others have grown, so that the total number of intercollegiate male athletes continues to grow.

The greatest drop in the number of men's wrestling teams occurred between 1982 and 1992, when it fell from 363 to 275. Similarly, during 1982–92, the number of men's gymnastics teams decreased from seventy-nine to forty. But over these years, there was little enforcement of Title IX. From 1981 to 1984, the Reagan administration dragged its feet on gender equity; then Title IX was eviscerated by the 1984 Grove City Supreme Court decision. The court held that only particular college departments that received federal funds directly were subject to Title IX. Thus, if a college's athletic department did not receive direct federal assistance, it did not have to comply with Title IX.

The power of Title IX was not restored until 1988. In 1987, Congress passed the Civil Rights Restoration Act, which asserted that if a college received federal assistance then, all of its departments were subject to Title IX. However, President Reagan vetoed the act. It was not until Congress overrode the veto in 1988 that Title IX became a viable instrument to promote gender equity in college sports. Yet Title IX enforcement languished during the George H. W. Bush administration, and it was not until 1993 that it was vigorously implemented.

Why, then, did the number of men's wrestling and gymnastics teams drop so precipitously during 1982–92? In the case of gymnastics the answer seems to be a concern with legal liability. Indeed, the number of women's gymnastics teams lost during this period was eighty-three, more than double the loss of thirty-nine male teams. Would anyone attribute the loss of women's teams to the enforcement of Title IX?

The explanation for wrestling appears to be a decline in interest, perhaps as young men have shifted their allegiances to the two most rapidly growing sports: soccer and football.

The U.S. General Accounting Office issued a report on gender equity in college athletics in March 2001. Considering all NCAA and NAIA institutions, the report found that the number of men's athletic teams increased by a net thirty-six between 1981 and 1999, and the number of participation opportunities for men increased by 12,000 over the same period. As of 2001, there were 163,000 women and 232,000 men participating in intercollegiate athletics.

Women have made enormous gains, but today they still represent only 41 percent of college athletes, and according to the latest NCAA gender equity survey, in 1997 women received only 21 percent of sport-specific operating budgets. In 1997, the average operating budget for men's sports in Division IA was $2.43 million, while for women's sports it was $663,000.

The NWCA's claim that Title IX represents a quota system is also misguided. Title IX implementation guidelines allow a college to be in compliance by meeting any one of three criteria. The first criterion alone is quantitative and states that the proportion of athletes must be roughly proportional to the share of students by gender. "Roughly" has been interpreted to mean within 5 percentage points. The second criterion states that a school must have a history of ongoing improvement with regard to the underrepresented gender. The third criterion is that a school can show it has effectively accommodated the interests and abilities of the discriminated sex. The possibility that a school can be in compliance by fulfilling either the second or third criterion—which are not quantitative—means that there is no quota system.

There is substantial waste in the current system. Football does not need eighty-five scholarships. Sixty would do fine. NFL teams have forty-five roster players. The average Division IA team has thirty-two walk-ons, plus eighty-five scholarship players. Cut the scholarships to sixty, and the average college would save more than $350,000 annually, more than enough to finance a wrestling team (average cost: $330,000).

But why stop here? The NCAA should seek a congressional antitrust exemption with regard to coaches' salaries. Currently, seventy-five Division I men's basketball coaches make $1 million or more, and there are dozens more football coaches in this category. Knock them down to $200,000 (which would put them above 99 percent of the faculty) and colleges would be able to add another three to six sports or, heaven forbid, reduce their large athletic deficits.

Colleges going to bowl games might also consider reducing the size of their traveling entourages (Nebraska took a delegation of 826 to the Rose Bowl last year and spent $2.3 million), eliminating the practice of putting the men's basketball and football teams up at a local hotel before home games, diminishing the size of coaching staffs, cutting the length of the playing season in many sports, and so on.

If U.S. Secretary of Education Rod Paige's task force does its homework properly, it will conclude that Title IX needs more, not less, enforcement.

The BCS Is Ripe for Reform

In July, the fifty-three Division IA schools that do not belong to the six elite athletic conferences formed the Coalition for Athletics Reform. Their goal is to open up the present BCS so that all Division IA institutions have an equal chance to compete for the national football championship.

Two weeks ago, the House Judiciary Committee held hearings on the BCS, asking whether the existing system is fair and whether it violates antitrust law. Last week in Chicago, Myles Brand, the new executive director of the NCAA, called together administrators from BCS and non-BCS schools to discuss whether the present post-season football competitions need to be restructured.

The BCS was begun in 1998 by arrangement among the sixty-four schools in the Big Ten, Pac-Ten, Big East, Big Twelve, Southeastern, and Atlantic Coast conferences. It was an improvement over the Bowl Alliance (1995–97), the Bowl Coalition (1992–94), and the unstructured system that prevailed prior to 1992, both because it provides a national championship game and because it shares roughly 5 percent of its bowl revenue with the non-BCS schools.

The BCS system, however, remains very imperfect and prejudicial. It maintains four major bowl games (Orange Bowl, Sugar Bowl, Fiesta Bowl, and Rose Bowl) and stipulates that the champion of each of the six BCS conferences will be guaranteed a spot in one of these games, leaving two of the eight spots for "at-large" schools.

These two berths are potentially open to any Division IA team with nine or more wins that ranks in the top twelve in the BCS ranking system. This system is based on seven computer ratings, coaches' and sportswriters' polls, team record, and difficulty of schedule.

If the champion of one of the six elite conferences finishes with a 7–5 record, while the champion of the USA, Mid-American, Mountain West, or WAC conferences finishes with an 11–1 record, it does not matter. The BCS conference champs still get guaranteed major bowl berths, and the non-BCS champs have no guarantee. In fact, in the five years of the BCS, no non-BCS school has received an invitation to a BCS bowl—not the 11 wins–0 losses Tulane University team in 1998, not the 12 wins–1 loss Brigham Young University team in 2001, not the 11 wins–2 losses Marshall University team in 2001 and 2002, despite the fact that each of these teams had better records than at least eight of the top ten teams in the BCS rankings.

Why can't the non-BCS schools get in? First, because Notre Dame, an independent football program, gets preferential treatment for one of the two at-large berths. If Notre Dame is ranked in the top ten or it has at least nine wins, it gets an automatic selection. Second, because if more than two teams qualify for the two at-large berths (usually five or six teams qualify), then the bowl organizing committees (members of the local chambers of commerce in the bowls' host cities) choose which teams are invited.

Each organizing committee wants the team with the most prestige to better promote its game and its city. If Utah, Wyoming, Ohio, or Tulane University qualified for an at-large berth, it would have next to no chance of selection up against a Notre Dame, Nebraska, Miami, or Oklahoma.

Third, the BCS ranking system is stacked against the non-BCS schools. One criterion is the strength of a school's schedule. BCS schools mostly play against each other. Thus, non-BCS schools see their excellent win percentages degraded because they are not playing against the "top" competition. Coaches and sportswriters, who have a voice in the ranking, see matters the same way.

Fourth, when BCS schools do play against non-BCS schools, they generally insist on playing at home. Between 1999 and 2002, the top ten BCS schools played seventy-six games against non-BCS schools, but only eleven of these were on the road—practically a six-to-one home-to-away ratio. Not only does the BCS school derive a competitive advantage from playing at home, it earns more revenue from the game.

Top high-school prospects know that they will play on better teams; have superior coaches, training facilities, and football fields; and garner more national exposure if they go to BCS schools. The BCS schools have earned approximately $500 million in revenue from BCS bowls since 1998, while the non-BCS schools have earned $17 million. These acutely disparate payouts and recruitment odds solidify the two-tier system. When the BCS commissioners say that they deserve to go to the top bowls because they have stronger teams, they are engaging in a self-fulfilling prophecy.

In all other NCAA divisions and in all other sports, each school has an equal shot at going to the national championship. Marquette University can go to the Final Four in basketball. Rice University, the smallest Division IA school, can rise to win the 2003 College World Series in baseball.

In Divisions IAA, II, and III football since the late 1980s, there have been sixteen-team playoffs to determine the national champions. In Division I basketball, there is a sixty-four–team playoff. Why not have a playoff in the top football division?

The apologists for the BCS say that it would destroy the tradition of the post-season bowl games and it would threaten the educational process. This is self-serving nonsense.

The tradition of the bowl games has already been changed, along with the bowls' identities, which are now adorned with the names of multinational corporations. Any playoff system could still incorporate the bowls.

If there can be football playoffs in the other divisions that don't disrupt the educational process and there can be March Madness in the middle of the second academic semester, there can also be a Division IA football playoff in December and January during the semester break. If the elite conference commissioners are still worried about disrupting the classroom, they can contemplate returning to the ten- or eleven-game regular-season schedule that prevailed until recently.

It won't be easy to change the existing system. Sixty-four of the 117 schools in Division IA benefit from it. Congress is unlikely to act. Antitrust precedent, while not prohibitive, is ambiguous. Myles Brand has little direct power and apparently less will to intervene.

But a disreputable Chinese politician once said: The long march begins with a single step.

Clarett Has a Compelling Case for NFL Eligibility

U.S. District Court Judge Shira Scheindlin is supposed to decide before February 1 on the request for summary judgment in *Maurice Clarett v. NFL*. Clarett, who will turn twenty-one in October, six weeks after the 2004 season begins, wishes to be eligible to participate in the upcoming NFL draft.

The NFL claims that its bylaws prohibit this and, moreover, that its bylaws are legal. Clarett's attorneys challenge the meaning and legality of the league's bylaws.

The NFL's collective-bargaining agreement with the NFLPA contains a provision that the union will not sue the NFL over any of the provisions in its bylaws. The 1992 bylaws included clause 12(E), which stated: "For college players seeking special eligibility, at least three NFL seasons must have elapsed since the player was graduated from high school." (Interestingly, the new 2003 bylaws omit this clause.)

The NFL says it restricts eligibility because the male body is not sufficiently developed at younger ages. Unlike baseball or basketball, the physical nature of football requires certain body mass and muscle development for safe and effective play.

Clarett's lawyers cry out for clarity and consistency. First, they argue, if the NFL were really concerned about physical safety, why does it not set a weight or muscle-mass criterion instead of an arbitrary "years out of high school" standard (which itself does not correlate perfectly with age)?

Second, they say, their client does not lack mass or musculature. Maurice Clarett is six feet tall and weighs 230 pounds, making him taller and heavier than Walter Payton, Barry Sanders, Gale Sayers, and Emmett Smith, among many others, during their NFL careers. Further, at the beginning of the 2003 season, there were eight NFL players who were only twenty-one years of age.

Third, the NFL rule has changed several times since it was introduced in the 1950s and has not been regularly implemented by the league. They point to several notable cases in which the NFL did not enforce the rule in effect at the time: Andy Livingston in 1964, Craig "Ironhead" Heyward in 1988, Barry Sanders in 1989, and Eric Swann in 1991.

Fourth, they argue that a reasonable interpretation of the rule from the 1992 bylaws would make Clarett eligible for this year's draft. Clarett graduated from high school in December 2001. The NFL's 2001 season elapsed in January 2002; the 2002 season elapsed in January 2003; and the 2003 season will elapse in January 2004. The *Oxford English Dictionary* defines elapse to mean "to slip by, pass away, expire." Thus, by the date of the 2004 draft, three seasons will have elapsed, and Clarett should be eligible to participate.

Fifth, if twenty- or twenty-one-year-old men are really not physically developed enough to be successful in the NFL, why not leave this judgment up to the teams? General managers are not forced to pick players who are not ready for the NFL.

Herein lies the larger point of the suit. By setting an artificial restriction on who can enter the draft, the NFL is imposing a restraint of trade. It is as if the different companies in the computer industry got together and declared that they would hire no person under thirty years of age or under six feet tall.

If the free market would lead to an NFL team drafting a twenty year old and the NFL does not allow this to happen, then the NFL is restraining free trade. By doing so, it is not only curtailing the rights of people like Maurice Clarett, but it is potentially reducing the quality of the players on the field, thereby harming consumers, a group that antitrust laws seek to protect.

Yet the NFL argues that it is protected by the nonstatutory labor exemption. This exemption allows a union to bargain away in arm's-length negotiating certain free-market rights that inhere to its members in exchange for other benefits. The NFL contends that the NFLPA agreed to the eligibility restriction when it signed on to the clause in the collective-bargaining agreement stating that there would no suits related to the league's bylaws.

The problem with this argument is at least twofold. First, the eligibility clause itself is not directly mentioned in the collective-bargaining agreement. Indeed, the existence of an eligibility rule predates the league's first collective-bargaining agreement in 1968. Therefore, there was no arm's-length bargaining over the rule, and it cannot be subject to the nonstatutory exemption.

Second, the nonstatutory exemption generally applies only to the union and its members. It does not allow the primary effect of a restrictive bargaining agreement to be on nonmembers. Clarett and other prospective draftees do not belong to the union.

On a different tack, the NFL argues that the nation's antitrust laws only protect competition, not specific competitors. In the case of the eligibility rule, they say that players' salaries are not affected because they are limited by the salary cap (which was negotiated at arm's length with the union). Further, the number of players is set at fifty-three per team, and this is also unaffected by the eligibility rule.

Since the quantity and price of the players is not affected by the rule, the NFL maintains, competition in the players' market is not damaged.

This, however, is only part of the story. If the quality of play is harmed, then so are consumers.

In this light, it is hardly surprising that the courts have consistently rejected league age- or school-related eligibility limits. This happened in Spencer

Hayward's case against the NBA in 1971 as well as in cases against the U.S. Football League in 1984 and the World Hockey Association in 1977.

The NFL also benefits from the rule because it helps to sustain the quality of college football. College football, in turn, serves as a free training, screening, and promotional vehicle for the NFL. It reduces the NFL's player-development and scouting costs. It helps the league to identify injury-prone players before putting them under contract. And it provides free promotion to the league's future players.

In many respects, the NFL is better managed than the other team sports leagues, and many of its rules advance competitive balance and financial viability. The eligibility rule, however, is a counterproductive anachronism. It is time to give it up.

*[**Note:** Judge Scheindlin found the NFL rule to be in violation of the antitrust laws, but the NFL got the ruling reversed on appeal. Thus, Clarett was not allowed to participate in the 2004 draft. After sitting out a year, he was drafted by the Denver Broncos in 2005.]*

Let Jeremy Bloom Ski and Play Wide Receiver

The California State Senate got tired of waiting around for the NCAA to enact some significant reform around its treatment of student athletes. Last spring, the Senate voted 26–10 to pass Bill 193, which would require state universities to provide several additional benefits to student athletes.

These benefits include providing a stipend to cover the full cost of attending college (around $2,400 extra for necessary travel, out-of-season medical expenses, clothing, and leisure activities); allowing athletes to keep income from work not associated with their sport; allowing athletes to sign with agents while in school; and allowing athletes to transfer immediately when a coach leaves a program.

Bill 193 is now making its way through the California Assembly's Committee on Higher Education. Meanwhile, the Nebraska, Colorado, Texas, and Oklahoma legislatures are also considering measures to increase the financial compensation to student athletes.

While any individual state legislation that contravenes NCAA rules would likely force local schools out of the association and wreak havoc on conferences, these legislative initiatives appear to be having a more productive side effect. The NCAA has heard the pounding footsteps and is studying new reform initiatives, including one that would introduce a full-cost-of-attendance stipend of $2,400 for student athletes.

Also banging on the NCAA's door is the unusual case of the University of Colorado's Jeremy Bloom. Bloom plays end on the school's football team and is a world-class mogul skier. In 2002, he competed on the U.S. Olympic team in Salt Lake City, and he hopes to train intensively enough to win a medal at the 2006 Winter Games.

The only problem is that serious Olympic preparation costs money for elite training, travel, lodging, food, equipment—probably $75,000–$100,000 a year. Bloom could get endorsement money to cover these expenses, but the NCAA won't allow it as long as he plays football at Colorado, not even if he puts the endorsement money in a trust and uses it only to cover his expenses.

The California bill would handle Bloom's problem, but the NCAA should take this on itself. Everyone knows that the NCAA system is a hybrid, with elements of intense commercialism and elements of amateurism. The system will likely remain hybrid, but it needs to be made less hypocritical and more efficient.

The NCAA has had a shifting definition of amateurism over the years. In the 1948 Sanity Code, the association allowed athletes to receive a scholarship, but only if the athlete was in financial need and only if the athlete met the same academic standards as the rest of the student body—and even then the scholarship was restricted to tuition. In 1956, the concept of amateurism morphed again, this time to allow scholarship money also for room and board, books, and $15 "laundry money"—and even if there were no financial need involved.

In 1964, the association introduced Rule 1.6 stating that the athlete had to have a high-school record that would predict a 1.6 GPA in college (basically, half C and half D grades). In 1972, the NCAA allowed freshman eligibility in football and basketball. In 1973, the association abolished the four-year guaranteed scholarship, allowing the coach to cut off an injured or poorly performing athlete from his financial support. This was followed by the entrance-qualifying rules Proposition 48, then Proposition 42, and Proposition 16, along with other legislation on satisfactory progress toward the degree and special-assistance funds.

In short, the NCAA has continually tweaked its concept of amateurism in response to political pressures. At the core of the concept is only one idea: Athletes may not be financially compensated directly for performance in their sport.

The association would be well advised to strip away all of the other extraneous rules. Let Jeremy Bloom play football and ski for his country in the Olympics. Let college basketball players sign with agents as long as they don't sign professional contracts. College players, after all, need agents to set up the team tryouts prior to the NBA draft.

Then let the student athletes enter the pro draft and return to college, even if they are drafted. The NCAA has an unnecessary restriction on college basketball and football players: If they enter the draft and are selected by any team, then they cannot return to college. Why place such a restriction before the athlete has signed a professional contract?

The answer is obvious. The NCAA is pandering to the NFL and NBA (leagues they already furnish with free scouting, training, and promotional services). If the association desired to help student athletes, then it would let them return to college if they (1) did not want to play for the team that drafted them; (2) felt they were drafted too low, given their talent; or (3) had a change of heart and wanted to return to college.

These days, with college football coaches earning $2.4 million plus handsome perks and some athletic directors apparently receiving packages worth $1 million, it is easy to sympathize with calls to offer student athletes additional stipends. The average Division IA football team earns about $16 million in revenue. How does it make sense for college coaches to be paid the same amount as an NFL coach (whose teams generate more than $120 million, on average)? It doesn't. Instead, it appears that the college coach is getting paid the money that his star players would get in an open market.

The problem with the enhanced stipend idea is that it can get very expensive with over 500 student-athletes on scholarship at typical DIA schools. The vast majority of DIA schools already are bleeding millions of dollars of red ink in their athletics programs.

The solution is for the NCAA to seek an antitrust exemption for NCAA coaches' salaries. If they were limited to the salary of the school president or a top-paid professor, the school could save $1 million–$2 million on the men's basketball and football coaches alone. If 500 student athletes were given cost-of-attendance stipends of $2,400, it would cost $1.2 million.

But the school could do even better than this by providing the stipends only to student athletes with financial need. The rest of the saving could support further progress with Title IX.

And, now, for the $450 billion U.S. budget deficit …

Curb Coaches' Salaries and Preserve Title IX Gains

Another exciting and contentious season of college sports has drawn to a close. One of the more remarkable events almost eluded media coverage altogether. Last month the Office of Civil Rights (OCR) of the Department of Education issued a new implementation guideline for Title IX.

The OCR overrode its own historical practice and judicial interpretations to change the meaning of prong three of Title IX compliance, which addresses the institution's obligation to provide participation opportunities that meet the interests and abilities of the underrepresented sex. If any one of three prongs is satisfied, then the school is judged to meet the athletic-participation-opportunity standards for gender equity in athletics.

The first prong states that the share of female athletes should be proportional to the share of female students. The second states that as long as the school shows an ongoing pattern of increasing the participation of the underrepresented sex, then it is in compliance.

The third prong states that a school only has to fully accommodate the interests and abilities of the underrepresented sex. The new guideline turns the tables on judging whether these interests and abilities are accommodated. It allows schools to conduct an e-mail survey to discern the level of women's interest as the sole assessment of interest and abilities and to count nonresponses to the e-mail survey as lack of interest. It thereby puts the burden of proof on the underrepresented population rather than on the institution, as it previously did.

In the Brown University case of the early 1990s, the courts ruled that interest surveys used alone were insufficient. Among other things, a proper survey represented nothing more than the female student body's interest level at a particular time. If a survey had been done in 1972 to discern women's interest, then women's participation might have been frozen over the last thirty-three years at a woeful level.

The new OCR guideline is issued three years after Education Secretary Rod Paige commissioned a year-long study. At the conclusion of the study, Paige stated that he would recommend no substantial changes to Title IX's implementation.

This approach stood until President Bush gained reelection. There was no new study that supports the present OCR guideline. If it stands, the advance of women's participation in athletics will be stopped or even reversed.

Title IX critics never say that they are against women's participation in athletics. They acknowledge that such participation has beneficial social, psychological, physical, and vocational effects. But, they say, Title IX has been pursued too zealously and expensively, and in the process, men's participation has suffered.

There are lots of juicy questions here, but one stands out: Why don't those concerned that men have insufficient participation opportunities argue for controlling other costs in college athletics?

Take coaches' compensation. There are probably more than 100 head coaches today with compensation packages worth over $1 million, and there are more than a dozen with packages approaching $2 million or more.

Consider, for instance, Bob Stoops, head football coach at Oklahoma. He has a guaranteed seven-year deal, with built-in annual increases, that can rise to more than $3 million with bonuses. The bonuses are varied and include $250,000 for winning the national championship. There's also a token $10,000 bonus if 70 percent of his players graduate within six years. On top of this, Stoops get perks galore.

We are told that Stoops and others are merely receiving what the market will bear. Perhaps, but what kind of a market is it? First, the players themselves are not paid, so Stoops is getting part of the value they produce.

Second, college sports benefits from numerous tax benefits that are premised on their activity being amateur and educational.

Third, college athletic departments are not profitmaking entities with stockholders demanding bottom-line performance. Any revenue generated by men's football or basketball finds a way to get spent.

Fourth, the athletic director hires the coaches. The more the coaches get paid, the more responsibility rests in the athletic director's job, and the more he gets paid.

Apologists for these compensation levels will argue that if a top coach brings his team to the BCS or the Final Four, it has a value to the school far in excess of the coach's pay. This may be true in some cases, but successful teams depend on a lot more than just the head coach. They depend on the school's reputation; its facilities; the assistant coaches, who do much of the recruiting; good luck; and, alas, athletes. Should all of the incremental value really be attributed to the coach?

But also keep in mind that only ten schools make it to the BCS and four to the Final Four. The others don't bring in the big bucks, but the coaches still get their handsome packages. LSU's Saban, Texas's Brown, Tennessee's Fulmer, Kansas State's Snyder, Georgia's Richt, among others, all earn $1.5 million–$2 million, plus luxurious perks and golden handshakes.

The Southeastern Conference in college football has the highest average team revenues, at $26.9 million. The average NFL team has revenues of more than $130 million (increasing to more than $150 million with the new TV contracts). How can the top college coaches be making as much (or nearly so) as the top NFL coaches?

The first step to sanity is straightforward. The NCAA (and others) should lobby congress for an antitrust exemption to impose limits on coaches' salaries. College presidents get handsome compensation, generally between $200,000 and $700,000. What about limiting coaches to the level of college presidents?

If such a rule were applied across the NCAA, the good news is that there would be no effect on resource allocation. That is, those best equipped to coach college football would still do so. The universities would save significant money—more than enough to save the men's wrestling team and then some. And best of all, the educational priorities of our universities would become better aligned.

Final Word: Million-Dollar Contracts for College Coaches Make Little Sense

The new year always brings many rituals. One of them for me is getting a dozen or so media calls about the growing commercialism of college football.

One question I always get is: Why are the top Division IA football coaches paid $1 million–$2 million (and sometimes more) when the top-paid college presidents are paid $400,000–$800,000?

The standard rationale in the trade is supply and demand. That answer begs the question.

Think of it this way. How much do you think MLB managers would be paid if every major-league team was exempt from taxes; it was supported by million-dollar operating subsidies from both a university and a state budget; and the players' salaries were constrained by law to be no higher than $40,000 annually (roughly the value of a full grant-in-aid at a top school)? And further, what if the team president were told that the more he pays his manager, the more he would be paid. This in effect is what happens to college athletic directors with their football and basketball coaches.

The answer lies in the fact that each team would have gads of money that it could not use to compete over players. Instead, it would use the money to compete over managers. Managerial salaries would balloon. Yes, even Joe Torre would earn more than $5 million a year—a lot more.

But the larger point is about resource allocation. Since Adam Smith's *Wealth of Nations*, the marvel of the marketplace has been perceived to be its ability to allocate resources automatically according to consumer wants. When consumer demand increases for some products, the prices of these goods rise, and producers are induced to shift resources toward increasing their production. Thus, thanks to supply and demand, resources are used efficiently or are put to use where they are most valued.

But suppose there are certain resources that are already being used where they are most valued. For instance, suppose that, if Ron Artest did not play in the NBA, his next best job possibility would be as a high-school basketball coach earning $35,000 a year.

In theory, and holding other things constant, to induce Artest to pursue an NBA career he would have to be offered only a $36,000 salary by some team. The society would not need to offer Artest $6.2 million to have his talents displayed in the NBA.

The difference between the $6.2 million Artest is paid and the $36,000 he might require is known as economic rent. It is payment to a resource that does not affect resource allocation. That is, it does not interfere with the market's ability to direct an efficient use of resources.

In this context, consider the multimillion-dollar compensation packages offered to dozens of college football and basketball coaches. There are thirty-two NFL and thirty NBA head coaching jobs. These jobs are already taken.

What would be the most remunerative alternative employment for Pete Carroll if he did not coach at the University of Southern California or for Mack Brown if he did not coach at the University of Texas? Of course, the answer to this question will depend on the skills, background, and interests of each coach.

But for argument's sake, suppose there was an NCAA rule stipulating that no head coach could be paid more than the university president at that school. Would Carroll or Brown find another job that paid him more than, say, $500,000? Probably not.

If not, the decision by Carroll or Brown, or any other Division IA head coach, to dedicate his efforts to intercollegiate athletics would not be affected by such a rule. Resource allocation would not change. The only thing "supply and demand" produces in the world of top college coaching is economic rent for the coach.

I don't begrudge people seeking whatever the market will pay them. But given that (1) the market for college coaches is rigged by tax exemptions, subsidies, etc.; (2) paying the head coach more than the school president sends the wrong message about a university's priorities; (3) the star athletes on the basketball and football teams are not allowed to receive cash salaries; and (4) resource allocation would not be affected by a salary-limit rule for coaches, it would make eminent sense for the NCAA to pass such a rule limiting head coaches' compensation.

The solution seems straightforward, but there are two significant impediments. First, its elevated rhetoric notwithstanding, the NCAA basically functions as a trade association of athletic directors and coaches. Why would they vote to reduce their own compensation?

Second, such a rule would require Congress to pass an antitrust exemption for this market restriction. I can think of no good reason why Congress would not cooperate on this, if asked by the NCAA. There's the Catch-22.

VI

Media and the Regulation of Steroids

Extreme Is Mediocre and
XFL Is the Name

Last fall, Vince McMahon's World Wrestling Federation (WWF) knocked *Monday Night Football* from its pedestal atop the television ratings on Monday evenings among the twelve- to twenty-four-year-old male demographic. This is a key demographic not only because its members do a lot of consuming and they are relatively easy to target, but because it is an age group when lifetime habits are formed.

If McMahon knows the way into the hearts and minds of twelve- to twenty-four-year-old males, then maybe his new XFL, to begin play in four months, will become a permanent fixture in the U.S. professional-sports landscape. NBC's Dick Ebersol is betting that it will, though these days that may engender more skepticism than confidence.

NBC has partnered with the WWF to own the eight XFL teams, purportedly as a single entity. Among other things, single-entity status will mean that within the league there will be no competition for the players. That is, XFL teams will not bid against each other for the better players, and the league plans to set players' base salaries at $35,000 for kicking specialists, $50,000 for quarterbacks, and $45,000 for all other positions. In addition, the XFL will give each player on the winning team of every game a bonus of $2,500 and a bonus of $25,000 per player for winning the league championship game (to be played on April 21, following a ten-game season).

The XFL plans to present an in-your-face attitude. McMahon calls the NFL the No Fun League. XFL players will have fun, we are told. On the field they will be encouraged to flaunt their individualism—dancing or spiking footballs after touchdowns. No more sissy rules, such as two feet in-bounds, fair catches where the receiver can't be tackled, or prohibitions on helmet-to-helmet contact. And in case you haven't picked up the vibe, all this will be fun for fans, too. Just to make sure, the XFL will run a thirty-five–second play clock and limit halftime to ten minutes so games will last no more than three hours—unless, of course, it takes more than a few seconds to remove each immobilized player with a spinal-cord injury from the playing field.

But it is not these gimmicks, or McMahon's transcendent connection to the psyche of twelve- to twenty-four-year-old males that gives the XFL its best chance of success. Rather it is two developments in the telecommunications revolution. The first is the expansion of national television networks beyond the big three. Ever since the NFL signed up ABC to televise Monday Night Football in 1969, the league has partnered with ABC, CBS, and NBC, making it very difficult for a rival league to get the type of television exposure and rights fees it would need to compete with the NFL. In 1987, the NFL added ESPN to its broadcast partners, and in 1990 it added Turner. Now, with the emergence of Fox as a bona fide national network, and with Fox replacing NBC in the NFL broadcasting mix, one network was left out in the cold, opening the door for the XFL.

The second development is the advent of TiVo and Replay—new, simplified digital recording devices for use with television sets. These devices make recording television shows as easy as Monday morning quarterbacking. It's bad news for TV serials and movies because consumers can now "tape" the shows they want to see with the touch of a button and replay them at their leisure, skipping over commercials. As TiVo and Replay technology becomes widespread, the value of prime time will diminish, as will the value of all shows that are not time-sensitive. The value to advertisers of *West Wing* and similar hot shows will fall because viewers can tell their TiVo systems to record them and then watch them on their own schedule without commercials. Not so with sports programming. Fans want to watch games as they happen. This phenomenon will further enhance the cachet of live sports competition on television.

And this helps to explain why NBC is willing to take a gamble on the XFL. Instead of investing $1 million per show for some serial or a Saturday night movie, NBC is going to put on the XFL. The ratings don't have to be as good as they are for the NFL; they just have to be as good as they would be for the alternative Saturday night programming. The XFL, then, is football as software rather than as sport.

XFL salaries will average about one-twentieth the salaries in the NFL, and it is no mystery which league will get the best players. Fans will respond accordingly. This doesn't mean that the XFL will be without a following. It does, however, suggest that the XFL's fans largely will come from the WWF, the Canadian Football League, and the Arena Football League (AFL), and that live attendance and television ratings will be modest. The latter two leagues have average salaries below those projected for the XFL, and we should anticipate some competition for salaries among these three "minor" leagues (although the playing seasons of the XFL and AFL do not overlap, and each league will allow its players to play in the other). This competition should drive salaries up but not enough to begin to challenge the supremacy of the NFL.

McMahon may think that the NFL is the No Fun League, but unfortunately for him and NBC, there are tens of millions of fans who feel otherwise.

*[**Note:** The WWF has since changed its name. It is now called World Wrestling Entertainment (WWE).]*

The Increasingly Complex Sports Media Landscape

It has been a tumultuous first quarter of 2002 in the sports-broadcasting business. News Corporation announced that it is taking a $909 million writeoff on its long-term contracts with the NFL, MLB, and NASCAR. Morgan Stanley issued a report projecting that the networks will lose an estimated $1.17 billion on their sports programs during 2001–2002, in contrast to a profit of $294 million in 1997–98. NBC dropped the NBA. And the sports media pundit Neal Pilson averred that all this was "a clear signal that the networks are tapped out for any significant rights-fee increases in future years."

The NBA inked a new six-year deal with ABC/ESPN and Turner that will bring it less revenue in 2002–2003 than it is receiving in 2001–2002 from NBC and Turner (though there is a modest nominal increase over the course of the deal). The new contract marks the first time since 1983 that the NBA has not experienced at least a doubling with its next national TV deal. And perhaps more important, to squeeze the average $766 million annually out of the new deal, the NBA had to agree to a schedule that will put roughly 90 percent of its games on cable.

Because cable reaches fewer households, many wonder whether the NBA deal is sacrificing long-term growth for short-term revenue. Others wonder whether the NBA deal will be seen as violating the 1961 Sports Broadcasting Act, which permits leagues to make package deals only for over-the-air television.

Does the NBA deal denote that the broadcast networks, with their single revenue stream from advertising, will cede the sports market to regional and national cable stations, which benefit from both advertising and license-fee revenues?

Some say a new paradigm is on the horizon that was adumbrated by the AFL deal with NBC signed in early March. NBC pays the AFL no rights fee. Advertising revenues are split evenly between the league and the network, and capital gains from franchise appreciation above $12 million are shared with NBC.

There are certainly negative factors affecting the value of sports rights. Sports ratings are drifting downward, as are ratings for all shows due to the increased competition from channel multiplication and the Internet. The ad market has been sluggish at least since the first quarter of 2001. And it is unlikely in the extreme that WB, UPN, or PAX will attempt to become an elite network, as Fox did several years ago by aggressively bidding for top sports programming.

Sports Business Journal, April 1–7, 2002

Yet the sky is not falling. First, the economy (and the ad market) is emerging out of its doldrums. Second, sports programming will become relatively more precious in the coming years as TiVo-type systems are hard-wired into new television sets. (Viewers will be more willing to watch *West Wing* than a Yankees–Red Sox game on a delayed, fast-forward-over-advertising basis.)

Third, News Corporation's decision to write down its sports contracts does not mean that these investments did not pay off indirectly. Fox's link to the NFL, MLB, and NASCAR has helped to build it into one of the big four networks. Its successful sports programming also has spillover effects by raising ratings on its lead-in and lead-out programming, as well as via promotional benefits for its other shows. Further, companies often take writeoffs during downturns when they are more routine and to get bad news quickly out of the way to show rosier results in future quarters. Such a strategy also saves in the present value of a company's tax obligations.

Fourth, national television ratings for eight-man, fifty-yard arena football haven't risen above 1, even for the championship game. There's little threat to the established leagues from the NBC–AFL deal.

None of this is to suggest that there won't be challenges ahead for the sports leagues. Even if rights fees don't fall, they are not likely to continue their meteoric ascent. There will also be the strategic issues of how to develop Internet programming, satellite distribution, and international markets. The growing dependence on regional and national cable in the context of the nation's shifting demographics poses additional conundrums.

The largest challenge, however, will be to develop and maintain sound management practices. Healthy media contracts and strong sponsorship support depend on peaceful labor and effective community relations. Nothing can replace enlightened central-office and intelligent local-team leadership.

No Easy Answers for MLB's Steroid Scandal

Two weeks ago, I was working out in the Smith College gym when I overheard a conversation among three boys, probably in their early twenties. They were talking openly and in graphic details about using steroids and their workout regimens and boasting about their new muscle mass.

When Senator John McCain says that he's not worried about what Barry Bonds and Jason Giambi do to their bodies, he's worried about how drug use by professional athletes infuses a harmful culture of body building among future athletes, he's got a point. Of course, the culpability goes well beyond today's sports heroes. Part of the problem is our culture of narcissism and materialism. And part of the problem lies with the U.S. government.

If there was more disturbing news than the admissions of Bonds and Giambi before the grand jury, it was that their confidential testimony before the grand jury leaked out. What good are government guarantees of confidentiality if testimony becomes public? How will this leak affect the ability of future grand juries to do their work?

Last March, Senator McCain issued his first warning to MLB that the league needed a tougher drug policy or he would introduce federal legislation to impose one. A few weeks after his warning, federal agents seized the specimens from the 2003 drug tests of the players. Those tests, according to the collective-bargaining agreement, were supposed to be confidential. The players' association has been fighting—so far unsuccessfully—for the return of the results.

The government's behavior in each of these matters is not conducive to the players' and owners' entering into a new agreement.

Also not conducive to an effective agreement is Senator Orrin Hatch's Nutritional Supplement Act of 1994. The bill allows a host of supplements to be sold legally over the counter. While these sales handsomely pad the revenues of U.S. drug companies, they also greatly complicate MLB's task of enforcing a drug policy.

Many of these supplements are contaminated with steroid precursors. Thus, players using these over-the-counter supplements could be tested and found to have failed their tests. Is it fair to give such players a strong penalty?

To be sure, earlier this year the Food and Drug Administration removed the prohormone andro from retail shelves (though andro analogs remain). And a new bill, which has passed the House but still sits in the Senate, bans andro and its analogs. Sadly, the bill explicitly omits a ban on DHEA, which is marketed to older people as a fountain of youth but becomes andro in the body and is converted into testosterone. Clearly, new legislation that tightens these categories, bans supplements that function as andro surrogates, and promotes spot testing of laboratory procedures is needed.

Last week, Senator McCain issued a new warning to MLB. This time, he indicated that, unless MLB and the players' association adopted a new drug program similar to the one that Commissioner Bud Selig introduced unilaterally in 2001 to cover the minor leagues, he would offer legislation to mandate this in January.

If Senator McCain or any of his colleagues were truly interested in promoting integrity in baseball, they also would address the government's breaches of confidentiality and the problems of the 1994 Nutritional Supplement Act.

McCain is calling for MLB to emulate its minor-league policy. This policy is certainly a substantial improvement over the current major-league policy because it includes year-round random testing, twice as many random tests, a longer list of banned substances, and immediate penalty for the first offense. It is an important first step for Major League Baseball to take.

Down the road, it would be desirable to see the policy strengthened. The penalty for the first offense in the minor-league policy is only fifteen days. Compare this with the mandatory two-year suspension in the World Anti-Doping Code that is employed by the International Olympic Committee (IOC). (Of course, the IOC does not have to negotiate its policy with a union.) To be sure, when a player is caught and "outed," there is significant public-relations damage to his career. So a fifteen-day penalty has symbolic value and is not trivial. But fans are forgiving, and fifteen days is insufficient.

Another issue with the minor-league policy and current major-league policy is scientific. Daily permutations of steroid compounds and growth hormones and new delivery systems that reduce the time period when the drugs are detectable in the blood stream to a few days or sometimes a few hours make it extraordinarily difficult to stay ahead of the curve.

The science behind doping grows more sophisticated and complex every day. In a few years, gene therapy for performance enhancement will also be possible.

MLB's current drug policy relies on a Health Policy Advisory Committee to identify new molecules, compounds, and procedures. This committee consists of two doctors, each top experts in the field, and two lawyers. Again, while this committee is an important step in the right direction, it is questionable whether it is sufficient to keep up with rapid pace of innovation in the world of nutritional supplements.

The World Anti-Doping Agency (WADA) has an extensive team of doctors working on a regular basis to follow scientific developments and evaluate new doping molecules. As has been suggested by Dr. Gary Wadler, the best path for MLB might be to use WADA or another independent scientific body to establish the appropriate standards and update the list of banned substances.

Thus, if MLB's drug policy for the minor leagues is implemented for the major league, it will represent very important progress. But more progress still needs to be made.

Reflections on the Super Bowl

When it comes to national cultural rituals, the Super Bowl is it. It is New Year's Eve and then some.

Consider this: Some 21.5 million households were expected to host Super Bowl parties this year that would be attended by 54.6 million people. Another 9.9 million trekked to bars or restaurants to watch the game.

Since 1972, television ratings for the Super Bowl have exceeded 40 every year except one. The exception was 1990, when the then dominant 49ers blew out the Broncos 55–10, and even then the ratings reached 39.

There's nothing else like it. Ratings for neither the World Series nor the NBA finals have reached as high as 20 in the recent past, and the NHL's Stanley Cup finals, when they happen, do not hit a 4.

With 110 million television households in the United States, a 40 rating means that 44 million households are watching the game. Add the people in the bars and restaurants, figure in the parties, and it implies 120 million–150 million people watching in the United States alone. Estimates for the worldwide audience go as high as 800 million—second only to soccer's World Cup finals, which have an audience in excess of 1 billion.

Another interesting feature of the Super Bowl as cultural ritual is that it crosses religious, ethnic, and gender lines. Just about everybody watches: old white men, young white men, women, African Americans, Hispanics, and more. Former Presidents George H. W. Bush and Bill Clinton participated in the pre-game show, and needless to say, the champion Patriots will be feted at the White House.

In fact, you don't even have to like football to watch the Super Bowl. A recent survey found that 34 million people will watch the game for the advertisements. This is the annual coming-out party for advertisers. It's a national advertisers' fashion show where the ad industry struts its latest, most creative products.

And no wonder. If a company is going to spend $2.4 million for a thirty-second ad spot, it has to make sure that each second of the ad is well used. That's why the average cost of producing Super Bowl ads is estimated at nearly $1 million a shot. And a million bucks produces a quality ad.

Some companies, of course, buy more than one spot. Anheuser Busch purchased ten of the fifty-eight spots on this year's Super Bowl. Anheuser Busch actually had twenty-five potential ads produced before selecting its finalists.

When one does the math, Super Bowl advertising at first blush seems too expensive. After adjusting for the number of viewers, ad rates are so high that the cost per viewer on the Super Bowl is still double or triple the norm for prime-time programming. Many companies, however, figure it's worth the premium. Unlike other shows, where during commericals people channel surf, go to the kitchen or the bathroom, or press the skip button on their TiVo control, viewers intently watch and discuss Super Bowl ads.

It's a formula that works well for the NFL. Ratings are converted into ad revenue, which is converted into rights fees. This year, each of the NFL's thirty-two teams will receive about $90 million from national media revenue. With the new TV deals, that number will soon jump to $120 million or more annually per team. Not only is this a lot of money (the total revenue from all sources of the average NBA team is about $90 million), it is money that is equally distributed to all NFL teams.

In part because of the NFL's equal revenue distribution and in part because of the league's salary cap, the NFL is supposed to be a league where a single team cannot dominate year in and year out. Yet the Patriots, as well as a few teams before them, seem to put together multiyear streaks.

Part of this is good fortune, part is that success breeds success, and part is effective management. When teams win, everyone is happy, and players such as Tedy Bruschi, Troy Brown, and Matt Light give hometown discounts to stay with a championship team.

But certainly, much of the team's success rests with its owner, Robert Kraft, who not only traded a player to get Bill Belichick as his coach but also stepped out of the way and allowed Belichick and his staff to run all aspects of the team.

Robert and Jonathan Kraft also set a purposeful team strategy. An important element of this strategy has been to have a steady cap-level payroll each year. Many teams spend big in some years to sign marquee players with large signing bonuses, surpassing the payroll cap, and then have to make up for the excess in one year with a shortfall in another. In contrast, the Pats have attempted to come in around the cap consistently. This strategy has fostered steady performance.

A key to the NFL's and the Patriots' success is that both emphasize the collective over the individual. For the NFL, it is the league over the team; for the Patriots, it is the team over the player.

Even though a former disgruntled Patriot, Lawyer Milloy, recently called the Krafts cheap, the team in fact has been in the top twelve in cash spending over the past five years. The Krafts are anything but cheap. They built their new state-of-the-art stadium entirely with private funds and are even reimbursing the state for its modest $70 million infrastructure contribution.

Cheap organizations don't win three Super Bowls in four years. Intelligent organizations do.

In Steroids Hearings, Congress Has Its Eye on the Wrong Ball

Don't these guys ever get embarrassed? Their constituents apparently find discussion of Social Security reform too confusing and have tuned out. To tune them back in, members of the House Government Reform Committee decided to haul baseball stars and bereaved parents into its hallowed halls to stage a CSPAN gala event.

The members asserted that the purpose of the hearings was twofold: first, to call attention to drug abuse and begin to set young Americans straight on the dangers of steroids; and second, to investigate the extent and roots of steroid use in baseball.

The first motive is laudable. But it is not best accomplished in the hysteria whipped up by Jose Canseco's book, during spring training when players are trying to prepare themselves for the season, and in an antagonistic context wherein Canseco's accusees receive subpoenas. Congress, someone should remind these members, is part of the legislative, not the judicial, branch of government. It is not its role to judge possible transgressors innocent or guilty.

A more effective way to reach America's youth is to appropriate funds for a steroid-education program and then seek baseball's cooperation. I suspect it would flow copiously from the union, its players, and MLB headquarters at 350 Park Avenue.

The second motive is curious. It is next to impossible to get to the bottom of such a complex issue during one day of public hearings. Why would a player who had used steroids confess to the same in such a hearing or rat on his teammates—unless, of course, he were trying to sell copies of his new book? Present-day players would risk having their multimillion-dollar contracts nullified. Shouldn't the hearings at least have been preceded by investigations and reports from the Congressional Research Service, the FBI, or other agencies? And if baseball players were using illegal steroids, wouldn't it have made sense to call the FBI to testify at the hearings to explain why it hadn't made any arrests or conducted any sting operations?

But the real embarrassment was to come after the hearings. Pressed by the media about what they might do, the members and some of their colleagues in the Senate engaged in that hoary political ritual: They threatened to take away MLB's antitrust exemption.

That ritual dates back to the Celler Committee Hearings in the U.S. House of Representatives in 1951 and has been practiced more or less on a triennial basis ever since. Members of Congress pretend to be outraged by MLB's latest behavior, and MLB pretends to be under serious scrutiny. Members get to show their constituents that they care about baseball's possible monopoly abuses, and baseball, in exchange for keeping its antitrust privileges, receives a scolding.

Until 2005, however, there was always at least some logic to the process. Members would call hearings when, say, their local team was threatening to relocate to a new city if it didn't get a publicly supported stadium. In such a case, the team's bargaining leverage is enhanced by MLB's monopoly power, and lifting baseball's exemption might be an effective means to diminish this leverage.

Similarly, when the last hearings on baseball's exemption were held in 2002, MLB had just announced that it was going to contract by at least two teams before the next season. That is, an industry whose revenues had been growing at 15 percent a year over the previous seven years was threatening to reduce its output—monopoly abuse pure and simple.

Not in 2005. This time, members brandished the lift-the-exemption sword if baseball didn't toughen its steroid policy. It would be as if President George W. Bush threatened to invade North Korea unless Congress passed a measure to privatize Social Security.

And just to let the members of Congress in on a little secret: If they want to get baseball's attention, there's a more effective way to do it than with the exemption. They could threaten to curtail the special tax treatment sports teams get by being allowed to amortize their players' contracts (indeed, all intangible assets since last year's legislation), to disallow tax-exempt bonds for stadium construction, or to prohibit deductibility for luxury-suite rentals.

Then again, starting this week the members of Congress will have more constructive things to do with the baseball industry. They'll be going to fundraisers for their next campaigns at Camden Yards and RFK Stadium.

Anti-Doping: Settle In for the Long Haul

The drug issue in professional sports, it seems, just won't go away. Congress has tried to point the finger at Bud Selig, Don Fehr, and individual players. The *Boston Herald* journalist Howard Bryant focused his finger pointing on Commissioner Selig.

But there are no villains. There is just a very complicated problem.

To be sure, Selig and the other commissioners may have acted with greater foresight and force, while Fehr and the other players' association directors may have been less legalistic and recalcitrant.

Players, until recently, did no more than respond to market incentives and attempt to improve their performance on the playing field. And they did so at a time when their sports had no, or weak, anti-doping policies, and the dangers of performance enhancers were not well known.

The most productive way to grapple with doping in sports is to design policies and procedures for moving forward, not to focus on the past. Bud Selig took an important step forward a few weeks ago when he endorsed both stiffer penalties and implementation by an independent agency.

Specifically, Selig stated: "We must increase the levels of discipline to fifty games for a first offense, one hundred games for a second and a lifetime ban for a third. And, probably most important, we must turn over the administration of our program to an independent authority to, once and for all, end the debate about the transparency of our policy."

An independent agency, such as the U.S. Anti-Doping Agency (USADA), can identify new compounds, insure proper random testing, and guarantee unbiased interpretation of test results and codified imposition of sanctions.

It should be emphasized, however, that even if Selig's proposal were carried out, the doping problem would not disappear. New molecules can be introduced. Masking agents can be used.

More significant, each of the major team sports leagues today—MLB, NFL, NBA, and NHL—all depend solely on urine samples to detect players' use of drugs. Currently, there is no urine test for human growth hormone (HGH), an important performance enhancer.

The only test for HGH is with a blood sample, and the prevailing view is that taking blood is unacceptably invasive. While it is certainly more invasive than taking urine, taking blood is not a big deal. The World Anti-Doping Administration (WADA) provides for the use of any biological material collected for purposes of doping control, including blood. This code is followed by the IOC as well as by the Association of Tennis Professionals.

Baseball is funding an effort to find a urine test for HGH. But at present none exists, and it may be years before one is found … if ever.

Without blood testing, any player can simply migrate from identified steroids to HGH with impunity. This is hardly an assurance that a sport is clean.

Until this year, even the blood test for HGH was of dubious accuracy. The scientific community, however, has now embraced a test, and sufficient antibodies are being produced to administer it.

Unfortunately, it won't be a simple matter politically to introduce blood testing. So far, the various sports' commissioners have not called for it, and even if they do, it is likely that the players' associations will resist.

Congress has made noises about legislating a mandatory anti-doping program for the leagues, but it is unclear whether it would include blood testing. In any event, the congressional remedy is suspect because of the Bill of Rights.

The Fourth Amendment to the U.S. Constitution, ratified on December 15, 1791, states: "The right of the people to be secure in their persons, houses, papers, and effects, against unreasonable searches and seizures, shall not be violated, and no Warrants shall issue, but upon probable cause, supported by Oath or affirmation, and particularly describing the place to be searched, and the persons or things to be seized." Thus, any law mandating testing may be in violation of the Fourth Amendment. Such a law would probably be challenged by the union and ultimately found unconstitutional (though there may be ways to legislate indirectly using the commerce clause or public stadium funding as pretexts for intervention).

Given the traditional union position on random testing, it seems improbable that blood testing could be collectively bargained in the near-term.

Civil rights are protected from government action, not private-sector action. It would thus be more likely to pass the Fourth Amendment legal threshold if each sport simply set its own rules of the game. Employers, for instance, can limit the freedom of speech of their employees within a company and random drug testing by companies, when job-related, has been upheld in certain courts. Unilateral action by a commissioner, however, would still be thwarted by labor law, as Commissioners Pete Rozelle and Peter Ueberroth learned in the 1980s.

All of this suggests that there are no easy answers. Indeed, answers will become still more elusive when gene doping becomes a reality several years from now.

It also suggests that we will have to live with some ambiguity—and the periodic bursts of media outrage that ambiguity engenders. In the meantime, if members of Congress are truly concerned about the effect of professional athletes' doping on the habits of America's youth, they should think about devoting energy and resources to drug education. This is an area where, I suspect, they will get full cooperation from commissioners, owners, and players' associations.

Index